THE ROGUE ARTIST'S

ART MARKETING GUIDE
PUT YOURSELF OUT THERE!

WRITTEN BY

RAFI

DEDICATION

THIS BOOK IS DEDICATED TO MY PARTNER, MUSE, AND MY WIFE, KLEE. SHE HAS HELPED ME PUSH THROUGH SO MANY INSECURITIES IN DOING THIS WHOLE THING. I ALSO DEDICATE THIS TO OUR ROGUE ARTIST COMMUNITY WHO HAVE BEEN MORE SUPPORTIVE THAN I CAN EVER EXPLAIN IN WORDS. THANK YOU.

TABLE OF CONTENTS

TABLE OF CONTENTS

FOREWORD BY KLEE ANGELIE

Hello, and welcome! My name is Klee Angelie Galligan. I am wife and partner in shenanigans to Rafi Perez, as well as co-editor of this book.

Our journey with this book began a couple of years ago when Rafi uttered the last words any spouse or partner ever wants to hear. "My next book is going to be on marketing." Frozen in terror, but always willing to have his back, I managed to squeeze an "Okay" out of my throat.

If you had asked me back then, I would have told you definitively that I despise... er, didn't have much interest in marketing. I didn't get algorithms, didn't post "effectively" on social media, didn't care for the traditional methods of "selling," wasn't a "closer," and generally wanted to keep the taste of all of it out of my mouth.

"That's exactly why I'm going to write this book." Rafi said, knowing my level of resistance. "Those things aren't at all what we've done over the past decade, and I'm tired of artists being made to feel like that's the only option for them."

Of course, he wasn't going to write a stuffy "how-to" book on marketing. Over the years we have done so many fun, silly, harebrained, excellent, complete flops, make it work, and "Huh?" things to put ourselves out there.

I'd love to tell you that I was always super psyched to do these things, but sometimes I had to be, uh...nudged into them. Regardless, they all made for a fulfilling and dynamic creative journey because we were doing it our way.

Here we are today. A couple of years since Rafi embarked on writing this book -- filled with much writing, much editing, a hurricane or two, a community of really awesome supportive creatives, and a cross-country move.

Reading it for what would be our final edit, I found myself not only engaged and entertained, but inspired and empowered. "This book doesn't even remotely suck at all!" I exclaimed. For me, this book is genuinely a breath of fresh air.

With that I leave you, awesome creative humans, so you can get on with reading this book. I hope you enjoy the journey, and also find that it "Doesn't even remotely suck at all."

DA MOON!

ARTISTS WHO CONTRIBUTED ART

If you read my last book, you know that I love sprinkling in some entertaining doodles to add something special to the context of what I am saying. With this book, several amazing artists from around the world contributed their silly doodles, sketches, and beautiful artwork to help bring this book to life. This is my awkward standing ovation to them.

Tina Colbourne, https://linktr.ee/TinaColbourneart
Christopher Rhoads, www.instagram.com/rhoads.j.christopher
Kelly Sterr, https://www.kellysterrgallery.com
Esther L Jones, https://estherljones.com
Sarah Molyneux https://www.sarahmolyneuxart.com/
Jason Boushard https://linktr.ee/NannuArtworks
Ethan Kirkman, www.instagram.com/indigowoodcrafts
Sara Neville, https://www.saranevillerogueart.com
Rachael Kerr www.rkerrart.com
Chris Shopland / Extempore Art, https://www.youtube.com/c/ExtemporeArt
S M Scott https://www.instagram.com/jellybean3302/
Rhonda Smith Withers Art https://linktr.ee/rhondasmithwithers
Chris "Chumpy" Lyons https://www.allmylinks.com/chumpyssketchbook
Holly J Cat: https://linktr.ee/hollyjcat
Marianne Hasseldal https://www.instagram.com/weirdlyuntimely/
Cindy Diel https://www.instagram.com/dielartful/
Teresa A Gagnon https://www.instagram.com/tagteresa/
Gingah Snaps https://linktr.ee/GingahSnapsArt
Corey Johnston https://www.coreyartusimagery.com/
Christopher Doll https://christopher-doll.com/

YOUR IDEAS MATTER

1. DON'T SEEK APPROVAL WHEN YOU SHARE YOUR IDEA.
2. DON'T SHARE YOUR IDEA UNTIL IT HAS LEGS.
3. JUST GET STARTED, IT WILL EVOLVE TO PERFECT.
4. TWEAK & MEASURE HAPPINESS AS YOU GO.
5. DON'T BE AFRAID TO GO IN A NEW DIRECTION.
6. REMEMBER THAT IT IS IMPOSSIBLE TO FAIL (UNLESS YOU GIVE UP)
7. CHECK CONSISTANTLY FOR GENUINE REASONING.
8. HAVE FUN & ENJOY YOUR CREATION
   -RAFI

Art By RAFI

INTRODUCTION

Welcome, creative human! We are about to enter the weird and wild world of marketing… In other words, we are going to talk about putting you and your art out there. Don't worry, this isn't one of *THOSE* books. Instead, this book is meant to empower artists all over the world to share their powerful message and story.

Interestingly enough, I had no intention of ever writing a book on marketing. I've never really been into any of the boring stuff people insist is "marketing". For most people, marketing is a blackhole of analytics, spreadsheets, fancy acronyms, and stretching the truth in order to get what you want. It can leave a really bad taste in your mouth if you follow the typical approach. However, marketing can be so much more than that. It can be art in and of itself. As it turns out, marketing can be all about creativity, powerful mindsets, and practical ways of approaching the world with your creations. It can be meaningful.

As artists, we have a superpower when it comes to putting ourselves out there, yet most of us try to follow boring and "proven" strategies to try and sell our art. This cookie cutter way of putting yourself out there can really stifle your creativity and lead you on a path to nowhere.

Marketing can actually be simple, fun, and quite exciting when you make it part of your own creative craft. In this book we are going to cover a straightforward and practical approach that will leverage your unique creative abilities – thus using your creative power vs. trying to make you fit in a marketing box.

That doesn't mean it is going to be all unicorn farts and rainbows. In the process of putting myself out there for over a decade, I've run into some roadblocks. Things are going to seem to be working against you sometimes – bad timing, glitches online, crashes, bad weather, opportunities disappearing, and lack of any support.

You must be exceptionally stubborn. Luckily for me, I was *VERY* stubborn and not willing to stop going for it. I bumbled through it and eventually made it all work. I created a life that I love. Not by hustling or chasing an algorithm, but by remaining true to myself. I make a comfortable living and I enjoy what I do. I create what I want to create, and I didn't jump through anyone's hoops to get here.

The more I did this whole art career thing, the more I realized typical marketing was mostly a dog and pony show. It rarely works for artists, not really, not in the long run. In fact, for the most part, typical marketing felt disingenuous and smarmy. Much of the hustle culture tactics that are preached are measured by fast and unsustainable results.

Here is something you should know before reading on. If you are looking for typical information about analytics, engagement, bounce rate, churn rate, conversion path, CPL, CRO, CAC, NPS, PPC, ROI, SEO and all the other fancy marketing acronyms out there, then you are SOL (So Out of Luck). Also, if you think you have to cheat, lie, or pretend to be something that you are not to get ahead in life, then you are going to hate this book. If you are into hustle culture and it's all about closing the sale, then this book may seem like scribbles from a mad man.

Rogue marketing is simple — it's all about building long-term mutual excitement, and cultivating human relationships and trust. That's it. The truth is that no matter what you do, you are always marketing the crap out of something. It could be your art, a brand that you like, your grandma's delicious lemon cake, or anything else that excites you. It may not feel like what you are doing is marketing, but it is.

Believe it or not, even when you are too shy to share your work, commenting on someone else's post, or walking down the street, you are marketing yourself. Everything we do tells a story about us. Our personal rhetoric, excuses, and reasonings all tell a story. You don't even have to come up with a story — being human and being your weird self is a unique story in and of itself.

As artists, we are like mythical creatures trying to fit into a world where they want us to believe magic is a thing of the past. An artist trying to do typical marketing is like asking a powerful wizard to post in the classifieds instead of using magic to promote their next feat of magic.

That being said, there is nothing wrong with the word "marketing". It's just a word. In essence it means to *put yourself out there*. However, the magic is lost in the way most people try to use it.

The problem is when you call it "marketing," it's attached to all kinds of shticks of "proven methods, for a limited time, two for one, free shipping, free introductory rates, or sign up for a free this or that." Everyone seems to be marketing…well, marketing. Despite what a lot of marketing courses, marketing people, marketing gurus, and your Uncle Steve have to say, marketing IS NOT A SALES TACTIC. It can be so much more than that.

So why am I taking on the subject of marketing and writing this book?

If I'm being real here, my time would be better utilized creating art and not taking on this challenge. However, I look at marketing as an art in itself and honestly, I am tired of the bullcrap information that is out there. I am sick of seeing artists or creative business owners fall for the same marketing rhetoric wrapped up in neat little bows. I'm writing this book for every creative individual in the world who feels confused, discouraged, and deflated by all the hustle. I'm writing this to demystify artists out there who think there is some secret to getting your work out in front of the "right" people. I'm writing this book because it is what I needed to hear when I was lost in the jargon.

The fact is that a "proven" method is not going to set you apart from the crowd. Great marketing is tailored to showcase the personality of the person putting themselves out there. This means that no marketing information is going to have an ultimate answer for you. This book is not a step-by-step guide on how to market your art. You are going to have to think for yourself. I'll share mindsets, techniques, and strategies that I have used to put myself out there, but you'll have to come up with and act on your own way of doing things. That's where your power lies.

If you read my last book, *The Rogue Artist's Survival Guide*, then you already know that I am not a fan of cookie-cutter, step-by-step ways of sharing ideas. We are all unique and we all have our own approach to the world – embracing that is your ultimate challenge.

My goal with this book is that you walk away feeling confident in your ability to put yourself out there and let people find you. I want you to have a solid footing when it comes to marketing yourself. Most importantly, I want to show you how marketing can be a creative adventure that you can enjoy and have fun with.

THE STRUGGLE IS REAL.

It is not an illusion that being an artist is challenging. As it turns out, trying to make a career of being an artist is an easy way to feel like you are stuck in a never-ending loop of craptastic nothingness. It's like walking around in the dark, feeling for barriers that you never knew existed.

When it comes to putting yourself out there, you might as well be on another planet trying to sell vegetables to alien trees who only eat meat. That's a terrible analogy, but it's how I felt when I started desperately trying to sell my art.

The worst part is going through the emotional anguish of putting your work out there, only to have nothing happen.

As a hopeful young human, who had his creative dreams squashed out of him for many years, it seemed like an impossibility to truly pursue an art career. I would have brief moments of inspiration, but I was lost when it came to putting my art out there. It wasn't for lack of trying, I would nervously share my art, only to walk away feeling ignored and stupid.

WHAT AM I DOING WRONG?!!!

That's the problem – you face the fear of putting yourself out there and then no one notices. No one listens. It can make you feel small and meaningless. This kind of experience can fuel doubt and the insecurity that although it is possible for someone else, you are simply not good enough.

Before I became the rogue I am now, I was painfully shy, insecure, and lost in the rhetoric of what the art world is *supposed* to be. I had the unbearable tendency to quit my attempts to be an artist more often than I like to admit. I didn't believe I had what it takes to make my dreams a reality. I bought into the lie. The truth is we all have what it takes to make our dreams a reality even if we don't know it yet.

Many years ago, I didn't understand that we either pave our own road or jump through confusing hoops to get where we want to go. As a result, I ran in circles and bumped my head on the same obstacles over and over. One of my attempts to put my artwork out in the world was so demoralizing that I quit creating art for almost two decades. At the time, I managed a coffee shop in the River North area of Chicago.

The area was filled with upscale restaurants, hundreds of shops, and – more importantly – fantastic art galleries. I dreamed of one day selling my art there.

It came to my attention that a few of my part-time employees were artists and they were making good money from their art creations.

This both annoyed and inspired me. I couldn't grasp how they were doing it, but I figured it was my opportunity to finally get into the art scene in the area. I invited artists to show their work in the coffee shop, and I put up a few paintings myself.

Location! Location! Location! Is one of those things we hear in marketing all the time, and I was primed and ready for success. The store I was managing was in a prime location.

There was a lot of foot traffic from art seekers, so I banked on the assumption that some would be interested in owning my works. I figured the only reason the other artists were making money was because they already showed their art in the area. I expected the big bucks to roll in. I had *FINALLY* made it to the big leagues.

However, months went by, and I sold nothing. People admired my art, but everyone seemed to be deathly allergic to buying it.

One of my employees, *he who shall not be named*…or *John*, was selling his art consistently. Just about every week, one of his pieces would be in the hands of a smiling human exiting the store.

Meanwhile, I wasn't smiling. I hate to admit it, but I secretly loathed his success. John unwittingly became my arch nemesis.

Confused and desperate, I took a closer look and noticed that his (and others) art prices were significantly lower than mine. In fact, thinking back, my pricing was a little ridiculous.

I was under the impression that art was only taken seriously when it was expensive – and I mean *VERY* expensive.

I priced my work like a seasoned artist who showed art at high end galleries, but the reality was I had no track record. No one knew who I was. I had never participated in any prior art shows, I had no collectors to speak of, and there was zero demand for my work.

In other words, no one was knocking down my door to get their hands on my art. Yet I priced my art as if I was at a high-end auction house.

I look back at those times and recoil a little at my pricing. I struggled with pricing because of the perception that real art sells for hundreds of thousands of dollars. This concept is bullcrap, but no one talked about practical business when it came to art. Most of the lingo I heard was about 'starving artists' starving to death or 'elite artists' making millions. This distorted my point of view drastically and I had no idea where to start with pricing. Everywhere I looked, the advice was confusing.

If No One Knows Who You Are, Then Why Would They Buy Art From You?

The truth is, I was trying to prove myself to be a "real" artist by pricing my art at what I thought were "real" art prices. However, instead of setting myself apart as a "real" artist, all I managed to do was repel people. The other art selling in the coffee shop averaged $300 - $1000 each. So, I did the only thing I could think of that made sense. I dropped my art prices to an average of $250 each. That's right, I decided to undercut all the other artists in the shop. Admittedly not my finest moment, but at the time, I thought I was brilliant.

I knew that penetration pricing is a marketing strategy used by businesses to attract customers to a new product. My art was a new product, so I figured I would offer a lower price during its initial release and watch the green stuff roll in. John wouldn't know what hit him. In my imaginary rivalry I felt like I was about to finally show him who was boss by beating him at his own game.

The next day, I eagerly awaited the droves of people who would be ignoring the now overpriced work and flock to my discounted art.

I sold nothing.

To my horror, three of the now "overpriced" paintings belonging to John were purchased by smiling happy humans and exiting the coffee shop. At this point, I felt defeated. I figured it was either a conspiracy, or I was *really* missing something.

Finally, in an act of desperation, I pulled my arch-nemesis to the side and asked him what the secret was to selling art. What was I missing?

John smiled, "There is no secret. I've been putting myself out there for years, and people are familiar with my work and my story." I nodded my head and pretended to understand what he meant. He continued, "I've made a lot of friends through my art, so they collect my work and support what I'm doing. It's not rocket science."

This didn't answer my question. I wanted the secret, and I felt he was lying. I was putting myself out there, and no one cared. Stupid John.

Looking back, his words make absolute sense now. At the time, however, I could not wrap my mind around what he was saying. I didn't understand what it really meant to put yourself out there.

I had been playing it safe and thinking short term compared to John and his simple notion of connecting with people. I just wanted people to give me money for my art so I could feel like a real artist. I was blinded by my need for validation and eventually it would bring everything crashing down.

After three months of not selling anything, I took ALL the work off the walls. I figured my art wasn't good enough, I wasn't good enough, and it felt like there was no point to any of it.

Back then, I felt so lost. As an artist, I wandered around aimlessly, desperately trying to find someone to validate or approve my creativity. I drove myself crazy trying to figure out how to get people to pay attention. I bought into the myth that I had to be tortured and misunderstood to pursue something I love.

Back then, I connected to Van Gogh. I believed this was a tragic story of an artist who loved to create beauty, and no one appreciated how he saw the world. No one paid attention to him until after his death, and I felt that my fate would be the same. However, unlike Van Gogh, I gave up, set my brushes aside, and vowed never to paint again. End scene.

I'm not telling you this story to discourage you. In fact, quite the opposite. Like Van Gogh and other starving artists, I perpetuated my own lack of success by how I approached putting myself out there. I did it to myself, although at the time, I was blaming everyone else. I blamed my parents, society, the art world, teachers, the world, stupid John, and anyone else I could point a finger at.

It was easier to believe that it was someone else's fault than to admit that I was standing in my own way. The fact is, I was the one who thought the way I did. I had given up, and I believed the myths that would lead me nowhere.

The concept of the "starving artist" is a myth. Art being appreciated only after someone dies is a myth. "Only the lucky ones succeed" is a myth. Living a tortured misunderstood life as an artist is a myth. Falling into obscurity is a myth. It's all like a depressing Grimm's fairy tale with a tragic and horrible ending. However, in reality, it is a silly narrative that we repeat to ourselves to keep us from REALLY going for it.

The truth is that as creatives, we hold our destiny in our own hands, and we do not need anyone's permission or validation to be successful.

I had to throw away everything I thought I knew about the art world, marketing, and why people buy art. Most importantly, I needed to stop listening to all the regurgitated advice on marketing that people love repeating.

I'm talking about *ACTUALLY* putting yourself out there. This is the stuff that made Van Gogh famous after his death. It's the reason you know who Banksy, Warhol, or Picasso is. Understanding how successful artists innovate and create their own marketing tactics is how I went from being clueless to making a living with my art.

Most marketing is based on the idea of finding a need, creating a product to fill that need, and then using typical advertising to proclaim that you have the best solution for said need. This is a very cookie-cutter approach to marketing your goods, products, or services. There's nothing wrong with that.

I GOT WHAT YOU NEED!

The approach persists because in the arena of general goods and services, it works. It's like two gladiators battling in a colosseum with cotton swabs to prove which product is superior. The cotton swab that becomes champion will be the most sought after and colosseum goers will have cleaner ears because of it.

This is Marketing

Unfortunately, it doesn't really work that way for artists. It makes no sense to battle for dominance with the unique art we are creating. We are not selling mass produced goods and no two artworks are alike.

We have a much more significant advantage over what typical marketing can offer. We are creative, scrappy, innovative, unique, and bold. We already stand out, and don't need to sacrifice our integrity to get attention.

As a *Rogue Artist,* you are not jumping through hoops to get ahead or seeking validation. This sets you apart from everyone out there using "proven" methods, templates, and roads that are most traveled. Like a breath of fresh air, you will bring something new and much more exciting than typical marketing.

Let's Get Luck Out of The Way

Before we proceed into more marketing nitty-gritty, I want to touch on something VERY important. Successful artists are told all the time that they are lucky to be doing what they do for a living. To be honest, I always feel a little insulted by this.

I personally struggled for many years to get to where I am, and I still struggle. The truth is that anyone who is doing what they love has to work to get there. Most of this work goes unnoticed and many times it is built on multiple failures.

It is common to claim luck as a reason why someone succeeds. In fact, it is so common that most times people say it as a compliment. They'll say things like, "You are so lucky to be doing what you love" as if it just fell out of the sky one day and chose me.

The only thing that ever fell out of the sky and "chose me" was bird poop... and hilariously enough, people like to say bird poop landing on you is lucky too.

I call *bird poop* on all of that. As a Rogue Artist, I realize that the choosing is all up to me. I must choose my destiny and go for it every single day.

The truth is that you are either persistent enough to be at the right place at the right time or you are not. You are either pushing out of comfort zones and reaching for new horizons, or you are sitting around hoping to get lucky.

Claiming "luck" as an excuse sets unrealistic expectations of the commitment required to make an art career work. It is a waste of time and energy that you could be using to improve and grow.

"LUCK" IS A WASTE OF TIME.

I think it is detrimental and creates a limitation of possibilities. Whether you are waiting around to get lucky, or you think someone else was lucky, it is just a distraction from the truth. Many people argue that luck has everything to do with it.

This is because their run of "bad luck" will make sense of why they haven't made it yet. It's easier to blame it on luck than to take responsibility for your own actions, but it won't get you anywhere. It's easy to point a finger and say, "Yeah, that guy got lucky" without acknowledging how much work it takes to succeed. It may be easy, but it completely takes away any sense of power to shape your own destiny. Instead, you may become held hostage by the fickle nature of luck.

No matter who you are, who you know, or how talented you are, it's not going to be easy. You have to put yourself out there and face the arena. You have to go all the way and not timidly approach the world from the sidelines.

"Don't be them, be you"

"Post everyday, comment on everything"

"Where's your niche? "Don't be you, be them"
FIND IT!"

"Shove it in their face, grab their
wallet and run"

"Do exactly what I'm doing"

"Give me money and I'll give
you nothing and tell you it's
everything"

"Be original"

"Give me more money and I'll
tell you what really works"

"It's one size fits all"

"Don't waste time on painting...
network, network, network"

"These methods are golden"
- Alexander Fatpockets McDouchebag

WHY IS ART MARKETING SO CONFUSING?

In our modern times, when we want to know more about something, we look it up online. There is a vast sea of information on the internet about marketing yourself. Unfortunately, most of it can be deceptive.

As a hopeful and bright-eyed artist, you may turn to the digital landscape to find answers. This usually leads to more confusion, overwhelm, or being pointed in the wrong direction.

When I type *HOW TO MARKET MY ART* into search, all the results dominating the first five pages are articles from website builders, art marketing gurus, vanity galleries, or paid courses on marketing.

There is always a link to find out more and they all seem to want to sell you something.
At the end of the article or blog, you'll find a service that promises to better your future as an artist:

28

"Want to learn more about art marketing? Click here to buy our magazine!"

"Click Here to Request a Demo and see how (and why) thousands of artists are using X to grow their fine art businesses."

"Join X's Discovery platform to connect with art collectors and art enthusiasts around the world."

"Visit our Gallery Representation and Artist Promotion page for more information on how you can succeed."

This, my dear friends, is called *CONTENT MARKETING*. The content is the information you read on *how to market your art;* the marketing is them trying to sell you their marketing service. This is usually a blog or article page with some information that sounds smart and expert-like. It is meant to target a market that is most willing to purchase its products and services.

The target market in question are artists who are desperately trying to figure out how to market and sell their art. Considering you are reading this book, that might be you.

Unfortunately, this market is VERY easy to target. Many creatives are looking for a secret to selling their art, and if it seems like someone has an answer, they are most willing to jump at the opportunity. Each article will have some seemingly good information that will make the person writing it sound like an expert, but it will leave you wanting more.

This is by design. That's because experts make us dumb, but more on that later in the book.

One of the biggest roadblocks that artists and creatives run into when it comes to the world of marketing is that it can be so convoluted. The other roadblock is that most marketing strategies leave you feeling a little dirty and inexplicably ashamed.

Most of the information you read on marketing on the internet is just fluff. Have you ever wondered why some articles or blogs sound incredibly like one another? Is it because it's so true that people agree and thus make it the best advice? No…it's mostly regurgitated horse crap.

A couple of years ago, in my attempts to learn more about marketing, I accepted a freelance job as a content writer for an online marketing firm. I was also doing it for extra cash while navigating my art career. I found myself writing six articles a week on exterior construction and decorative elements.

COMPOSITE BORED… BOARD

I don't know anything about exterior construction, so I was asked to look up articles or blogs about the content I was writing about. The marketing company only wanted to make sure that I changed the writing so as to not plagiarize someone else's material. They would also provide additional notes suggesting a link back to a company's product but emphasized not mentioning the company by name.

They mostly wanted a compelling story from a human point of view that would relate to others. The title and content had to grab the person by relating to their situation.

In doing this kind of work, I realized that just about every helpful article on the internet is copied and altered from somewhere else. The more I've searched for information, the more astonished I am at how common this is. Content writers write *content* and most times they don't know much about the subject they are writing about. As a content writer myself, I realized that the quicker I came up with something, the more content I wrote, and the more money I made. Educational and helpful information wasn't necessary as long as the articles had an eye-catching title and some smart-sounding stuff written underneath.

In passing, I told a friend at the marketing company that companies like theirs are the reason information on the internet is so confusing. They are just putting a bunch of information out there without really checking sources.

She laughed and said, "Oh yeah, that stuff is just crap. We hire writers to do it and if it is eye-catching and sounds good, that's all we are looking for."

The internet is a marvel of human information, but along with human information comes a human trying to sell you something. It makes for a confusing and contradictory road that will leave you feeling stupid and lost if you are not informed on how it works. The fact is, most of the information we find on marketing online is all about getting your attention. It is marketing to you.

"Content Is King!"
"Influencer Marketing!"
"Clickthrough Rate!"
"Growth Hacking!"
"Advertainment!"

"Sure... BUT, WHAT DOES IT MEAN?!"

"Do you have five minutes for a free consultation on what we can offer you?"
Let's be honest. Most people that talk about marketing are trying to sell marketing. I personally don't think there is anything wrong with that if they

are helpful. The problem is that most times they will sell you the same type of marketing techniques that got you to sign up with them in the first place. Selling a marketing service to desperate artists is a very easy niche to target. Marketing *art* on the other hand, is so subjective, all encompassing, and unique that it is virtually impossible to use an existing niche, demand, or need. Let's face it, there isn't a group of desperate art collectors chomping at the bit to buy the first work of art they see. Most of the time, we are going to have to create our own niche, demand, or following.

Therefore, I am VERY skeptical of art marketing mentors and gurus. I can see the irony here. This is an art marketing book. Luckily for you, I'm just some schmuck who sells art and has no interest in opening an art marketing company. Besides, I don't have a secret answer for you, you are going to figure this out yourself. All I can do is be supportive and brainstorm some ideas.

No one has the answers for you, only you do. Despite this fact, a lot of people are going to claim to have answers for you – some are well meaning, and some just want your money.

I received a letter recently from somebody who had departed one of the many "art marketing mentorship" programs currently online. She stated that the marketing mentor instructed her to focus on only one kind of art.

This didn't sit well with her because she liked creating in multiple mediums. She said that the mentor wanted to put her in a tiny niche that she didn't like. She told him she had built up a following for over a decade and sold her art just fine. She just wanted to know how to grow her art business.

She went on to say, "His attitude is that not following his rules means failure. He gets rude instead of listening and figuring something out and just says, suck it up."

Upon reading this line, I immediately wanted to punch the "mentor" in his giant forehead. I'm not a violent person, but I don't react well to bullies. Especially ones who are full of themselves.

Over the years, I've been contacted by several artists who have had similar experiences. Many have taken online art marketing programs and have been very unsatisfied with the results.

Because I am someone who is skeptical and does extensive research into "Art Selling" opportunities. I checked backgrounds and found that, interestingly enough, this particular art selling mentor isn't even an artist. He's never sold art in his life, however, he sold a book on art marketing. To me, that is ridiculous. How can someone teach you to sell your art if they have never had to sell art themselves?

Unfortunately, even many *actual* artists that sell marketing courses struggled and had their financial luck turn around once they started selling "proven" art marketing courses to artists. Most of them stopped creating art once they started marketing their "art selling" courses.
I'm not here to say that all those programs are crap, but I think you should look closer at what you're getting into. Look at their background, especially

if you're going to be giving somebody your hard-earned money. If they know how to sell art, they should be making that maximum of their income from selling art, just saying.

The truth is that there are a whole bunch of people out there claiming to have the answers for just about anything that someone wants a quick fix for. That's because the quick-fix is the EASIEST product category to advertise and do marketing for. We live in a quick-fix culture. Everyone wants to:

- *Lose weight fast.*
- *Gain muscle fast.*
- *Meet a soulmate fast.*
- *Cure this or that fast.*
- *Make money fast.*
- *Learn to draw like a pro fast.*
- *Sell art fast. Make $100K in your first year.*
- *Become popular fast.*

Quick fixes are ultimately easy to market because people believe these things will bring them happiness. It is like Jack trading his cow for magic beans.

"Stop my boy! I'll swap your cow for magic beans. They'll bring you lots of joy." Jack thought this was a great offer and replied, "You've got a deal!"

- Jack and The Beanstalk

Most of us want to take the magic beans and move on with our lives to bigger and brighter days. Because of this, artists who are desperate to make their art career a reality are ripe for the picking. However, quick fixes rarely work and end up discouraging them further.

Creative types are notoriously filled with a churning sea of insecurities. Heck, not a day goes by that I don't have a bout of imposter syndrome or feel like what I do is meaningless. We live on a tightrope held together by strands of uncertainty. We may find ourselves drawn to the security in someone claiming to know the secret straight shot to circumvent failure.

Unfortunately, those answers are often dependent on you fitting into a mold that was never designed for you. You either force yourself to fit, cutting off bits and pieces of your creative soul, or you walk away feeling like an even bigger failure. Either way, you may lose in the end.

Many of these courses make it sound like they have the ultimate answers to all of your struggles. They may claim a proven method, secret formula, or insider information. Usually, it is touted as something they discovered that no one knows anything about. Honestly, none of it is all that revolutionary. It's all common marketing tactics that may get you a little more attention, but that's about it. It's all stuff you can do on your own.

Think of what makes sense for you and the art you create.

For example, if you sell wine paintings or paint vineyard landscapes, it makes sense to contact wineries and places that sell wine. You may want to go to wine culture hangouts, wine groups, and wine tasting festivals.

You would find out if there are ways to display your art at any wine events. You would also want to find online groups and become part of that culture.

It's just common sense. It is a specific niche, and it is easy to target that market, because the market already exists. In other words, it is a group of people that have a common interest in what you are selling. It is marketing 101.

Typical marketing isn't terrible for artists who create art that already has an existing market. I think people who are timid about putting themselves out there may benefit from taking some of these art marketing courses.

However, when you niche yourself and only focus on creating one type of art, you may end up eliminating other possibilities for yourself. When I think about putting my art out there and the way I market myself, I realize that most of the rules in marketing do not apply to us crazy creative types.

We are all in a league of our own and what we create reflects that in several ways:

- Mass Products and Fine Art don't work the same.
- As Artists, we are not in competition with anyone. Artists establish themselves and their art as a unique brand. The only way to compete is to copy another's art exactly.
- Artists are more innovative than most marketing people that are out there.
- Artists evolve and grow, and thus the way they put themselves out there will evolve and grow as well.
- Artists are busy, and don't need extra complicated crap to do or think about. We want to be creative. Most cookie-cutter marketing is not clever, not creative, and it is tedious.
- As artists, what we create matters to us. We are not just going to make what is considered popular in our area if we hate doing it. Any artist who has experienced this knows what kind of private hell that could be.

- As artists, we are nonconformists who have the creative ability to blaze our own unique trail. There is NO ONE out there that knows better than us how to put ourselves out there.

- No matter how much someone tries to niche us as artists, we are like a round peg in a square hole. It is just not sustainable to the creative spirit, so stop telling us what to be.
- We can create our own market. The goal is to have a market of collectors that collect your art. Doesn't matter what it is – they do not collect it simply because it is vineyard art, pet portraits, abstracts, or falls into an existing market, but because it is the art that you created.

We all can be extraordinary in what we put out into the world, but we have to throw away the myth of what marketing and sales are supposed to be. We must throw away the stereotype of what we think we are capable of as artists. We must stop looking on the internet for answers and trust in our own creativity to make a splash.

Plenty of people will say that they are experts in marketing and will tell you that there are rules of engagement. They will say you can't do it without them, but they are wrong. You are in control of your own destiny.

Do not leave your fate in someone else's hands. Be skeptical about who you allow to have input in your art career and how you put yourself out there. No one will care about it as much as you do, so if someone tells you to "suck it up" and do it their way, ask them to eat a *bag of shirts.*

So, beware of the experts because the only reason you are listening to what they have to say is that you deem that they are an authority. Chances are, you think they are an authority because that's how they marketed themselves. The only expert in your unique art career is you and no one else. That includes me, so take everything I say with a grain of salt. I am giving you my **opinion**.

That really is the only thing anyone can give you. It is ultimately up to you to take what works for you and throw out the rest.

Things in the marketing world are constantly in flux, and everything gets mixed up in the word marketing. You have traditional marketing, digital marketing, influencer marketing, content marketing, and fifty other types that all fall under the marketing umbrella. In addition, people come up with new names for their marketing style to set themselves apart, and thus, you can add another name to the expanding list of types of marketing.

If this book becomes popular, countless articles will talk about Rogue Marketing written by people who probably never read the book but copied some information from some blog.

ROge... Rouge... Roog... Rogue.

The marketing world is confusing because of the lingo, buzzwords, and misinformation. I want you to just forget all that crap and focus on the simplicity underneath all the jargon. Honestly, all it takes is creativity, imagination, and persistence to put yourself out in the world in a powerful way.

These are qualities that artists have in spades. Besides, you are *ALREADY* putting yourself out there, whether you know it or not.

YOU ARE A CHAMPION!

WHY IS ART MARKETING NOT CONFUSING?

Despite everything in the last chapter, marketing is not actually all that confusing once you look at the core of what is behind ALL marketing. The simplicity of marketing understands that every time there is a possibility of interacting with another human, it is an opportunity to inform them of who you are and what you do. Whether it is virtual or in-person, if you realize that everything you write, say, record, paint, photograph, comment on, have a conversation about, or act on is marketing, then you understand what it's about.

Everything we say, do, and share is part of our brand. Everything.

1. A conversation in an elevator is marketing.
2. A comment on a video you like or dislike on YouTube is marketing.
3. Your body language when talking to someone is marketing.
4. Who you talk to and hang out with is marketing.
5. The meaning behind the art you create is marketing.
6. How much art you create and share is marketing.
7. The clothes you wear are marketing.
8. The hobbies you have are marketing.

Marketing, at its simplest form, is communication. How you communicate to the world is ultimately what will represent how people see you and your art. Because of this, I try to remain as authentic as possible.

EVERYTHING YOU DO MATTERS.

Let me take a moment to explain what authenticity means to me. The fact is, that when you are being yourself, not everyone is going to like you. Whether it is you or someone else, we all have our passive aggressive moments where we are less of a representation of who we actually are or want to be.

We may have moments where we fear losing control because we are angry, we feel insecure, or lack self-esteem. We may be feeling stress, anxiety, depression, insecurity, or be dealing with rejection or some conflict. We might be holding a grudge or feel underappreciated at that moment. This is why before I say, share, or do anything, I ask myself some simple questions.

What does this say about me?
Is this who I am?
Is this who I want to be?
Am I being real?
In my opinion, being authentic does not mean that you air all your dirty laundry or throw daggers at other people. Being authentic means living

your life according to your own values. Other people may have differing opinions than you on how to live, but you're ok with that because you live life to your own tune. Put simply, authenticity means you're true to your own personality, values, and spirit, regardless of the pressure you may be under to act otherwise.

I personally think that people who are genuinely authentic:
Don't try so hard to make people like them.
Accept their mistakes and embrace them.
Don't waste any time judging other people or themselves.
Reflect on who they are and what they want often.
Give without expecting anything in return.
Respect everyone's opinion, even if they disagree.
Speak their mind without being confrontational.
Are transparent about their motives and have no hidden agendas.
Are reliable in how they behave.

Everything you put out into the world, say and do, says something about you. So even a troll that might be harassing your social media page, being rude and obnoxious, says more about them than about you. Think about it, that troll's advertising only appeals to people who may be trolls. Everyone else will most likely be repulsed by it.

However, your response to the troll will say everything someone needs to know about you and not the troll.

Think about it this way. If someone is walking down the street and other people can see them, they are communicating something. They wear what they wear, they walk how they walk, they look at what they pay attention to, what they say, who they talk to, their facial expression, and anything else people can observe. It all tells a story. This story is your brand image. If you see a young person assisting an older person across the street, there is a story there, even though you have no real idea who these people are.

Before you freak out because you think you are constantly being watched, remember that this is already happening. This is how we all navigate the world. We are continually communicating. The question is, are you aware of what you are saying?

If your personality is hateful, optimistic, negative, pessimistic, joyful, hopeful, suspicious, discouraging, encouraging, apathetic, or whatever, you will attract more of the same you communicate into the world. You will find your people. It's not about being one thing or another. It's about being who you are and figuring out what you are all about, whatever that may be.

It is simple.

Everything you communicate with another human is your marketing and represents your art and your brand. Your brand is you. So, keep that in mind when putting yourself out there. Ignore the specifics that marketing experts are trying to sell you that confuse the situation.

Keep it simple and remember – everything you publicly say, don't say, do, don't do, create, and don't create is your marketing.

Ask yourself these four questions when you are unsure what you are saying when putting or not putting something out there.

What does this say about me if I put it out there?
What doesn't this say about me if I put it out there?
What does this say about me if I don't put it out there?
What doesn't this say about me if I don't put this out there?

360 DEGREE PERSPECTIVE!

Marketing is everything you do to put yourself out there and how you do it. The act of putting yourself out there is the most terrifying, awkward, and powerful experience a creative human will ever have. It is an essential part of our creativity. Our art takes on a new life once it is unleashed onto the world.

Therefore, I am not a big fan of hiding behind a screen and purchasing ads or deciphering analytics. If your focus is on the numbers and not the emotional aspect of communication, you can get lost in it. The numbers have nothing to do with actually putting ourselves out there. This is why most art marketing programs are popular. The act of purchasing a program may make you feel proactive, but you might still be hiding. It's easy to hide when you are being told what to do and how to think.

The problem with this is that you must be willing to not follow the same tactics that EVERYONE else is following to set yourself apart. If a method is "proven," it means *everyone is doing it*. No one wants to willingly put themselves in front of the firing squad of critics. So, they may hide and toss their stuff out in the world with no personality attached to it.

We are artists, which goes against the very nature of cookie-cutter. The most important thing I have learned from watching successful artists is how they turned marketing into a part of their creativity, innovation, and communication. It became an art form in itself and allowed them to say something to the world.

The truth is that we are all experts at marketing when it's not our own stuff. We say things like, "You should read this book, I think you'll really like it." or "You should try the food at this restaurant, it's delicious." All of that is marketing. We already use marketing and sales every day. One reason we may not associate this with marketing is because it is honest. We *REALLY* think that particular person will like or benefit from what we are suggesting.

And that my dear friends is the ultimate reality of marketing. The things you are really excited about, are the things that you will share with others. Whether it is something you are wearing, using, looking at, saw somewhere, read, or created, you will tell others about it. You will wear it, share it, exclaim it, talk about it, show it off, and recommend it. If another person connects, they will share in that mutual excitement and do the same exact thing. That is how things go viral. However, it starts with one person's excitement and desire to share.

Do you walk the walk? Do you talk the talk? Do you excitedly share your art for the simple fact that you are excited about your art? Either way, you are telling a story. So, what story are YOU telling?

TELL YOUR STORY.

WHY DOES MARKETING MAKE ME FEEL DIRTY?

Remember that time in the last chapter, when we covered how readily and excitedly we share stuff we love with other humans? Most of the things we buy are recommended by someone out there who is excited about that particular thing. We, for the most part, love the art we create, yet may not talk about it with much vigor. Why do we feel comfortable recommending things we like, but would rather staple our eyelids shut than talk about our own creations with the same enthusiasm?

A whack perspective and motive.

Let's talk about this. When you recommend or give a shoutout to a thing you like, you are doing it from a buyer's perspective. You experienced the benefits and want to share those amazing advantages with the humans you're recommending it to. You're not doing it for financial gains or personal glory (unless you're an influencer… just kidding… mostly…that's for a different book). No matter how you look at it, the only real gain you get from recommending something you love is passing on the benefit to someone else. Your motives are crystal clear.

A lot of creatives feel dirty sharing or promoting their art because while they may understand the benefit they experience in creating it, they're less certain of the benefits gained by the person that might want to own it, or whether it benefits other people at all. Artists get all crazy in their mind when they look at their own art through someone else's eyes.

In other words, creatives sometimes have a hard time putting themselves in the perspective of the potential collector and understanding how and if what they make has value. This means that putting it out there feels like a selfish, self-serving act. Throw potential financial gains into the mix (you made the thing, so if someone buys it, you get money) and suddenly, your motives feel downright muddy.

It can be tricky to put yourself in the perspective of the collector and understand how they would benefit from what you create.

You're not the only one who struggles with it. Large companies have spent billions trying to understand what humans value and benefit from, and how best to tap into that.

Assuming you don't have billions to spend, or a research team at your disposal, here are some questions you can ask yourself to gain a deeper understanding of how your art can benefit the people that might connect with it.

- Am I putting my art out there because I want to share it, or am I simply trying to sell?
- How would I talk about my art if I knew the person was going to buy it?
- How would I talk about my art if I knew the person was not going to buy it?
- How would I talk about my art if I knew the person would benefit from it?
- How would I talk about my art if the person viewing it was in tears because the art really touched them in a powerful way?
- What if this was art by another artist and I LOVED it, how would I talk about it then?

I think marketing became a little more twisted over the years when people had to learn to sell products that they don't believe in. I mean, c'mon, how passionate could you really be about selling carbonated brown sugar water? That's where deception became a standard in marketing and sales. This is one of the main reasons that marketing can feel dirty.

However, as artists, we are selling something we cultivate and believe in.

That's why most marketing doesn't apply to us creative folks. Most marketing relies on setting some kind of imaginary bait and sucking the potential customer in with a ruse. Whether it is an exaggeration, puffery, or a false promise, it all relies on some kind of scheme.

It's all about convincing someone past their skepticism to believe that the product is what you say it is.

For example, if I said that this book will help you achieve your dreams of being a successful and highly paid artist in six months, you may not believe me. However, if I say that I achieved success, money and awards in four months using the secret techniques that the elite artworld doesn't want you to know, some of your interest will perk up. If I follow that up with video testimonials from hundreds of artists who read my book and became mega successful within six months, then I might have you in my evil clutches.

Obviously, there is nothing I can say in this book that is going to make you a mega successful artist, that is clearly up to you, but false promises are so common in marketing that they have become the standard.

Speaking of standards, as humans, we are all very well-versed at playing these mind games as well. We are all experts at trying to get our way and sometimes going so far as to lie in order to get what we want. It is a rough truth, but unless you are aware of this fact, you may not even notice it. We may make excuses for it, like calling it a white lie, or saying it was necessary, but it's a lie nonetheless. This is marketing in a nutshell, and it is all around us. We are steeped in it every day. You know it so well that you use it in everyday life.

For example, If you have kids, you may be trying to convince them to clean up their dirty room. How would you market that concept? How was it marketed to you as a kid? Is it ok to lie in that situation? By the way, these are ALL marketing tactics.

- **You can offer incentives** like, "We'll go to the movies when you finish cleaning your room."
- **You can offer a checklist** on what to do with rewards for each item done. Yup, still marketing.
- **You can threaten punishment.** Believe it or not, this is marketing too.
- **You can turn cleaning the room into a game and promise a big reward at the end.** Also, marketing.
- **You can try bribery.** This is called a kickback and is used in marketing all the time.
- **You can use a personal fear against them**, such as, "When your room is dirty like this, it attracts biting snakes, and I know you are terrified of biting snakes. Luckily, biting snakes hate clean rooms." Again marketing, also, as a side note, awful parenting.
- **You can use social comparison to threaten.** For example, "Santa is going to bring you coal if you don't clean your room."
- **You can post a post-it note** that reads "Clean this" on their door and every area in the room that needs attention. This is still marketing.
- **You can repeat**, "Clean your room" for ten minutes until, at wit's end, they engage in the process. Yes, still marketing.
- **You can make them a false promise**. Tell them that their favorite superhero cleans their room, "You should be more like Thor. He always cleans his room. How do you think he got those muscles?" You guessed it, marketing.
- **You can compare them** to the "better" sibling or friend. Start a competition by saying, "Don't you want to be better than John? Because right now, John is better than you." This is marketing… and just plain wrong.

- **You can offer to upgrade something they own.** Just say, "The new (fill in the blank) came out, but only kids with clean rooms can get the new one." You guessed it, marketing.

- **You can use the 'this or that' method** by saying things like, "People on the other side of the tracks may not clean their rooms, but we are not those people… do you want to be THOSE people?" It really doesn't matter what side of the tracks one is on, just as long as someone points a finger to the other.
- **You can call them lazy and ungrateful and tell them this is why they don't have nice things** in the hopes that it will guilt or demoralize them to change. You guessed it, still marketing.
- **You can be overly nice until they change their behavior because they don't want to disappoint you.** Indeed this is marketing.

These only scratch at the surface, but ultimately every tactic works to one extent or another. However, just like typical marketing, it doesn't work all the time. Another tactic that is very effective in marketing is playing *the long game*. This is the marketing that goes unnoticed. The same tactics are used in brainwashing, so it is very elaborate and involves a lot of propaganda. Luckily for us, most parents aren't *that* dedicated to clean rooms.

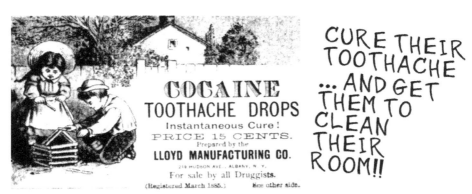

Most companies that dominate right now and advertise the most have been advertising to the underlying narrative for generations. It's been layering perspectives for years.

Sounds ridiculous, right? However, we have all been inundated with marketing since before we were born. It's been there for generations, and

51

it may have molded our thinking to one extent or another. Who in your family swore by some product that you now use?

It may not be creepy parents trying to mold us into comfortable room cleaning robots, but we have been bombarded with tactics that we may not even recognize as marketing from day one. This is because marketing and sales underneath the tactics are more about how the brain works and what makes people think.

Advertising and sales are a byproduct of this. It explains why people sign up for "get rich quick" scams, even though we all know they are fake. As skeptical as we are, we are also extremely trusting of a compelling story and can get funneled into buying it.

THE SALES FUNNEL

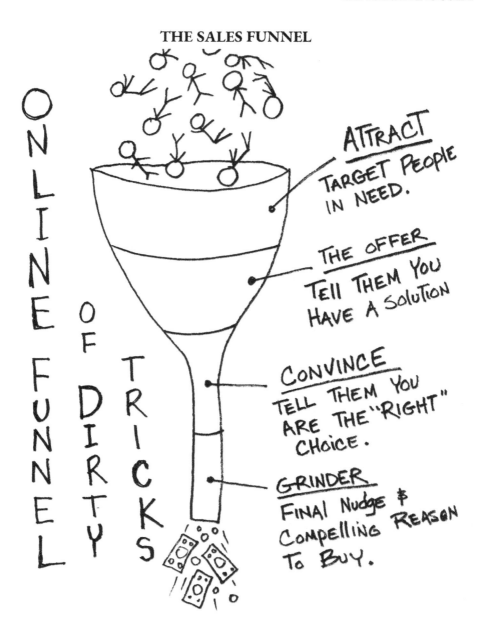

How Sales Funnels Work

I want to share a quick aside on how a sales funnel works. I'm sure you have heard this term by now, and most likely it was being touted as a *fix all* for your creative business.

Honestly, it's just a way to get people from one place to another if they are interested. Unfortunately, many times, they become the annoying reminder that you should have never signed up for that free eBook.

The goal with most marketing funnels is to turn leads into customers. In reality, this isn't how business works, but it can work depending on what kind of business you have. For example, if you are offering to teach people the secret of making $1000 a day by opening their own course, then this will work. Everyone wants to know how to make $1000 a day using their own skills.

Offer a free eBook or course and collect an email. For example, this is taken from an actual ad online:

Create Passive Income with a Simple Online Course [FREE Workshop]
Make $1000 dollars a day! Discover how 21,382 average people are
creating real passive income with their own online courses, including
how they:

Become the trusted expert in any niche using the "1 Step Rule"
Generate sales around the clock using a simple "1 page funnel"
Get (virtually) unlimited traffic from today's #1 traffic source...
Launch in 7 days (from scratch) without a team or complicated tech

As you can see this ad is VERY enticing. I mean, if an average person can do this, so can I. This is the perfect example of marketing to an emotional need where there is an easy fix to all your financial problems. These ads always look good as an example of what marketing is supposed to look like and yes, you can attract people, but ultimately what you are offering is what matters.

A marketing funnel is just a way to use the attention you are getting to find an easy way for them to get from point A to point B. So, how does it work?

Awareness: This is the point where they become aware of you with something compelling you put out there. This could be an event you did, some advertising, festival, blog post, online class, postcard, social media, search, and more. Honestly, ANYTHING that gets a person's awareness.

Interest: Next, they show interest and want to learn more about you, your art, and what you are about. This is also where you would ask them to sign up for your blog, newsletter, video channel, or anything. A lot of marketers will suggest offering something free for an email which I'm not a fan of. In my opinion, you can ask them to sign up, but don't bait and switch. Giving an email is a relationship building thing, if you offer something free, I feel it shouldn't cost an email.

Consideration: At this point, because someone showed interest, a marketing company will see them as a qualified lead. This is when the automated emails, targeted content, case studies, free trials, and all kinds of other things start showing up in the inbox.

Intent: most people will delete and unsubscribe at this point. However, there will be some people that will still be interested and will become heavily targeted. Something becomes the convincer. It could have been a survey, a product demo, or an item lingering in the shopping cart that they are still on the fence about. This is where a marketer would let the person know that the product is the best one for them.

Evaluation: At this point the person is making a final decision whether or not to buy. This is typically where a discount or something is offered to gently nudge the person off the fence.

Purchase: Boom! The person finally buys what the marketer is selling.

MAKE THAT MONEY!

Honestly, most times funnels are used, they are selling something where the person needs to be strongly convinced that it will benefit them, or it will work. Many times, it doesn't. As Rogue Artists, we create benefits in everything we do, including our marketing and all of this happens automatically.

When putting yourself out there whether online or offline, collect emails so you can stay in touch, but use them to build a relationship. Write blogs and newsletters that bring the person a benefit in reading them, not just you trying to push your product.

Honestly, this will create much more long-term loyalty than trying to funnel humans through your cone of sales tactics.

Many of the sleazy, annoying, or boring tactics in marketing can be spotted on the surface. Underneath all of that, It is about being human. It's understanding human behavior and why things work in context. Before I scare you off, marketing and sales are not sleazy unless you are a sleaze. If you are selling something you believe in and love, you should not feel bad about marketing your creations to your people.

I think it is important to understand marketing on a much deeper level than just buying ads.

People will say things like, "I never fall for marketing." If you are part of the group that proudly proclaims this statement, I hate to break it to you, but you have no idea what marketing and sales are actually about.

We ALL fall for any marketing that gets past our skepticism. Some of it is from before our time and the perception is still alive today.

HALITOSIS IS A MADE UP WORD.

IN THE 1900S LISTERINE MADE IT UP. THEN THEY SAID THAT 1 IN 3 WOMEN HAVE IT.

LUCKILY THEY HAD THE REMEDY.

Some of the most prominent and most influential companies have shaped ideas and culture since the early 1800s. They've had time to perfect the narrative. If you doubt this, here are a few obvious and innocent examples of how marketing can shape minds and change the culture.

- "A Guide to Casual Businesswear" was a marketing campaign launched by Levi Strauss & Co. in 1997, which is why khakis are business casual, and sweatpants are not.
- A diamond is forever and is used as a symbol of marriage because of marketing in 1948.
- Guinness beer launched the "Guinness is good for you" campaign in 1929, and to this day, some people believe the beer is healthy for you.
- The hearty American bacon and eggs breakfast is the standard because of marketing in 1920.
- Orange juice is a breakfast drink because of a massive marketing campaign in 1907.

Marketing works because it can make us feel something and may shape our thinking. As artists, we create stuff from our imagination. Everything we create evokes an emotion.

So, when you are thinking that you have no power in shaping minds and hearts, I want to make it very clear that as creative people, we wield an extraordinary amount of power.

It's not dry businesspeople following some cookie-cutter structure coming up with methods to successfully market products for big companies. It is the creative, innovative, and divergent thinkers that change the world. That is why the best marketing agencies hire creative people.

As a *Rogue Artist*, you recognize the immense amount of responsibility you hold in your hands. Once you let go of the idea that there is a structure of rules to marketing and trust your own creative thinking, you will be unstoppable.

However, with great power comes great responsibility. Once you understand your creative power and influence, remember to benefit those that are listening. There are too many people in the spotlight spewing garbage, drama, and strife in exchange for popularity. Use it wisely, don't fall into the trap of chasing popularity by any means.

YOU'VE GOT THE POWER

We are masters of innovation, determination, do-it-yourself-ness, self-branding, publicity stunts, and creative thinking. We are experts in beauty, culture, and human behavior. Just the fact that artists exist is a rare oddity that compels people to look closer. We can't help it. We are fascinating creatures that live in a world that most people have never experienced.

However, the most common and repeated myth is that creative people are bad at business, sales, and marketing. Artists constantly tell me that they have a hard time with sales and marketing because their minds don't work that way. Honestly, this is horse-crap.

The problem is that most business courses, mentality, and tactics are uncreative and boring. There is nothing there to capture the imagination, which is what the expression of art is all about.

In most marketing, people get caught up in analytics, consistency, and information collecting. This could be extremely tedious and dull. Marketers will tell you to keep track of the numbers because they matter, and they do, but not as much as one would think. At least not for an artist.

If you rely on typical marketing by paying for ads, building your lists, social media, or product promotion, then yes, it's essential to keep an eye on the numbers. This, however, can cause you to quickly lose sight of the art of what it takes to actually put yourself out there. Ultimately, what creates a successful campaign isn't statistics and analytics. It's the excitement, innovation, creativity, passion, and deep belief in what you are doing.

Artists are some of the best marketers out in the world. Not because we are good at logical thinking, but because we are good at being authentic, unpredictable, and illogical. We can easily infuse our creative marketing strategy with drama, divergent thinking, performance, meaning, color, music, and passion. We can create and design our own materials and think beyond the scope of the ordinary. Once we start putting ourselves out there and face fears, we can become an unstoppable force.

YOU'VE GOT THE POWER!

I'MA RES SOU RCE FUL MOFO

That's why many marketing people will study artists, musicians, comedians, dancers, thespians, YouTubers, and others who think outside the box and innovate. We are creative geniuses who can think beyond the typical methods and develop new approaches. We are the creative directors of our own brand.

As creative people, we have a vast wellspring of resources at our disposal. We not only communicate in words, but we can use vibrations of sound and color to express what we want to say. We create communication through all the mediums. Marketing is communicating to the world that you exist. As artists, we communicate with color, music, and methods that can excite all the senses.

1. As visual artists, we create visual communication.
2. As a sculptor, we create visual and tactile communication.
3. As musicians or writers, we create audio communication.
4. As filmmakers, we create visual and audio communication.
5. As culinary artists, we communicate through touch, taste, and smell.

Every sense that is affected tells a story.

CAN YOU SMELL WHAT THE FROCK IS COOKIN'!

If there is any part of you that still thinks creativity and business don't mix, then you will have to push out of that box. The companies that do exceptionally well do so because they value creativity. I think as artists, we forget that. We undervalue our ability to approach the world from a creative perspective. Yet, people in business that are successful value their own creativity above anything else. Even Warren Buffett, who at the time of writing this book is an American investor, business tycoon, philanthropist, corporate rich guy, and the chairman and CEO of Berkshire Hathaway, says, *"I am not a businessman. I am an artist."*

SING TO YOUR OWN TUNE.

We lose sight of our power as creatives because we view things like marketing as a standardized process. We think there are rules and ways that you are *supposed* to market yourself. However, excellent marketing is like the standing egg challenge. If I asked you to make an egg stand on end without any assistance, how would you go about it?

Would you desperately try to balance it? Most people would find it absolutely impossible. Maybe with many hours of practice and effort, you might achieve it, but it is unlikely. Chances are you would give up at some point because it would be too tedious and time-consuming.

As Rogue Artists, we break the rules and think out of the box. With a small crack on one end, the egg will stand upright on its own. That is where innovation happens. We make up our own rules because we don't have the time or energy to deal with uncreative tediousness.

DO IT THE ROGUE WAY! YOUR WAY!

Here's what is interesting. Once that trick is performed, anyone willing to break the rules will achieve balancing the egg. You showed them how to do it, and eventually, that became the standard. The more people do it, the more it becomes the rule.

Everything that we know about business and marketing comes from innovative and creative people breaking the rules. The tactics are the result of a creative approach to problem-solving, not logical persistence. It is the creative mind that will always find the solution. Even Einstein relied on his imagination to figure out some of the mysteries of the universe.

The problem comes later. Someone tries to make sense of the innovation with spreadsheets, analytics, and data. This is when a myriad of contradictory rules on how to properly stand an egg start to show up all over the internet. They tell you the rules of how the egg should be cracked, what size the egg should be, and at what angle for the best results. They take something potentially fun and turn it into a tedious chore. Creativity is not something that can be distilled and bottled, and once it becomes a rule that everyone is following, it loses some of its magic.

That's why, as a creative individual, you must be willing to take what exists and tweak it to work for you. Your unique way of seeing the world will bring innovation if you are not simply following the rules like everyone else.

The same applies to marketing.

Our advantage as creatives is something to embrace and use to its fullest potential.

- A creative person can see the world from multiple perspectives. Understanding that problems can have more than one solution.
- A creative person thrives in the absence of rules and limitations. Whereas logical people tend to freak out a bit.
- A creative person improvises and is flexible when problems, circumstances, and opportunities change.
- A creative person doesn't rely on words or numbers to explain everything they know. They can see outside of that box.
- A creative person knows that minor changes can have significant effects.
- A creative person can inspire and describe using more than words.
- A creative person makes up their own rules because living in a box can cause them to become stagnant.

Many creative people may underestimate their power because they fear failure, unpredictability, conflict, and a lack of knowledge. Yet all innovation and things that haven't been created yet will face failure, be unpredictable, conflict in certain areas, and are unknown. To embrace creativity is to embrace risking failure. How you respond to failure is ultimately what matters.

It can be a work in progress, and you can learn from it. It can also be your reason to quit and lick your wounds. Ultimately, it's up to you.

To keep going means to embrace the creativity that lives and breathes within you. It means turning the idea of putting yourself out there into the most creative thing you can do and embracing everything that comes with that. This includes embracing failure.

FAILURE IS A WORK IN PROGRESS.

Not only is failure only a work in progress, but failure is a necessary ingredient for success. If you want to succeed at marketing yourself, you must be willing to fail. Many artists are timid in their approach because they are afraid to fail by having their efforts be ignored. Ironically, they may spend their time running away from failure because they don't realize failure is the path to succeeding. Innovating, experimenting, and trying new things that have not been done before will mostly crash and burn. Putting yourself out there in different ways will end up not working at first, but it is all part of the journey in finding your unique voice on your path to awesomeness.

To innovate, stop telling yourself that you can't do marketing. You can. Blaze your own trail and create your own marketing campaigns. Don't wait around for someone to tell you how. Do it now with the tools, resources, and brilliant creative mind you have at your disposal. Most importantly, remember that you are a person who is selling something of original value. How you put yourself out there should be original as well. You are a Rogue Artist. That means that everything you do is creative. The way you live your life, see the world, approach adversity, and put yourself out there is a creative occasion.

Stand up for the occasion that is your life by blazing your own trail and not waiting for someone to tell you how.

TYPICAL MARKETING

1. ~~CHECK LATEST STATS.~~ ← BORING!

2. (CHECK MENTIONS & REPLIES.) ← INTERACT WITH MY PEEPS

3. ~~MONITOR~~ BRAND MENTIONS. ← CHECK & SEE WHO SHARED YOU ☺

4. SET DAILY ~~GOALS~~. TRY TO POST OFTEN

5. ~~CHECK CONTENT SCHEDULE.~~ ← I DONT HAVE TIME, SO I'LL POST WHATEVER Im DOING

6. ~~CHECK MARKETING PLAN.~~ ← BORING

7. ~~CHECK YOUR COMPETITION.~~ ← STUPID.

8. FOLLOW INDUSTRY TRENDS. ← SEE WHAT SILLY STUFF IS GOING ON IN THE ART WORLD.

9. (CREATE) ~~A FOCUSED REPORT.~~ ← YES CREATE ART & COOL PROJECTS SO YOU CAN HAVE SOMETHING TO SHARE.

SO, WHAT'S YOUR STORY?

That's right, the most dreaded question you can ask an introverted creative person is to share their story. I have seen artists locked in terror at the very mention of the word *STORY*.

You've probably heard people in marketing talk about the importance of telling your story. Heck, I'm constantly going on about how important it is to tell your story, and I'm not even a marketing person. Anyone that knows anything about putting yourself out there will tell you that story matters. Earlier in the book, I pointed out that we always tell a story whether we mean to or not by just walking down the street. But how important is it really?

I'm going to say something very taboo right now, and a lot of you are going to gasp in disbelief, but I have to be honest with you. When it comes to art, the story is more compelling than the quality of the art.

Before you throw this book in the garbage, let me explain. This is one of the most powerful lessons I've learned. I'm not saying that the quality of your art doesn't matter, because it does. However, it can really only matter to you. We challenge ourselves to create better and better art, because we keep leveling up our own quality. However, no one else will agree on what that means, they see what they see.

When you look at one of the many priceless works of art from the great masters, you may be left in awe. However, as artists, we tend to look closer at something else when examining a work. We may see the nuances, brushstrokes, and technique. This allows us to catch a glimpse of the human who created it. Many times, we can identify areas where they might have gotten lazy or rushed the painting. As artists, we realize that although the world sees certain art as perfect, all art could be better. However, there is a perfection to that imperfection. In many cases it is in those cracks that we find a compelling story.

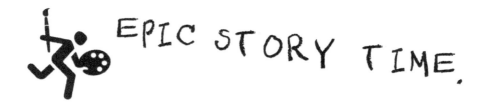

We get a genuine impression of another creative human's life with a snapshot of a moment in time. All those imperfections are what make it perfect.

Yet, that is the story most artists are afraid to tell. So instead, they try to compare their art to other people's art.

Countless artists love to point at a Jackson Pollock and condemn it as not being "real" art. They make up labels and hold art up to an unreachable standard, but they completely miss the point. It's completely worthless to criticize anyone's art, including your own.

Honestly, you are either creating art or pointing fingers from the sidelines. If you are creating and putting yourself out there, then you have a compelling story already. If you are finger pointing, then you may be too busy with someone else's story and probably don't have your own.

What is your message when you are finger pointing and criticizing? What does it say about you?

Whether you are selling fine art or a bottle of "this morning's fart," what ultimately matters is your story. Picasso, Van Gogh, Pollock, Dali, and any other artist you know by name have been popularized by their story.

"Story" is so powerful that large companies come up with stories for what their products stand for. A coke can teach the world to sing in perfect harmony because otherwise we wouldn't relate to an inanimate object. It is the story and association to that story that we relate to. As artists, we don't need to come up with a story – we are the story.

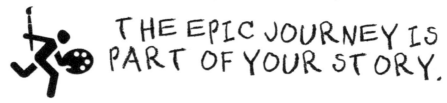

THE EPIC JOURNEY IS PART OF YOUR STORY.

This is the point where I've had artists angrily exclaim that they don't have a story. However, you do have a story, and it is still in the making. The simple act of putting yourself out there becomes a significant plot point in your narrative. When you go out there and face rejection, fear, being ignored, criticism, and keep going despite all of that, your tale becomes an epic saga.

Imagine for a moment if Dali, Picasso, Banksy, or Warhol quit when they ran into their first or second roadblock. Every one of these artists were ignored for a vast portion of their life, yet never settled for living a life where they faced no obstacles. What if they traded in their paint supplies for a stable job and security? What if they didn't push the envelope and themselves through the financially rough times? What if they quit? There would be no story.

Be Yourself. Be Real. Be Personal.

Your story may not feel like it is compelling, but it's not over. When you put yourself out there, the elements in life that put you where you are now will play a significant part of that narrative.

However, every good epic needs hardship and growth. So, when we embark on our journey to put ourselves out there, we create our own compelling story. Our novel is less of a hero's journey if we avoid rejection, fear, being ignored, criticism, and pain.

For example, here is my story:

As a kid, I dreamt of being an artist. I was a quiet and timid child in a very rambunctious and loud family. For most of my childhood, the adults were worried that there was something wrong with me. I would usually walk around quietly with a sketchbook instead of playing sports and roughhousing like the rest of the kids.

As a teenager, my dream had expanded to art, writing, music, and movies. I wanted to be a polymath creative and pursue living a creative life, however I was expected to work for the family business.

I remember telling my dad that I was going to be an artist, and he pretty much shot me down and laughed in my face. Around the same time, I blew an art scholarship by telling my art teacher off. At that point, I settled into the life that was handed to me.

Years later I had left the business and entered corporate life. The dream of being an artist burned inside me, but I stuffed it down as an impossibility. At this point in my life, I barely created any art and when I did, it was dark, depressing, and sad. It reflected who I was.

Someone who had given up on their dreams. Someone who bought into all the negative voices telling him he wasn't good enough. Someone who settled into the life he was told he was *SUPPOSED* to live.

Ok, let's pause for a moment. What if my story ended there? Honestly, it's quite the mood killer. Unfortunately, this story is way too common.

It's not compelling because this is just everyday life for a lot of people.

There's no hero's journey. Luckily for me, it wasn't the end, here's the cliff notes version of what happened next in my life.

Decades passed and I was sitting in a hotel room on a business trip and caught a glimpse of myself in the mirror. I didn't recognize the miserable human looking back at me and I realized life was too short. I decided to pursue my creative career no matter what obstacles would come my way.

For over a decade, I pushed through countless failures, rejections, financial struggles, and mistakes. With every step I took I faced biting winds of fear and doubt but kept moving forward.

One day, years in, I was sitting in a room and happened to catch a glimpse of myself in the mirror. I saw a bright-eyed artist who was living his dreams. I continue to face every struggle that comes my way head on, knowing that the life of your dreams doesn't fall in your lap. You must reach for it and happily push through the suck in order to make your own dreams a reality.

The most significant shift during my career as an artist was realizing that life wasn't typical for artists. We are like mythical beasts and heroes in an epic tale. Our lives may not make sense to most people because we willingly put ourselves in the crosshairs of critics and rejection.

Sadly, not too many people are willing to pursue their dreams, so just the act of putting yourself out there is compelling. Artists are creative, divergent thinkers, rogues, and pegs that don't easily fit into the social status quo. We can have a powerful narrative, but we must be willing to live that story.

The art I created, the blogs I wrote, the shows I did, the people I met, the conversations I had, and the hardships I faced all became part of my epic saga. As a Rogue Artist, I realized that putting myself out there *IS* my story, and my story is my creation. My story is just another artform. We are surrounded by these stories.

If you are reading this book right now, you have spent your entire life shaped by the storytelling around you.

Most of the things you know as valuable, cheap, important, frivolous, and possible are because of clever storytelling. The clothes you wear, the car you drive, the food you eat, and even some of the things you believe about the world can most likely be traced back to some story.

Growing up in the jewelry business and watching customers appreciate one thing over the other was fascinating. For example, when you open a Rolex or Timex watch, you find that they are made of similar materials. However, someone will spend thousands on a Rolex because of a story that has been carefully crafted since 1905. Marketing in and of itself is clever story telling.

Stories are so powerful that they defy logic. If you look at the phenomenon of Veblen goods, you'll get a great example of awesome storytelling in marketing. The story creates a demand, and the demand increases the price. Then the demand increases as the price increases.

The price increase becomes part of the story. So, the more expensive it gets, the more people want it. It's the weirdest thing ever, and it is entirely illogical.

Most materials that go into art are cheap when you consider it. The idea of value has more to do with status and belief behind a story. If an expert says it is worth 12 million dollars simply because this *famous* person from the 1940s owned it, then we all agree that it must be true. We buy the story, not the art itself.

How is that logical? The art hasn't changed. The materials haven't been magically imbued with this famous person's essence. However, it just is what it is, not many people will question it because the narrative is compelling.

We think we are rational creatures, but we make decisions based on emotional and illogical reasons. Therefore, an emotional story is more powerful than a list of facts or a "buy now" button.

An artist contacted me the other day because he was having a difficult time getting any traction on his social media posts. When I reviewed his posts, I saw beautiful art pictures with a caption that said, "on sale now!" and that was it. Every picture, every post, and everything else he shared had no other story than a desperate attempt to sell his art. You can feel it a mile away. No one is going to connect with that. In fact, it's going to repel people.

COMPELLING STORIES
SPREAD QUICKLY.

Maybe you still doubt the power of a story, so let's do a thought experiment.

You are looking to buy a guitar, but don't want to spend too much money on it. You walk into a reputable dealer and find the guitar section. You have two identical guitars in front of you that are for sale.

One is $400, and the other is $1500. The $1500 guitar has a noticeable scratch. They are similar in every single way and crafted beautifully.

Would you buy the $400 guitar right away, or would you pause? Would you wonder what's wrong with it? Would you ask what the reason for the price difference is?

At this point, you are asking for the story.

The shop owner says, "They are the exact same guitar, but this one was the guitar Elvis used in 1956 on "The Milton Berle Show." He brings out a photograph, and there is Elvis with a scratched guitar. He then shows you the small markings of Elvis's signature on the back.

Is the value of the guitar going up in your mind? Does $1500 actually sound like an excellent deal? Why do you think that is?

It's not logical, even if you try to make sense of it after the fact. It's still the same guitar, but this one has an incredible story that you can now become a part of. This guitar will give you bragging rights, higher status and add value to your own identity.

You will be able to say, "Only two people have owned this guitar. Me and Elvis."

You are not paying for the guitar. You are paying for the story.

As humans, we are captivated by good storytelling. We love art because of the story it tells. We are fascinated by certain people because of their life stories. We think some artwork is more valuable than other artwork because of a story. Marketing at its simplest form understands that you are telling a narrative with everything you put out there.

This includes context. When you are looking at the context, you are looking at the whole story. Context is your surroundings, what you are wearing, your body language, and everything unspoken.

You may be wondering, "How much does context actually impact the story of the value of art?"

Let's take Banksy. You know him as the faceless rogue who loves fighting the art world system yet somehow still makes millions in the art world. Just about everyone in the world recognizes and knows about his story. The alleged man is a legend.

Banksy once posted on social media, "Yesterday I set up a stall in the park selling 100% authentic original signed Banksy canvases for $60 each." with a video of an old man with an art booth around New York's Central Park.

So, what happened with the expensive art taken out of context?

- Hundreds of people walked by, ignoring the expensive art that they could have bought for pennies on the dollar.
- His first sale came mid-afternoon, and the woman rudely haggled two pieces down to 50% off.
- A man bought a couple paintings an hour later to fill his empty walls, utterly oblivious of what he was buying.
- Later on, after passing by the booth several times that day, a woman asked the old man, "Are these Original Banksy's?" And when he said, "Yep." She hesitantly bought two.

Some estimates say that in total, $225,000 Worth of Art at the Central Park Stall sold for $420. It is the same art, two different tales. One story is attached to Banksy's narrative, and the other is just an old man selling Banksy look-alikes.

The fact is, Banksy did not do this stunt because he wanted to sell art and make money in Central Park. He did it for the story. This story will spread and take on different meanings, but at the end of the day it says something about Banksy's character, and it is worth more than $225,000. It is priceless.

On a side note, can you imagine Banksy desperately trying to sell art using all the typical marketing crap that art marketing courses try to sell artists on? I don't know about you, but I have a hard time picturing him hunched over a computer trying to purchase boring ads on social media.

Ultimately, part of it is perception. price, status, brand, quality, and personality. However, how you put yourself out there and what you are saying is a major part of your story.

Also, what you are *NOT* saying is part of your story. This is where being authentic comes in, making sure that the narrative is true and not just a desperate attempt to get something out of a person or get attention.

If your story is a deceptive attempt to get recognition, validation, money, or respect, the *underlying* story will always seep into the narrative. Make sure your motives are true.

As a Rogue Artist, you rely on your own narrative to create your own economy. Never compromising your values or jumping through hoops to be accepted, you create your own opportunities with the tools at your disposal.

BLAZE YOUR OWN TRAIL!

You put yourself out there and persist through the bull-crap. You are telling a story of resilience and innovation. But, most importantly, when you have fun coming up with creative ways to put yourself out there, you are setting yourself apart. It's all about you and what you bring to the world. You are either bringing something that has meaning and sets you apart, or you are just trying to sell something like everyone else.

Don't get me wrong, I want you to sell art. I want you to make a living doing something that you love. However, it starts with you and how you put yourself out there. You are either approaching the world walking on eggshells and feeling small, or you are being bold.

The thing that is important to remember here is that we are *ALREADY* bold. The moment you create something that didn't exist before, you have entered the realm of exceptional. Your story is exceptional, you are exceptional, and you have all the tools you need to share your fantastic story.

How you share your story doesn't matter. We have been storytellers since the beginning of time and since then, we have used many of the same methods that are used in advertising today.

Pompeii, circa 35 C.E.
Umbricius Scaurus and his family produce and sell four different Roman fish sauces, including the relatively famous garum. Garum was a popular seasoning that tasted much like the fish sauce found in Thai and Vietnamese cooking today.

Scaurus' garum was said to be so top notch, Pliny himself described it as "The fruit of the sea."

Mosaic patterns on the wall of his shop were decorated with images of amphoras boasting the brand and the quality.

"Only from the shop of Scaurus."
"The flower of garum, made of the mackerel, a product of Scaurus, from the shop of Scaurus."
"The best liquamen, from the shop of Scaurus."

I'm sure Scaurus also painted murals, signs, and paid or sponsored influencers (gladiators and Olympians of the day) to market his products and build his reputation. So even thousands of years later, we can picture Scaurus being a big personality.

He signed everything with his name, had giant mosaics advertising who he was and what he did on his home. He was larger than life. Even now, Scaurus's marketing story is compelling. If I went back in time and tried garum, I wouldn't settle for anything less than Scaurus.

Late Song Dynasty Ancient China.
A copper printing plate was used to print posters. These were square sheets of paper with a rabbit logo holding a needle.

It read "Jinan Liu's Fine Needle Shop" and "We buy high-quality steel rods and make fine-quality needles, to be ready for use at home in no time."

I wanted to share these with you because I wanted to examine the idea that you don't need anything special to put yourself out there. As creatives, we can have fun creating materials to share our story. We already do it with our art. Why not turn our marketing into an art form of storytelling.

Scaurus used mosaics and murals. The needle shop used the first printing on a copper plate. These are ALL artisan creations used in order to share a story of what they did and how to find them. They all promoted their name triumphantly through time and space. Putting yourself out there is all about finding creative ways to do it big, bold, and beautiful.

Artists will often ask me if they should sign their work. My answer is yes. You are your brand, and your signature is your brand, and your brand name should be on everything you create.

Speaking of which, Euthymides was an artist in Athens *circa 500 B.C.E.* who wrote "Euthymides painted me, as never Euphronios could do." on one of his vases. I find this absolutely hilarious.

In a thousand years, what evidence will there be of your putting yourself out there? What will your story be? You know more about what you create and who you are than anyone else on the planet.

Only you are qualified to choose how you are going to introduce yourself to the world. Think beyond typical played-out marketing tactics. Think bigger and broader in how to share your creative saga with the world.

Will you be remembered for a bunch of annoying social media ads?
Will you be remembered as inspiring?
Will you be remembered as authentic?
Will you be remembered as greedy or desperate?
How will you be remembered?

You can choose to leave a legacy of authenticity, creativity, imagination, and persistence. Of course, it takes the willingness to put yourself out there and risk embarrassment, rejection, and failure. It also requires you to remember that everything you put out there is speaking for who you are.

Changing your perspective about marketing, advertising, and sales will open up opportunities for you that you couldn't see before. First, as a creative individual, you are powerfully equipped to excel at sharing your creative journey. Second, you have spent your life honing a creative skill that most marketing firms crave. Finally, you can get people to pay attention because you are not ordinary. You are a unicorn in a world that craves the fantastical.

People pay attention to things that interest them. They buy something that they emotionally connect with. You are an artist. You are one of the most exciting creatures on the planet. People are fascinated by whatever your story is. It may not seem attractive to you, but it is.

TELL YOUR STORY.

As artists, most of us get so wrapped up in the idea that we have to find a good gimmick or magic formula to sell our art that we rarely stop and pay attention to what is actually going on. This *SELL SELL SELL* and *hustle* mentality that is so common can honestly feel a bit hopeless and overwhelming. It's like you and a hundred fishermen are on a lake containing a single fish.

Will it be the person with the shiniest lure? Will it be the one with the quietest boat? Will it be the most skilled? Will it have everything to do with proximity? In the end, even after the fish is caught, no one will really know why. Everyone will have an opinion, but that's all they will be, just opinions. There are a lot of "Proven Methods" out there. Things like funneling, gimmicks, and paying for ads are sold as the quick fix to all of your marketing needs, but at the end of the day, it is the compelling story that will make or break any tactic you apply.

When you stop and contemplate the question, "Why do people buy art?" or, more importantly, "Why do people buy anything?" Chances are you may have a jumble of reasons floating around in your noggin that sound good, but they're probably not getting you anywhere.

We may think that we evaluate price points, quality, and other factors, but most of our choices come from an emotional place. I'm talking like a subconscious type of emotion deep down inside of who we are.

Ultimately, emotion makes us buy stuff because feeling is what controls our decision-making in general. This is why storytelling is so powerful. This is the reason things like clickbait can exist. If we were all rational decision-makers, no one would click on an ad promising some compelling story.

It's interesting how storytelling is at the core of all marketing, but most of us don't make that connection. We think a company is advertising a product, but in actuality they are selling us on a story.

For example, if you see an ad for a yacht, most likely you will see a picture of luxury. In reality, the product is a giant expensive yacht that will require a lot of upkeep. However, the ad is going to showcase the story of self-worth, acceptance, and status in the world.

We all know that when you look at a yacht you immediately think of wealth. The bigger it is, the more wealth you think you see. It's *all story*, but a yacht is typically seen as a symbol of affluence. However, my dad once bought a yacht on eBay cheap.

The reality is often not what the story tells.

Reality Ad: This phone is… well. They all pretty much have the same features.
Story Ad: This phone offers a connection with friends, family, and a broader network of people. Also, if you own our phone brand you are part of the cool kid club because the other phone brand is for lame people.
Reality Ad: These athletic shoes are created in a factory out of the same material as other athletic shoes.
Story Ad: These athletic shoes inspire adventure and glory through the act of competition. You know, just do it.

As you can see, each of these ads is telling a compelling story. It's all promising a certain lifestyle that will make you feel included and awesome.

Art, music, clothing, jewelry, furniture, food, and just about EVERYTHING else in life can make us feel something. Likewise, your art and story make people feel something. So do not undervalue your fantastic tale. You have a compelling story.

To tell a compelling story, you need to understand the compelling reasons why you do what you do. Unfortunately, some creative people haven't really explored this on a deeper level. Sure, some may say, "It relaxes me to create." but I want to know why.

1. What is it relaxing you from?
2. Why does it relax you?
3. Why do you want to share what you create with others?
4. What are you trying to say?
5. Why do you do what you do?

Honestly, I get a little infuriated with some artists who play it down and lose their power simply because they don't look a little deeper into the emotional reasons they do what they do. That's where you can find your story.

When you don't have something compelling to share, it is easy to blame other people for not connecting with you and your art. However, it's all on you if you're not giving them *ANYTHING* to connect with.

DIG DEEPER AND FIND YOUR STORY.

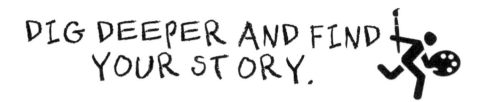

Recently, an artist who painted old cars told me that he doesn't have a story to tell. His paintings were beautiful, and there seemed to be a common theme in his art. Every time I asked him to dig a little deeper, it was like pulling teeth.

He said, "I just like painting old cars."
 "Why?" I asked.
 "I don't know. I just do."
Trying to reveal something more profound, I asked, "Why do you think you like painting old cars and I don't?"
 "I don't know. Maybe you don't like old cars."
I paused, "I like old cars just fine. I just don't have the desire to paint them. Why do you think that is?"

 "Don't know."

A month later, he reached out and told me he was quitting art and going back to focusing on his full-time job.

This kind of thing bothers me because I spent a significant portion of my life reciting the same lingo and not going deeper. I guess I was afraid that I would discover that it was all meaningless or vapid. Ultimately, I didn't bother to put in the time to make it worth it.

Honestly, it doesn't matter if it has a profound meaning or it's just something you find pretty. What matters is that *you know why you do what you do.* This can be anything you create and can be for a myriad of reasons.

In a culture of burying your emotions until your eye twitches and you explode, it should be no surprise to imagine that everything we do in life has some sort of meaning underneath it all. Sometimes, it's unconscious and we don't easily find the answer on the surface. Whether we draw stick figures or old automobiles, there is a reason for it.

Therefore, after I create a work of art, I'll ask myself, "Why did I create this?" I then stare at the details of the work to find answers within myself. It doesn't have to be profound, it just has to make sense to me.

Getting an understanding of my motivation will make it personal to me. It's like putting together a puzzle where every work of art reveals a little more about who I am. It reveals your intention and the direction you are heading. If you don't bother figuring out why you are creating art, how are you supposed to genuinely talk about your art?

THERE IS SO MUCH MORE TO YOU!

Know your art, know yourself, and know why you do what you do. As you grow and evolve this will change and reveal more and more.

It is the only thing that will fuel you during the less-than-ideal times that dominate the different stages of an art career. Your reason for doing what you do becomes your anchor and lets you make strong choices that will keep you going.

89

In the case of painting old cars, it could mean anything.

- It can represent a symbol of love.
- It can represent the simpler times and when things were made better.
- It can represent longevity and immortality.
- It can represent car culture and like-minded people.
- It can represent pride and power in something rare.
- Again, *IT* can represent *ANYTHING*.

So how do you find the story in what you create? Your overall life story will be tied into everything you do, that includes your art. If you want to find out what you are saying, you will have to sit with your creations.

Look at something you have created and ask yourself these questions:

Why do I create what I create? Why did I create this, what was I feeling?
What am I feeling now that I'm looking at it?
What do I enjoy about it?
Why do I share it with other people?
What do I want them to get out of it?
What am I saying with this art? What is this art saying to me?
What do I care about?
What would my inner child think of this art?

Don't overthink it. Your reasons could be as simple as creating things you think are beautiful or making people laugh. It could be more profound if you want to dig deeper and ask why, but it is unnecessary to lay out all the details at first. It will evolve as you grow.

By the way, if your answer for any of these is "money," then dig a little deeper than that. As much as I love money, it has never been a great long-term motivator.

Find something more substantial that will motivate you to keep going when things look bleak. Unless you are willing to put your art out there and announce, "I only create art because I want to make money" then there will be more to it.

It is important to say three things here:

- Don't turn this into a serious mission, have fun, but don't disparage your purpose and message by saying it is meaningless or that you don't have one. We all do.
- Your purpose will change and evolve as you do organically.
- Don't tell people your purpose to try and get validation. It is for you. Share it because you want to.

Creative people tend to feel powerless when putting themselves out there because their ideas can get squashed by people with good or bad intentions. If you are constantly trying to defend your reasons to create art, you won't spend any time doing it.

Your story will connect you to people who have similar stories. It will connect your art and who you are to the world. There will be plenty of people out there who don't connect. Don't waste your time coming up with a narrative to get validation from them, just be who you are.

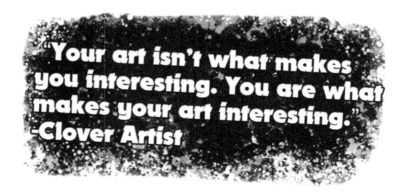
"Your art isn't what makes you interesting. You are what makes your art interesting."
-Clover Artist

THE STORY OF VAN GOGH'S FAME

When many people find out that I am an artist, they picture me living a tortured life, eating paint, having no money, no friends, and suspect I'm off my rocker to live that kind of lifestyle. This is the starving artist's widespread myth and is somewhat romanticized by the naysayers in the world. They imagine a life like Vincent van Gogh.

"You can't make money with art until after you die!"

92

"Van Gogh was a great painter; it didn't work out for him. What makes you think you'll make it?"
"Hahahaha, you'll have to eat paint to survive."

The idea of the tortured artist goes back to Plato's writing, but no artist embodied that stereotype more than van Gogh. The perception is constant torment due to frustrations with art, other humans, or the world in general.

It is often believed that creativity and severe mental disorders are necessary ingredients for creative genius. It is also thought that it will always eventually lead to some sort of self-destruction. Obviously, this is a myth, but Van Gogh is the typical stereotype of a misunderstood genius. The truth is that we are *ALL* weird and unique – some of us just embrace it more than others. That being said, feeling like you don't fit in and thinking there is something wrong with you because you don't, can drive us to madness.

Van Gogh is an interesting example of powerful storytelling that I see slightly differently than what is commonly associated with him. He is known as an artist who struggled his entire life to be recognized. The truth is art creation wasn't his first, second, or even third choice for a career.

He started creating art only ten years before his death, yet he poured everything he had into it, thus we remember this great man. The funny thing is, that is not the whole story. Despite being self-taught, which at the time was frowned upon, he was on his way to being recognized for his art.

Let's rewind a little for context.

Vincent shared his name with a dead brother who had been stillborn a year earlier. This, along with a looming grave on the property that read "Vincent Willem van Gogh" probably messed with his head a bit. If I was staring at a grave with my name on it every day growing up, I'm sure I would be questioning my own identity. His cold and unloving mother telling him that the *"good"* Vincent is in heaven most likely didn't help matters.
His mother would not win any "Mother of the Year" awards considering

she rejected him throughout his life, and even after death, possibly burned a crate of his paintings.

Later in life things like poisoning from drinking turpentine, ingesting lead paint, smoking tobacco, catching syphilis, and being introduced to absinthe probably weren't helpful in coping with his upbringing.

His personality was, dare I say, abrasive. Many of his fellow impressionists spent most of their time partying hard until they needed more money. They only really worked on art when they were broke. Vincent spent a lot of his time arguing vehemently against their lazy approach to their art. This is most likely when he was introduced to absinthe by his lazy friends.

Eventually, he went off (after suggestions from his peers) to live in the

French countryside. That's when he started creating some of his most famous paintings. The only problem is that Vincent started to feel loneliness, and he began to deteriorate severely.

His brother sent Paul Gauguin to live with him. Vincent, being super excited that his friend was coming to live with him, filled the house with sunflowers. Unfortunately, all they did was argue. They could barely withstand being in the same room.

Vincent later had a breakdown and pulled out a knife, at which point they both stared at the weapon in disbelief. Paul Gauguin then promptly left, never to return.

The famous ear-cutting incident happened soon after, leading to Vincent checking himself into an asylum. Eventually, he left the asylum, and found a certain peace in a small village in France. He soon began painting prolifically again. Sadly, two months after arriving, Vincent died.

As you can see, van Gogh persisted through a lot of suck. He wasn't that great at communication or connecting with people. His argumentative style was off putting, to say the least. He had substance abuse problems and felt worthless a lot of the time. His art wasn't appreciated and for the most part, you could say he was wasting his time. Yet, he kept painting and creating art.

Van Gogh is considered a failure during his lifetime. However, right before he died, he had just sold a painting for 400 francs. His work started to gain recognition amongst the avant-garde, and his paintings were being exhibited in Paris and Brussels. He was on the cusp of the next part of his creative journey.

Van Gogh had many struggles throughout his life, but despite all these setbacks, those ten years of creating art led to his career becoming what we all recognize today as a success.

During his time as an artist, he created countless works of art. There are

850 paintings and nearly 1,300 works on paper that we know of. He experimented with color and created a style that was all his own.

I have run into artists who give themselves a few years to try and "make it" in an art career. Some try it for a few months and quit because they are not being recognized or validated.

This is why I never recommend you put a cap on how long you are willing to move forward without recognition. There is no way to predict where this strange creative journey will lead us and how long it will take.

Van Gogh had some serious struggles and insecurities and yet he persisted out of the love he had for art. That is inspiring, that alone makes him successful in my book.

However, his story doesn't end there. After his death, interest in his art waned. So how did Vincent become world-famous? *A compelling story.*

His brother's widow found herself with nothing but crates of Vincent's work and most importantly Vincent's letters to his brother.

There were hundreds of letters, and they told epic stories of his life, his thoughts, and his art. Once she published his letters, a fuller picture of Vincent's life was revealed, and his art became a sensation.

Everything I shared with you in this chapter about his life comes from those letters. Van Gogh's fascinating life story is the reason why his work gradually took the whole world by storm.

However, had he not persisted, had he not shared those details with his brother, and had the letters never been released, there would be no story. I highly doubt any of us would know the creative genius that was van Gogh.

We all have a story, we all have something to say, and we all have the stuff to share that means something to us. It may not be as tragic as van Gogh's life, but every life has meaning, and every life story is compelling.

Your story doesn't have to be elaborate. Like I've said before, we tell our story with everything we put out there.

Think of what inspires you to keep going and share your art in the world.
Think of what inspires you to create art.
Think of the words you share with the world, like letters to a loved one.

Take a look at some of Vincent's quotes and hear the story of his life in short sentences. Despite his abrasive behavior with his peers, his words are rather inspiring.

- "I would rather die of passion than of boredom."
- "I always think that the best way to know God is to love many things."
- "I put my heart & soul into my work and have lost my mind in the process."
- "It is looking at things for a long time that ripens you and gives you a deeper meaning."
- "What would life be if we had no courage to attempt anything?"

When I say to tell your story, I'm not saying you have to air your dirty laundry or expose your weaknesses to the world.

Share what inspires you. The fact of the matter is that a story of you will form nonetheless. While Vincent was alive, much of his narrative was told by other people.

STORIES CAN SPREAD QUICKLY MAKE SURE IT IS YOUR STORY THAT IS BEING TOLD.

He was difficult, hard to deal with, and a danger to himself and others. Only his brother really knew the beautiful narrative behind Vincent's life and his art. It wasn't until those letters were released that the rest of the world was able to enter into his beautiful story. Even now, there are exhibits that mesmerize us by allowing us to physically enter his mind and see the world through his eyes.

This is why it is important to tell your story. To share your narrative and not let the world come up with their own conclusions of who you are. Share your inspiring thoughts, share why you keep going despite the obstacles, and share what your dreams are.

Tell your own story and be persistent. Share that adventure. Everyone loves a hero's epic through the obstacles. That's what makes van Gogh's story so remarkable. He was putting himself out there and persisting. As artists, the simple act of putting ourselves in the arena, facing obstacles, rejection, and hardship is inspiring.

Most people don't know what it is like to really experience something like that. Your story will always be worth sharing, so share it. Don't wait around until you are gone in hopes of someone else telling it.

BECOME A BRAND LIKE PABLO

Anyone that knows anything about marketing is familiar with branding. Branding is one of those marketing concepts that everyone talks about but can still seem vague and confusing, even for people who claim to know marketing.

Back in the early days, branding developed to burn marks into livestock to denote who owned them. Also, shop owners would use branding to symbolize their business for illiterate peasants or plebians throughout history. For example, a boot would represent a cobbler, and a loaf of bread might represent a baker.

It evokes the idea or image people have in mind when thinking about what you sell, your services, and any activities you participate in. Effective branding is both practical such as "Rafi always meets his deadlines," and emotional such as "Rafi's art and content makes me feel powerful". Basically, it is a story about you that pops into someone's mind when they see your brand.

It's not just logos and letterheads, but also the feelings people develop towards you, what you do, and your art. The physical and emotional message is experienced every time a person is exposed to the name, logo, art, visual identity, or message the artist communicates. This happens by remaining consistent in your message whenever you share your brand.

No matter what you may think of him, Picasso was one of the first artists I know of who thought globally about his branding. He knew he was recognized as a great painter, but he also knew that recognition wouldn't be enough to propel him to stardom. So how did Picasso become one of the most well-known artists in the world?

Step one: Identify What Sets You Apart.
Every artist has at least one exceptional quality that makes them different from every other artist. This is something that sets you apart and identifies you to your following. It is something special about you that your audience can only experience with you.

This could be your distinct art, content, image, technique, schtick, personality, sense of style, where you are from, and the way you interact with your collectors and followers. Ultimately, it is what you want to be remembered for. The thing you want to be known for. Think about what that could be and identify what sets you apart.

For example, if I say the words "I'LL BE BACK!" or "GET IN THE CHOPPA!" in an Austrian accent, a brand will have entered your mind. Arnold Schwarzenegger took all the aspects of himself that people claimed would make him fail and turned it into a recognizable brand.

Picasso had a polarizing set of personality traits, yet somehow, he managed to create a powerful empire. He is remembered chiefly for pushing the boundaries in the art world and being outspoken. This is by design. He spent a lifetime driving himself to create art that had never been seen before. This, along with his questionable relationships and prolific obsession with art, made him one of the most discussed artists in the 20th century.
Pablo painted, drew, and made sculptures in a way no one had ever seen

before. In fact, he didn't create what was popular. Quite the opposite, sometimes it was highly unpopular even amongst his admirers. The thing about Picasso is that his outspoken temper, striped sailor shirts, stubborn Spanish pride, and machismo were larger than life.

The thing that sets you apart is more than the art. It is you, the whole package. Identify the things that make you who you are. Those things that make you unique.

Step two: Tell Your Compelling Story To Everyone.
Many artists will write a boring bio and leave it at that. It's usually a vanilla story that doesn't tell me anything compelling about them. They'll also write blogs, and post on social media some lackadaisical information about some work of art and say nothing of interest. This is a waste of everyone's time.

When you are putting yourself out there, EVERY opportunity to share your story should say something of interest about you and your work.

Your collectors and followers build a more profound relationship with you when they can relate to your personal story.
Write a bio that expresses your creative background. Make sure you

102

include life experiences that have influenced you in life and in your art. Your write-ups, blogs, posts, and website pages should give your collectors and followers a glimpse into where you've been and where you're going.

Picasso knew that he had to create an essence around him. He knew that it was essential to define himself beyond his art. He understood the need to prompt fascination and intrigue around who he was. People want an original back story. It's not just the "what" but the "who" that fascinates most art collectors. It builds an emotional connection between them and your art. If your narrative is authentic, everything you do in public will work in conjunction with the message of your art.

Step Three: Craft Your Image.
Your collectors and followers build their perception of you based on the story that your image evokes. Your brand includes how you present yourself and how you put yourself out there. From the art you create, how you interact with people online or offline, to your body language. All of it.

What does your image say about you?
Do you persist?
Do you quit?
Do you complain?
Do you overcome?
Who are you?
What are you saying?

Identify what style represents you and who you want to be. By style I mean not only your appearance but most importantly your character. Remember to remain authentic when developing your image and story.

Then identify how to best share that story any time you are putting yourself out there. Every photo you share, logo, content, and interaction should be imbued with your unique flavor. Make it something that is *REALLY* you, it's easier to remain consistent that way.
However, if you decide to create an alter-ego, try to make it as close to

your personality as possible. This way, it doesn't start feeling like a chore as you grow.

Picasso created a captivating brand personality with such staying power, that we remember him simply as "Picasso." He knew that this single moniker would set him apart from other artists, so he dropped the "Pablo Diego José Francisco de Paula Juan Nepomuceno María de los Remedios Cipriano de la Santísima Trinidad Ruiz y Picasso" and just kept the "Picasso." Simple is always better.

Part of putting yourself out there is controlling the narrative, and Picasso had developed into a master of storytelling. He knew he had to be in command of his tale. If Picasso didn't do it, someone else would, and he didn't want that with his reputation. He understood that becoming successful is the creative art of getting the media to tell your story, the way you want it told. Remember, this is before the internet, yet he succeeded in putting himself out there as a brand that is so powerful that it is still recognizable today.

It really starts with having a clear sense of yourself and what you want to stand for. Picasso boasted, posed intensely for every photograph, and created his own reputation by being consistent in his approach and remaining authentic to himself.
Step four: Be Consistent By Being Real.

If you stay consistent, your collectors and followers will quickly identify you no matter what you put out in the world. People should know what to expect in your behavior whenever they interact with you, your content, and your art. Who you are and what your message is will not bounce around and change day to day once you have identified it. Building trust and recognition are so important when it comes to building your brand. This doesn't mean your message may not evolve and change, but change happens gradually, and your audience will grow with you.

Years ago, a friend of mine who was a big fan of Steven Seagal found out that he was filming in Chicago. He went to the set with a poster, approached Seagal for an autograph and told him he was his biggest fan. Seagal was my friend's role model who inspired him to change his life. Upon hearing this, Seagal then proceeded to rip my friend's poster in half and call him a loser as he turned and walked away.

I know that sounds too awful to be true, but it happened and it's a really great example of what can happen when you're not authentic to your image. Maybe Seagal was having a terrible day, maybe he truly is that cold hearted. Either way, your brand image extends to everything you do, and this type of behavior would later bite Steven Seagal's career on the behind.

This is why consistency in who you are matters. If you don't know what you are saying overall, your brand becomes nonexistent. Artists like Damien Hirst, Banksy, and Jeff Koons are great at branding because they stay very consistent in their overall message. It's important to point out that these artists all work across several mediums. Consistency has nothing to do with what you create. It has to do with what you are saying.
Let me repeat that for the thousands of artists who have contacted me with

stories of some art marketing guru telling them they have to focus on one medium.

Consistency has nothing to do with what you create. It has to do with what you are saying.

Picasso worked on sculptures, ceramics, drawings, printmaking, ballet set design, costume design, poetry, and he authored two plays. He was an outspoken Spaniard living in France who continued to create, show his work, and put himself out there consistently. The only time he didn't show his work was during World War II, when the Nazis barred him from showing it. Even then, he kept creating art.

The thing about Picasso that really impacted his experience was his persistence to put himself out there and let the world know that he existed. He started in taverns and house parties. He put himself out there for 80 years as an artist, and even though his art changed, his message was consistent.

Step five: Be Authentic.
If I could summarize my thoughts on branding, it would be "do you." Your brand is who you are and what you stand for. Don't try to fit in. Don't jump through hoops for anyone else. Embrace what makes you stand out. Identify your artistic vision and message and persist. It will take time to build but stick to it.

By mid-career, Picasso had established his brand so firmly that he had the upper hand over the dealers who represented him. Picasso's work was so in demand that he would sell whatever amount of it he chose by allowing it to leave his studio.

What you personally feel about Picasso is irrelevant. What matters is that people are still talking about him. He was a significant influence in art and one of the most well-known artists on the planet.
He laid the groundwork and didn't wait around for someone to make him

famous. He made himself recognizable, put himself out there, and the opportunities came to him.

"Only put off until tomorrow what you are willing to die having left undone"
— Pablo Picasso

A fun way to figure out your brand is to think of yourself as an action figure or doll. Let's design the packaging and display for who you are. Have fun with this exercise and don't overthink it. You can design and redesign your avatar as much as you want.

What is the name on the box?
What does the logo look like?
What colors are on the box?
What color are the fonts?
What kind of font are you using?
What is your character all about?
What promise does your character stand by?
What is your character's personality?
What scene is around your character?
What description is on the box?
Are there any warning labels?
How is the character dressed?
Are there any accessories?

Once you design the box and your new action figure or doll, let's look at how we would market it out in the world using typical marketing. Again, have fun with this. The more ridiculous, the better.

What does the TV ad look like? What about the radio ad? What about the magazine ad? What do your outdoor ads and posters look like? What does the website look and sound like? How does your store display look and feel? What are your characters priced at? What is your consistent message? What is your tagline that describes your character?

Keep your tagline simple. Too many slogans try to say too much. You should explain what you are about in three to five words. Think of it as your motto. A motto isn't just about marketing. It's about letting people and yourself know what you are all about.

I know these questions sound ridiculous, but they will really help you visualize something tangible and consistent. It is often easy for us to see our brand in our art, and we forget that the brand is who we are.

Ultimately, just remember to be honest with everything you do in public, whether on social media, the internet, or in person. It will all evoke the idea or image that people have in mind when thinking about what you sell and who you are. It is much easier to stay consistent when you figure out who and what you stand for. This will, over time, build a relationship, and you'll have people paying attention and saying, "I'm rooting for you!"

Five important things I want you to remember when it comes to your branding:

- Take time to figure out who you are and what you stand for.
- Be consistent and remember that everything you do in the public eye is your brand.
- If you collaborate or work with anyone else, make sure they represent what you stand for.
- Control your narrative and don't argue, simply stand by your truth.
- Don't be afraid to show all the different aspects of you.

I think that any human on the planet could make anything happen as long as they take a leap of faith in themselves. If they create genuinely, investigate who they are, put themselves out there generously, and persist defiantly, they would be unstoppable.

Do you evoke a consistent idea or image in people's minds when they see anything you share with the world?

BANKSY GOING ROGUE?

I find it hilarious that some artists think that Banksy doesn't do anything that could be called "marketing." Upon the announcement of this book, one artist responded with, "Banksy doesn't do any marketing at all, and he's pretty famous. No one needs marketing. You just need talent."

The word talent gets thrown around a lot in the art world. You can easily say someone is talented and repeat the rhetoric most admirers of a "creative genius" say. You can also point at someone's art and call them a talentless peasant.

The truth is that the word talent is synonymous with popularity. The more popular you are, the more "talent" people think you possess. That being said, chances are you are popular because you spend a lot of time practicing your craft publicly.

However, that doesn't make everything you create gold. Some prevalent artists whose artworks are going for millions have some works that are more of a shiny turd than a representation of their talent.

Banksy doesn't follow the usual standards and rules we all associate with marketing, but it is marketing nonetheless. Putting yourself out there and letting the world know you exist is marketing, and he is fantastic at everything he does.

To be clear, I'm not saying Banksy isn't talented. He has created some really unique and compelling works of art, but at this point, he is also a millionaire artist who can fund some of his more exciting projects.

He didn't start out that way. He started with graffiti and stencils. It wasn't as "cutting edge" as people like to claim. There are thousands of exceptional street artists who create incredible works of art that no one knows about. So what set him apart?

A Consistent Message.

When we look at Banksy today, it can be hard to relate to him and what he does. He has resources that most of us can only dream of, and it is hard to remember that he had to start somewhere.

According to legend, Banksy started as a punk kid and freehand graffiti artist in 1990. During the next decade, he met a photographer who would eventually become his agent. Around this time is when Banksy developed the stencil style that he is famous for.

Banksy's consistent brand is openly and vocally anti-commercial and anti-establishment.

Everything he's done has a message and narrative. He's used murals, art, websites, video, documentaries, press releases, and most importantly, stunt and event marketing.

At the time of writing this book, it has been 41 years since Banksy started creating a masterpiece of creative marketing. You may not know who he is or if he even actually exists, but you know what he stands for, and that is the point. His message is featured in striking and witty images occasionally coupled with slogans. The stencils are often of rats, apes, policemen, soldiers, children, the elderly, and have a consistent message.

Slogans and taglines are a great way to advertise your art, and Banksy knows the staying power of a good image and tagline in controlling the narrative of what you are saying.

"Even if you don't come up with a picture to cure world poverty, you can make someone smile while they're having a piss."
- Banksy

Banksy makes his marketing look so effortless and spontaneous that most people don't recognize it as marketing. To me, that is the goal. To make your marketing part of your craft and total masterpiece, and most importantly, have fun spreading a message and having something to say.

Be Newsworthy. Just about everything Banksy does has been a publicity stunt. Even in the beginning, he was publicly displaying his messages for everyone to see with his murals.

While most of us think about toiling away in our studio and eventually having an exhibition on plain white walls in a gallery space with cheese squares and wine, Banksy thinks of the big picture.

Even after becoming famous, he knew his exhibition needed to stand out. Banksy did up an old warehouse and put a literal live elephant in the room.

The exhibition was called, "Elephant in the room."

Things that are out of the ordinary will always be newsworthy.

I couldn't get an elephant when I did my first exhibition. Still, I made it a point to have at least something out of the ordinary and significant in the form of a large hanging sculpture, interactive art, and several photo opportunities for guests. This gave people something no one had seen from me before and left them with a memorable experience. Most importantly, my art was saying something. Word of mouth eventually spread, and it made the local newspaper.

Break The Rules Like A Rogue. One of my favorite Banksy publicity stunts was in 2005 when he walked around the New York Metropolitan Museum of Art in disguise and quietly hung small pieces of his own art on the walls with double-sided tape. Of course, everything was caught on video. The "Hang and Run" artist continued to set up his own small works at top museums and art institutions in the U.S. and the U.K.

This is so brilliantly fun. These are the stunts that I love because they do not damage property but still give the stuffy institutions the middle finger in a playful way. Honestly, I'm a bit jealous that I didn't come up with the idea. I may have to try it, but I'll put my own twist on it.

Take A Stand. Whenever we read a quote, watch an interview, view some art, experience an art project, or hear about some stunt that Banksy is a part of, there is a consistent story.

He has always been anti-war, anti-fascism, and anti-consumerism. He loudly proclaims his dissatisfaction with certain aspects of society, certain political situations, or even certain decisions taken by world leaders.

Banksy is not shy to communicate this through his art, interviews, and writing. He controls his narrative with every method of communication at his disposal.

I'm not saying you have to be controversial or be like him but be aware of what you stand for and who you are. If you have a message, you feel strongly about, then it will be easy. I stand for self-empowerment and not buying into what other people think you should be, which is infused in everything I do.

A message of warning here, if you are the type of person that jumps on the bandwagon and points fingers at the other bandwagon, then I'm not sure expressing your group's rhetoric is beneficial. Sharing what you stand for is most potent when you stand back and look at the whole picture.

If you are embroiled in drama, hatred, discrimination, and anger, your message can get lost in cynicism. Of course, that's my opinion. You are free to do and think whatever you want, ultimately it is your choice how you live and what you want to share with the world.

When Banksy takes a stand, he looks at culture and society and points out the hypocrisy that he sees in it with humor and sobering imagery.

It is a brilliant way to take a stand and inspire a deeper look at an issue. Not telling people how to feel but allowing them to examine it from a different perspective.

A great example of how Banksy communicates this is his temporary pop-up art exhibition "Dismaland," where he poked fun at the manufactured friendliness of big corporations and institutions. It was billed as "the U.K.'s most disappointing new visitor attraction."

Be Consistent With Your Story. When you arrive at Dismaland, you are greeted by a sad-looking black-clad and pink-vested group who are snide and completely unhelpful.

They greeted you with a bored, "Welcome to Dismaland. Get rich or try dying. Enjoy!" The message is consistent with Banksy's brand, from when you try to buy a ticket on a crappy crashing website, the morose saggy mouse-eared attendants greeting you, to the dystopian-looking theme park castles.

Exaggerate Your Point And Make It Memorable. When people enter the park, they are forced through a security screening. Cardboard x-ray machines and crudely constructed security devices are used by rude characters. Then angry, power-mad guards order the guests to turn around, bend, hop and avert their gaze while being invasively checked for spray paint contraband.

Rewrite Common Experiences. The "Bemusement Park" has an artist creating keepsake caricatures, just like in any amusement park. However, unlike most caricatures, this particular artist will only draw the back of your head. Dismaland works with this theme throughout, playing on the expectations of commercialism and revealing the ridiculous to show a different perspective.

Focus On The Details. As soon as the Dismaland project opened, online ticket sales encountered nothing but problems, delays, and crashes. At the event, long lines, miserable workers, and disappointing announcements of cancellations followed.

The whole experience wasn't meant to pander. Every part of the experience and every detail was saying something consistent.

Whenever I do any event, whether it is an art walk, solo show, installation, or art show, I do several walk-throughs. I am looking at every step of the experience and every detail. I want everything to tell a story and say something. It is easy to lose sight of simple things like what you are serving or where the bathrooms are, but those are missed opportunities to surprise and astonish. Pay attention to all of it.

When you are doing an event, challenge yourself to consider ways to turn everything into an unforgettable experience. Don't over-hype and under-deliver on the occasion.

Always over-deliver on the experience and exceed people's expectations by bringing a little extra excitement into their lives. Surprise and delight will always live on with someone long after the event is over.

BE BOLD AND HAVE FUN!

Use Humor And Wit. Dismaland had carnival games which were somewhat depressing and completely unwinnable. Games like "Topple the Anvil" where you knock down a giant anvil, using a giant anvil that you can't lift. What do you get if you win?

A giant anvil you can't carry.

What matters here is consistency and attention to detail in how you express it. Banksy stencils are recognizable all over the world. That is only because before he even became famous, his art and message were consistent. Everything "Banksy" for the last 40 years on bridges, walls, streets, video, online, or anywhere is recognized because of what he was saying. This is what set him apart from other street artists who mainly were marking territory. He was saying something using humor, irony, satire, and creativity.

Even though issues in the world have changed and Banksy's career has evolved into stardom and wealth, his brand and message remain unchanged. This is how you build trust through authenticity and persistence. If your message is at the whims of society, it will get lost in its own contradictions.

Controlling The Narrative. When you look at anything produced by Banksy, whether a documentary, video, article, quote, work of art, graffiti, installation, exhibition, or anything, you will hear a consistent message. Everything he does controls the narrative.

He now uses his popularity as a way to spread this message. The video that circulated of an old man struggling to sell some Banksy canvases for as little as $60 from a vendor stall in New York's Central Park is a perfect message of the hypocrisy of the elite art world. I take it as a statement to any young artist struggling to sell art at a live event. Even Banksy's art would grapple with selling if no one knew it was his.

Using the fame of his art, he also unapologetically attacks art collectors and institutions. For example, when actors Brad Pitt and Angelina Jolie purchased his work for millions of dollars, Banksy stated, "I can't believe you morons actually buy this shit."

Everything he does and says is on brand and comes off as authentic because it hasn't changed in decades.

There are so many marvelous ways that Banksy has put himself out there that I can't possibly cover them all in this section, but I don't have to. Look closely at any famous artist you admire within and without the elite forum in the art world and find what their consistent story is. You may be surprised to see that it is in everything they do. Banksy just happens to be the most prominent and fun for me to investigate.

If you can fully grasp that every news article, every video, every quote, and anytime you hear about something unique or controversial that one of these artists did, it is by design. This is the only way to see the whole picture and think outside of the box.

"Think outside the box, collapse the box, and take a fucking sharp knife to it." - Banksy.

Think about it. Law enforcement on a worldwide scale has the equipment necessary to monitor all our movements.

Remaining anonymous is basically impossible, yet we believe the narrative and the fun of the mystery. It is all part of the marketing of the brand that is Banksy. It would lose the magic at this point if we knew who or what he was. That is by design.

In 2018, moments after the closing bid for a framed Banksy painting at Sotheby's, the artwork began to self-destruct. The damage came via a hidden mechanical paper shredder that Banksy had built into the frame bottom.

Some artists believe that the anti-establishment message in shredding a Banksy painting that had just sold at auction for 1.4 million dollars was a failed attempt to send a message. This is because it is consistent with the Banksy brand.

However, if he wanted to really destroy it all the way, he would have. Now he has something much more potent than a destroyed work of art. It became a half-shredded symbol of his brand and became a legend. It's brilliant marketing.

A good and compelling story will always have someone controlling the entire narrative. If you think I am full of crap, Banksy authenticated and renamed the new shredded work of art soon after it happened.

If anything, watching Banksy throughout the years reminds me to create a memorable experience with a consistent message in everything I put out there. Be defiant, think outside of the box, and be a rogue.

Events come and go, but an "experience" will last a lifetime. Why not have fun while we are doing this crazy thing called an art career.

Just remember to be who you are and don't try to be Banksy. The experience should be entertaining and engaging, but it must also be rooted in an authentic and coherent narrative. Every element should be consistent with what you are saying and who you are. Don't do some crap just to get attention.

As Banksy puts it, *"The time of getting fame for your name on its own is over. Artwork that is only about wanting to be famous will never make you famous. Any fame is a by-product of making something that means something. You don't go to a restaurant and order a meal because you want to have a shit."*

Remember that everything you do is a stepping stone to the next thing. Leave your audience wanting more and give them some mystery. If you take a picture or film a video of your stunt that could be anonymous, resist adding logos. Let your audience figure it out themselves.

They are intelligent and deserve the respect of not being spoon fed. People who don't know who you are will want to know. Banksy is exceptionally strategic when choosing where, when, and how his message pops up next.

People typically love audacity, originality, rogue-ness, cheekiness, fun, rebel-ness, and being entertained.

Have fun and take chances with your event and art. Push the envelope and take some risks. However, don't be stupid. If you put yourself or others in danger, it's not worth it. There is a big difference between doing something like Banksy to spread a message, and some of the dumb things people have done to get attention.

Before I plan anything, I question the experience to make sure I'm not doing anything fake or stupid. Always examine the idea and concept thoroughly. Ask yourself the difficult questions.

Why am I doing this?
What am I hoping to share?
Am I expecting something in return, or am I doing this because I believe it needs to exist?
Is it safe?
What are all the things that could go wrong?
How can I make sure that doesn't happen?

Don't Be Predictable. At one point, Banksy created a stenciled figure and text reading, "Better Out Than In – 2013." This was in Los Angeles, Yet a few days later, he revealed a month-long residency on the streets of New York City on a website and social media. It became national news because nobody knew where the following work would appear.

The press followed a daily city-wide scavenger hunt, and people were eating it up. From LA to New York, the internet, social media, network media, and newspaper attention this campaign received was massive.

BETTER OUT THAN IN

Don't Wait For Approval. Obviously, I'm not a fan of vandalism and destroying property, but I also don't wait for outside input on what work to make or how it should be shown when I am doing a public work of art.

When it comes to sharing my art, I don't follow an art world-approved formula. I don't need to get into the art world by following their rules. I am an artist who inhabits my own art world ecosystem. Banksy knows this. By exploring his own system outside the official art world, Banksy has created his own mystique and culture. The elite art world can't help but bend their own rules when it comes to him because of his popularity.

Live your life your way, don't do it to get noticed, do it because it is something you believe in. Life is too short. Put yourself out there and spread your message the only way you uniquely can. As Banksy puts it,

"What we do in life echoes in eternity."

Don't be small. Let your life and message echo in the world. Share your art, be bold, and put yourself out there.

"I've learnt from experience that a painting isn't finished when you put down your brush — that's when it starts. The public reaction is what supplies meaning and value. Art comes alive in the arguments you have about it."
-BANKSY

YOUR CREATIVE CULT... URE. CULTURE.

When it comes to putting yourself out there, it can feel like you are just going around in circles. Every time I attempted to put myself out there, I was usually left more confused than ever. My experience in the coffee shop, for example, only seemed to validate how unmarketable my art was.

Of course, despite popular belief, *ALL* art is marketable.

What I didn't understand at the time was that "John the artist" had built a culture around himself and his work. It was much more than just a marketing gimmick. It was organic.

Building a culture means that John conveyed his values, beliefs, underlying assumptions, attitudes, and behaviors through his art and the way he interacted with people. This happens slowly and results in cultivating a group of like-minded people that share a similar spirit.

The group of collectors that are cultivated will be loyal and want to bring that sense of culture home with them. The only way to build this culture is to begin to put yourself out there and let your people find you.

The truth is, no matter how offbeat or weird your creations and mission are, they will always have an audience. It may not be marketable to *ALL* audiences, especially if it is *VERY* different. However, in a world of billions, there will always be millions out there that will connect with what you are about.

This is why building your own culture is so important. The moment that enough people follow *YOU*, *your art* becomes mainstream.

When we ignore the culture we are building, we tend to default to the status quo. You see this all the time in the art world. To get started, you need an art degree or body of work, a resume of shows, some awards, some recommendations, and then a gallery or agent might choose to represent you.

In this scenario, you are a nobody until they validate you. Your livelihood belongs to someone else. You are part of someone else's culture.

Create your own culture, your own guidelines for what surrounds you and your art. This has an impact on other artists and collectors who discover this fantastic world you have created. Create an atmosphere that really embodies what you stand for.

This will guide your decisions and interactions with other humans. Embrace your unique path and blaze your own trail.

In my opinion, this is paramount because it will have a positive impact on everything you do and will give you the guiding principles to stay true to who you are.

BUILD YOUR OWN CULTURE.

I know it may sound silly or unnecessary, and maybe it is. I don't know you personally and have no idea what you want out of life. However, in my experience, this changed everything for me. It was the first step in seeing myself as more than an artist chasing a carrot. I was no longer looking for validation. It allowed me to really think about and construct what I wanted in life. I thought about the legacy I wanted to leave behind, way beyond just the artwork for the first time ever. It caused me to think bigger and reach for more ambitious goals than simply selling my art... I had something to say.

I could create my own culture and not rely on trying to fit into one created by other people.

My own culture of innovation.
My own culture of creativity.
My own culture of acceptance.
My own culture of persistence.
My own culture of empowerment.
My own culture of love.
My own culture of hope.
My own culture of honesty.

From this, Klee and I came up with the guiding principles of our mission statement and values.

BUILD YOUR OWN MISSION.

Rafi & Klee's MISSION
To inspire and encourage creativity and empowerment in the human spirit with everything we create and do.

Rafi & Klee's VALUES
We live these values in everything we put out there and everything we do:

- To point the lens on how beautiful and powerful a single human being is and how they can influence the world.
- To share what we've learned as artists and humans and do it freely and openly.
- To create a culture of creativity, laughter, empowerment, and innovation where everyone is welcome.
- To treat ourselves and others with humanity, love, understanding, and patience in everything we do.
- To have the courage to say no when something doesn't fit our values, but without arrogance or hubris.
- To not chase money, fame, likes, subscribers, accolades, power, or validation as a definition of success.
- To approach every personal or career challenge as an opportunity to grow and act with courage.
- To challenge the status quo and nurture a community without hierarchy – seeing EVERYONE as equal.
- To remain real, connecting with transparency, authenticity, empathy, and respect for all in everything we create.
- To keep humanity, ethics, sustainability, and the environment in mind in the choices we make for our business and art.

You may be wondering, "What the heck does any of this have to do with selling art?"

It's simple. This forces you to think about who you are and what you stand for. The how, what, and why of who you are is so important. It gives you something more than just selling art for the sake of selling art. You will be selling a powerful message with everything you put out there.

Your art will take on a vital role as the ambassador for what you are all about.

What is your mission? Come up with a sentence that explains what you are about and what you want to bring to the world. Then list your values. Come up with sentences that describe how you will interact with other people and why.

And finally, how will you put this message out there and share it with the world authentically?

One important thing to remember here is that you MUST put yourself out there as much as possible in order to communicate your mission. If you have a brilliant mission statement and it is stuck in a drawer somewhere and no one ever sees it or experiences you, then nothing will happen. That's what is always interesting to me. When someone talks about an artist they love, they say, "I discovered this wonderful artist that I (met, found, saw, etc.)."

No one will break into your house and discover you. You have to share your art and message to get noticed. It's simple. To be found, you have to put yourself out there. I don't just mean putting your art out there in a boring social media post that doesn't say anything about you. I mean, put yourself out there and *ACTUALLY* say something that has meaning to you.

SO HOW DO I CREATE A CULTURE AROUND MYSELF AND MY ART?

Interestingly, you can create a culture much in the same way one goes about creating a cult. No really. Think about it… cult.. uure. Stay with me… with a few *very very* important differences.

One- you're doing this for the benefit of everyone involved, not your own nefarious personal gains.

Two- you're not telling people what to think and believe, you are sharing your ideas and beliefs and encouraging everyone else to do the same.

Three- you're not giving yourself a title like "The Supreme Czar," even if one of the artists that is part of your group created a poster with your face on it. Use your newfound powers for the good of all artist-kind.

So, let's build a Cult—ure, shall we?

How To Start A Cult—ure.

Step #1: Determine what sets you apart, what is your message?
If we were in the business of recruiting followers, we wouldn't be very good at it unless we had a mission. A solid declaration of what we want to bring into the world.

If you were paying attention earlier in this chapter, you may already have your mission well established. If not, please refer to the earlier part of this chapter that you may have glossed over. We'll see you here when you have that sorted out.

(Removes finger from button for secret trap door under your seat).

If you doubt that a mission statement is necessary for building a culture, let's take a close look at one of the most dominating cults that exists in the world right now. Hmmmm, I may not be allowed to call them a cult, so for the purposes of this chapter we will call them Smartbucks Coffee that way they keep their anonymity.

Smartbucks coffee has a powerful, clearly written mission statement that guides not only their culture, but every decision they make as a corporation. They have used that mission statement to create their own language, atmosphere, and community of loyal devotees.

A word to the faint of heart, you will be the leader of your mission. That means that *YOU* will have to put yourself out there in your own awkward and charismatic way.

I know that for some of you, this is terrifying, luckily, we cover this in a later chapter when we talk about *ARTROVERTS*. The biggest mistake that I see artists make is thinking that they are separate from their art. They treat their art like a product that needs to be marketed and sold.

However, your art, your message, and *YOU* are inseparable.

130

If you want to build a culture around your art, you will have to push through some comfort zones. Luckily, you can be yourself the whole time and have some fun.

Step #2: Create some mutual excitement.

If you want your cult…ahem… culture to become an empire, you will need people to talk about what you are talking about. Like any supreme leader bent on world domination, you are nothing unless your message spreads. It starts with you, and your passion for what you're all about.

If you are not excited about what you are creating and the message you are sharing, chances are they won't be either. Imagine for a moment walking into an art show and asking about a particular work of art that you are interested in. The artist looks bored or disconnected, points at it and says, "meh, yeah, I like this one too." Would you go forth and tell the world about that amazing interaction? Probably not. You might tweet about it, but not in a way that's going to benefit the artist.

Our art will truly sell itself. However, if we are too salesy, too aloof, or desperate, we may kill the vibe and alter the meaning of the art to the person who wants it. If we are *ACTUALLY* excited about sharing our art, genuinely there to meet people, and are not focused on sales, the impact will be explosive. That excitement spreads and becomes its own force of nature. Honestly, why should you expect anyone else to be excited about your art if you are not showing your own excitement?

We have this idea that showing admiration for what we create is not humble or that we are full of ourselves if we share our excitement. That's ridiculous. That's like saying that a parent should introduce their kids as losers because being proud of them would be braggadocious. Be proud of your work and share your excitement. As a rule, however, make sure you are never lifting your work by putting someone else's work down.

That is not excitement, that's just insecurity being masked by your fake pride. There are no comparisons in the art world, just what we individually create, and it is ALL awesome.

Step #3: Spread the love.

So, cults have a reputation for weird versions of what "love" is supposed to mean. Honestly, it's a subject best not talked about in a marketing book. So, we are going to stay away from that nonsense. Instead, we're going to be expressing some genuine love and appreciation for the people that show up for you.

There will be times where you do an in person or virtual event and only one person may show up. I have seen some artists get hurt by this and ignore the person that *DID* show up to support them. The fact of the matter is that no one is required to show up, they are there to support you, so show some gratitude.

Klee was a lead singer in bands that toured for years and one thing she said that really stood out to me was, "No matter if there were 100 people or 2, we gave them the best show they had ever seen, we rocked that stage."

Remember one important fact – people have lives, and their lives don't revolve around you. Whether it is a thousand people or one person, always show your appreciation. Make them feel special for supporting what you do. They will return whatever feeling you send their way. If you ignore them, or spend your time focused on the people that didn't show up, then chances are they won't be at your next shindig.

Step #4: Interact with your peeps.

Have one on one distraction free interaction with your audience. Not so that you can ensure their maintained loyalty (gross), but because you recognize the awesomeness that is them and the value their ideas bring to the community.

Remember, most of the people that will relate to what you have to share will have common interests. It's like a special club of people that love what you bring to the world. It's like saying, "We have this in common and we're in this together."

Instead of standing on an unreachable pulpit pointing down at your devotees spouting off *"THE WORD OF YOU"* it's about having open communication and dialogue. Acknowledging what everyone brings to the mix and remaining relatable.

At the time of writing this we have close to 50K followers across all of our online platforms, we have hundreds of loyal collectors, and we manage our own membership platform for Rogue Artists. Obviously, that means we get a lot of messages across the board.

This can feel a little overwhelming, and it could be easy to ignore people reaching out to you. However, although it is impossible to be everywhere at once, I do recommend you find simple ways to stay in contact.

Klee and I have a *contact us* page for artists that want to ask us questions on our website. We are also highly interactive with our membership community. This is important, do not allow yourself to float off on your high horse and forget the people who have been there with you through the years.

Sometimes all it takes is showing a little appreciation and acknowledgment in what you share to get that message across.

Step #5: Have your own language and symbols.
Secret handshake anyone? Do you know the password? Of course you do, because you are one of the "in" crowd, one of the cool kids, you know what's up.

Every culture has their own lingo and meanings for things. Even if it is a small group of people who like each other. Think of the inside jokes, words, and names for things that you may have with your friends. This language may distinguish you from other groups. As Rogue Artists, we can have fun with the kind of information we put out there especially because we are paving the way.

As an artist, your art becomes symbols in themselves. When someone hangs your art on their wall, listens to your music, or wears your jewelry, they will be reminded that they are part of this special club. Anything you put out there, from clever names for things, catch phrases, to symbols, they all become your secret decoder ring.

You don't need to try too hard or overthink this. Honestly, this is something that happens organically when people spend time together and share openly.

It has more to do with a willingness to be your unique, awkward, nerdy, glorious, weird self and share that, than it does with some carefully or arbitrarily crafted set of "inner circle things". In this environment of sharing, others will feel comfortable being themselves, and the coming together in of itself will form its own language.

Step #6: Fight the enemy.
This is the most controversial step and one that is not easy to talk about. For the most part, if you are one of those scary cult leaders, this will be the glue that keeps people from straying from the path you laid out for them.

However, I hate to sour your plans on nefarious world domination, but in the end, it usually doesn't work out well for the villain. Many traditional cults demonize something in order to make their devotees feel shame if they take part in any outside ideas. They will shun anyone's outside perspective and push the idea that if something is not 'us' then it is 'them'. The last thing you want to be if you are part of a cult is to be one of 'them'.

The truth is that we are very used to living in a world of 'us vs them'. Whether it is a sports team, political party, or a dance off, we are used to having some sort of *bad guy* in our story.

People will relate to that. However, instead of being against something, you can have a cause that you stand *for* and it would be much more powerful. For example, Klee and I stand *FOR* empowerment, and bringing beauty and love into the world through art and what we share.

Our enemy is insecurity, disempowerment, and anything that might make someone feel like they are incapable of making their dreams come true. It doesn't make for very good "villainous leader" status because we are not shaming anyone for being different than us.

WE ARE IN THIS TOGETHER.

In my opinion, that is WAY more powerful. In other words, we're about inclusion and standing for who we are, rather than exclusion and standing against who we are not.

Step #7: Keep things familiar. Be consistent.
This is where we're really going to deviate from the cult mentality and practice of making the outside world feel unfamiliar and almost alien to anyone inside.

If your intention as a cult leader was to control people, this is where you would build a wall and claim that anything on the other side of the wall is dangerous. We are going to collapse the wall and build an actual foundation that matters.

"THIS IS ART... A!"

We are not going to shy away from or fear the world. Instead, from a solid foundation, a culture can embrace and communicate with the world. Your foundation will not be built upon fear or hierarchy, but upon genuine trust and dignity. In order to do this, your peeps need to know what to expect from you.

This means authenticity. This means keeping things real. This means actually doing good by and through your community, not just sounding good on paper.

This is what builds actual, real familiarity.

136

Step #8: Give your followers a safe place to congregate.

For the most part, being the supreme leader of a cult bent on world domination could be overwhelming. You need a place where you can give your villainous speech (followed by malevolent laughter) once without interruption or having to repeat yourself. A secret board room or diabolical underground lair might work. However, that can still be too much, world domination and giving villainous speeches is exhausting.

In my opinion, just setting up a safe place for people to hang out and share ideas is powerful. Throughout history, people who hold a common interest will always create a safe place where they can gather. Whether it is a secret temple with men in funny hats or a bunch of kids in a poorly constructed tree house, we all love to have a place to congregate.

Nowadays, we can create communal places in the virtual landscape giving people from all around the world the opportunity to become members. Whether it be your website, a dedicated server, a social media group, your living room, or a coffee shop, the ultimate goal is to have a place for discussion and brainstorming.

Your mission statement is again going to play an important role here. You begin creating a safe space by making known and staying true to your core values. Even those kids in the tree house usually had some club rules clearly stated somewhere.

I know, I know... "No girls allowed" is not a good example of a mission statement, but you get the idea. You continue nurturing a safe space by making sure your words and actions align with those values.

In essence, everything that we are focused on here is to create our own community or club of like minded people.

There are a lot of clubs out there, some are weird, some are exclusive, and some are snobby. I personally recommend you make your community of collectors and followers all inclusive.

Step #9: Leverage, make things easier, and be different.

If you are a morally questionable supreme leader, you'll watch your devotees closely… study them with a keen eye, learn what best motivates them and use that to bend them to your will. However, that's a lot of work and it's probably better for you and everyone else if you simply listen to one another and work together.

Watch and learn from what your collectors and audience are doing and the kinds of things they interact with the most. Listen to their advice and recommendations. Make it easier for them to do what they are already doing.

Give them access to valuable information they may be looking for. In other words, make it easy for your community to get what they want. How are your collectors talking about or sharing your creations? Can you make this easier for them?

This is where things really evolve into something of a collaboration that has never been seen before. Everything I recommend in this book is about shaping your career as an artist into something that has never come before it. Your uniqueness is what you bring to the world. If you want to achieve *cult status*, you will have to think outside the box in terms of how you put yourself out there and the way you communicate who you are. Your people will let you know what attracted them to you and you can build and evolve from there.

Step #10: Remember what matters.

Ultimately, when it comes to our collectors, followers, friends, audience, artists, or anyone, we want the best for them. We want them to grow, we want them to be happy. This is why we focus on the person and make it all about them. Not what we can *GET* out of them. Your brand is not about what you sell, it is about your relationship with people who relate to you and your art. It is about their experience, their enjoyment and what they get from you. When thinking about building an art career, remember that it will be built upon relationships.

You will have to take the lead in your art career and make it a point to give as much as you can. So much of the world is built on getting and taking whatever you can get. However, the most powerful thing you can do is give, and it will set you apart from most. If you are planning on building a culture and community around you and your work, make sure you appreciate and give more value than expected. Victory is ensured. *(Please insert evil laugh here).*

Free Range Art

NO ONE WANTS YOUR ART

A brutal truth I had to face was that no one was really interested in my art. In fact, no one is *actually* interested in anything they buy. I know it sounds pessimistically glib, and like I'm saying your art doesn't matter, but that's not what I'm saying.

People don't purchase things to own the item itself. Whether they are aware of it or not, humans buy stuff because they want what the item will do for them and how that process will make them feel.

This is why some artists have a difficult time separating themselves from the art they create. It has a meaning that runs deeper than just the art itself. Sometimes it is simply an emotional and social trophy that makes them feel like a good artist. In the case of a painting, the materials are mostly useless.

It may consist of some ground pigments, acrylic, oil, some canvas, and wood. You don't buy paint just to buy paint. You buy paint because it allows you to create, and when you create, you feel something. As an artist, you buy art materials because of what they could do for you and how that will make you feel.

Pick anything you own, and I mean anything. It could be something in your studio, office, kitchen, bathroom, or anything random. Make sure it is something you purchased and ask yourself these questions.

What does this do?
What am I able to do because I own this?
How does doing that make me feel?

If you can tap into the emotional reasons why you actually purchase things, you will have a profound insight into how marketing really works. This is at the most simplistic core of *ALL* marketing. It is so ubiquitous that we may not realize how influential our emotions are in buying something mundane like a stapler.

We are not buying a stapler. We are purchasing what a stapler can do and how we will feel better in doing it. Maybe you'll feel more organized, grown-up, or professional.

The color and kind of stapler will say something emotional about you too. Did you buy the small cheap one, a weird artsy one, or a fancy professional one?

Everything we buy and the reason we pay attention to it is that ultimately it will make us feel something.

As humans, we should be able to survive with our basic physical needs met. All it takes are nutrients, shelter, physical activity, sleep, and clean places to have bowel movements.

Yet the idea of tasteless gray food, an unadorned gray room with a basic bed, exercise equipment, complete solitude, and a toilet sounds like a nightmare. What would you buy for your gray room? How would you decorate it? Why? Would you find a way to connect with others? How would it make you feel?

You have a personality and a point of view reflected in what you buy, pay attention to, and create. When it comes to your art, you make what you like, and there is an emotional reason for that.

Getting that narrative across in the way you put yourself out there will be the foundation of everything you do. You cannot just sit on the sidelines and hope for the best.

You must get in there and get your hands dirty. Ask yourself the hard questions and look for answers.

Know what you stand for. Don't wait around for someone to tell you who you are and what your art represents. Take charge of your art career and your life.

Take control of what you are saying. I know this could be a terrifying step, and many of us avoid this, but if you are not speaking for yourself, then someone else is speaking for you and controlling the narrative of your life.

What do you and your art represent?
What are you about?
Who is this art for?
How would they benefit from owning my art?

Answering these questions will help you put both feet firmly on the ground and help you choose how to appropriately approach putting yourself out there.

At the end of the day, the best way to determine why people buy stuff is to look at how you make purchasing decisions. Here are the 7 steps to making a purchase.

Step 1 - Problem recognition. You identify a need. "Crap, I need to learn how to make sushi because it is too expensive to buy all the time." No matter what excuse we have, it will always come down to something emotional. It's not like I actually need sushi in my life... but I need sushi.

This could also be someone walking at an art fair and thinking, "I need some of this art in my life."

Step 2 - Product specification. You identify what precisely you need to make step 1 happen. After much research into making my own sushi, I make a list of all the tools and equipment I need to make my own delicious goodness.

This is when someone walks around your art booth investigating all the art, taking a closer look, and possibly asking questions.

Step 3 - Supplier search. At this stage, I am looking for the best and easiest place to buy what I need. I may be comparing price, information, quality, and general appearance.

When someone stops and compares your art in their mind. They may have seen art at another art booth that they liked. They will evaluate the price, quality, experience with you, and how the experience makes them feel.

Step 4 - Solicitation of information. This is the point where I have chosen a supplier for my sushi making materials. I go through and read the about page and find out a little more about them, just to see how the company makes me feel. If I get a bad vibe, I have a few other places in mind that I could go to.

This is where the person will ask you a few questions to determine if you are the right fit for them. After all, they are about to take a little piece of you home with them. If they get a bad vibe, or you are fake, there are other places they will go.

Step 5 - Pricing Evaluation. At this point, everything is in the cart, and I look at the price and determine whether it is worth it. I am comparing the cost of buying premade sushi to the money, time, and effort of making my own. Several emotional factors significantly influence my decision, such as the joy and pride of learning how to make my own sushi.

The person in your booth asks the price of your work, and they are evaluating several things. They are thinking about the cost of other work. Mostly they are thinking about bills and how much money is in their bank account vs. filling a space that the art would be perfect for. This is all emotional.

VALUE IS MORE THAN A PRICE TAG

Step 6 - Making the purchase. Yeah, it's sushi. I'm all in! At this point, I am looking at checkout and how easy it is. If there are too many steps to making a purchase, I will go somewhere else. I've had websites tell me that I needed to call them to make a purchase, and I rarely do.

The person is ready to purchase. They pull out a credit card, and you are either prepared to run it or send them to a nearby ATM. Make it easy for them. The experience is what it is all about and walking to an ATM sucks for most of us who don't use them anymore.

Step 7 - The review. At this point, I have made my purchase, and I review my experience. Was it enjoyable, helpful, educational, and easy? Is this going to be the place I trust and return to for all my sushi making needs?

The same thing happens in your art booth the moment the person leaves. They are reevaluating the entire experience, and all of it will determine whether they come back for more art. It's all about the emotional experience.

WHY DO HUMANS CONSUME ART?

One of the universe's biggest mysteries seems to be figuring out what kind of art sells when starting a creative career. People are constantly trying to guess what is trending so they can jump on that bandwagon early. I have had hundreds of desperate creatives approach me, wondering what kind of art they can create to make the big bucks.

This question is the equivalent of asking how many chickens it would take to kill a lion.

Is it a fat lion? How old is it? What kind of chickens are we talking about here?

I'm not necessarily saying it's a dumb question. There is just no absolute answer. There are too many factors to consider, such as area, economy, culture, population size, demographics, personality, and even then, there is no honest way of knowing.

When it comes down to it, all art is marketable, and all art is trending. It will *ALL* sell, but it needs to find the right person who wants to buy it. To fully understand what kind of art sells, you have to determine why people buy art in the first place. In fact, a great question to ask is, "Why do people buy anything?"

It amazes me that as humans living in all the diverse cultures we live in, our motivations are very similar when it comes to buying stuff. Yes, we may speak different languages, have unique quirks, and have different customs, but our urges are all rather fundamentally alike.

Contrary to popular belief, we humans aren't as savvy as we might like to think. You might picture yourself comparing brands, weighing out pros and cons, and evaluating options when choosing to purchase something. However, underneath all the posturing, our decision-making is not so complex.

We are social and emotional creatures who make all of our choices based on how that choice will make us feel. The hamster wheel in our head is wired to buy stuff because of the potential of how we will respond emotionally.

Our choices are so emotionally motivated that neuroscientists found that if brain areas that generate emotions are damaged, it will render us incapable of making decisions.

Whenever someone buys art, they decide to invest in the artist, but ultimately, they are investing in their emotional well-being. This is not rational decision-making.

This is essential to recognize if you are going to market your art. We often make the mistake of trying to persuade someone to purchase our art using silly tactics like logic and reason.

These tactics don't regularly work. Humans are driven to buy stuff because of how it will make them feel. Luckily, as artists, we deal in the creation and capturing of emotions.

However, if you are one of those creative people out there who doesn't investigate the emotional reasons you create the art you create, you will struggle with this. You must be willing to dig deeper and spend that time studying your art.

How do you expect anyone else to feel anything for your art if you don't feel anything?

Individuals are motivated by feelings. So if you want a potential buyer to recognize your art as something they want, the experience and interaction must be engaging, impassioned, and emotional. You must understand how the art may make someone feel by understanding how you feel about it. This is how anyone that is selling anything makes a sale. Think about it for a moment. What is actually being sold in most marketing campaigns?

- *Every luxury item is sold as reassurance of self-worth, acceptance, and elite status.*
- *All communication devices are sold as portals of connection to friends, family, and more relationships.*
- *All pairs of athletic shoes are sold as an adventure, a sense of worth, and glory through competition.*

They are not selling a product. They are selling how you may feel owning it.

Artists who are successful highlight the emotional response a collector will realize by owning the art. The quality, technique, style, and other technical factors are important, but ultimately the feeling is what matters.

When I look through my collection, I see what the art or series of art represents. I have art expressing potential feelings of love, relationships, sexual desires, empowerment, imagination, beauty, wonder, nonconformity, passion, overcoming, calm, and the list goes on. We sell the feeling evoked by the work, not the work itself.

Emotion is all part of the package. That's why I think about everything in an emotional tone. I ask myself, "How does this make me feel? What am I saying with this?"

For example, I think about the art I create, my logo, my homepage, my packaging, my displays, and how I present myself because it is all part of the emotional experience. I consider the words and messaging carefully when writing content, posts, creating a video, or anything I put out in public.

- How could this make someone feel?
- What am I saying with this?
- Am I being emotive and engaging with what I create and my interaction?
- What is the experience of the location where I am selling, whether online or off?
- Even if they don't purchase anything, what feeling are they leaving with?

Every interaction has the potential to convey a powerful feeling about your art and your creative brand.

Why would people buy your art? Because of how *YOU* make them feel. I think it's too common to lose sight of that and treat our art like a random product.

This is one of the many reasons typical marketing tactics don't work unless you have a handle on the impassioned side of things.

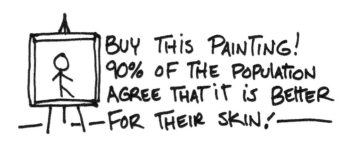

Suppose you are off trying to build your email lists, get new subscribers, and pay for ads on social media without understanding the emotional reasoning behind it. In that case, you are at the whims of an uncaring algorithm. You might as well be throwing a dart at a dartboard while blindfolded and standing on your head.

You may get lucky and hit the bullseye, but chances are you won't.

Remember the motivation behind the reason you put yourself out there. Even when purchasing an ad for your art, you are doing it for your own emotional reasons. Think about it for a moment. Do you just randomly buy ads for no reason? Did you buy the ad with exacting data on how many sales you will make? Does the ad have a money-back guarantee if you get no sales?

Or did you purchase the ad in hopes that it will attract new buyers and make some money?

BUY THIS!!! BUY IT NOW!!! NOW!!!

Believe it or not, buying that ad was an emotional purchase. There is absolutely no guarantee that paying for an ad is going to get you more buyers.

First off, unless something is compelling about your ad, no one is going to even notice it. Second, most ads are annoying and the equivalent of sticking your money in a slot machine.

Unless you are targeting a specific need that already has a market that you can advertise to, you are wasting your money by buying an ad.

Why would you logically do that? You wouldn't. You would, however, purchase the hope of better financial times and what the ad could potentially bring you, which is exposure, success, or money. This means you are chasing a sense of security.

Everything we purchase is because of deep emotional reasoning.

As an aside, I'm not saying to not purchase ads, but you need to understand the emotional stuff. Your ad should be creative and be more than a paid plea begging someone to buy your art. Most ads have typical lingo and a boring message. Don't do that to people. If you are going to force them to watch your ad, at least make it enjoyable and connect with them.

Humans will invest in you because of how you, your message, and your art makes them feel.

Someone may buy your art because it is aesthetically pleasing and makes them feel good. They may buy the art because it's an excellent conversation piece, making them feel unique.

There are so many reasons people buy art, but it always comes back to emotion. To share my experience, here are several reasons why people have purchased my art over the years.

Connected Art Collector: This is by far the most common in my experience. I have had people stop in their tracks and buy a piece of art simply because something about the work spoke to them. They will usually have a visibly solid emotional response to it.

These collectors tend to purchase art that speaks to them deeply. This is the art that is a visual expression of meaning in their life. I tend to engage in deep conversation with them about the art and how it connects to their story. This is by far my favorite interaction with another human being.

Life Change Art Collector: These personalities buy my art because it inspires them, and they feel alive owning it. I usually have long conversations about something they want to change in their lives. They tend to break through comfort zones, and the art evokes feelings of zeal to undertake otherwise challenging tasks. The art is a reminder to them of the life they want to achieve.

Decor Art Collector: These humans purchase art that helps make a room feel more beautiful. Art can transform any setting by giving it a character that is more engaging and enriching. This collector cares deeply about how their surroundings make them feel.

Art Gifting: Although art is a very personal thing, I've had many people purchase it for gifting to a loved one. This is one of the reasons I also sell small, easy to create pieces. They are buying the joy that comes with giving something unique and original.

Prestige Art Collector: Some of my collectors own my original art simply because they are part of the prestige of owning my art. They are proud to own an original "Rafi." In their opinion (and in mine) it gives them bragging rights. Some of them have been with me since the beginning and watched me grow to become popular in my area. Artwork can make people feel like they are part of an exclusive group. These collectors tend to challenge each other by the size of their collection of "Rafi" art.

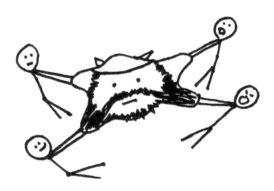

Love Of Art Collector: I've had people collect my art simply because they love art and found a work of art beautiful. For some people purchasing art for the love of the work is enough.

These pieces tend to be more minor and inexpensive. These collectors find joy and prestige in their diverse collections. I always enjoy our conversations because they talk about art as a whole.

Statement Art Collector: Some personages collect my art because it makes a statement. Some of my art is considered controversial, rogue, and inappropriate. Many of my collectors own it because it reflects their desire to be different. In displaying my art, they enjoy the controversy that it may bring. This art may make some people feel uncomfortable, question the status quo, and inspire self-expression.

The "YOU" Art Collector: Most of the art I sell goes to humans who enjoy interacting with me or what I stand for overall. I tend to have a lot of deep conversations with people, and we form a connection.

Because my art represents me and my belief system, once they connect with me, they connect with my art. They may find me online through something I wrote, filmed, or recorded. Many will start following me after interacting with me in person at a show.

As a side note: I tend to talk honestly and vulnerably because I like connecting with people. I don't go the vanilla route of only saying things I think they'll agree with. I don't enjoy fake surface conversations especially when it comes to my art.

Some people may be there to just buy something and you will not connect, and that's fine, but I think ultimately, you should always be yourself. Don't be agreeable just to sell something. You can agree to disagree. Just don't be a jerk about it.

Reminiscent Art Collector: Some people connect with my art because it reminds them of something that brought them great joy in their life. Something about the art reminds them of something unique that they experienced.

Empowerment Art Collector: Many collectors of my art purchase from me because of this reason. I spend a lot of time talking about living an empowered life and associating it with my art. By describing the feeling of the work such as, "This piece depicts the moment my blinders shattered when leaving the corporate world." I'm able to connect on a deeper level. These collectors use the art as a daily reminder of the empowering message they attached to it.

Niche Art Collector: I also have niche collectors who may purchase bird paintings because they are bird watchers or flowers because they love nature. The pieces are reminders of identity and a hobby they love.

Investment Art Collector: I've had people collect art from me because they believe I am going somewhere with my art career. These are collectors whose sole intent for buying art is to build a collection that will yield some kind of financial return. Their collections usually involve many artists, and they may not be loyal until you make it big. This gives them emotional bragging rights, prestige, and the ability to show that they make good investments.

Of course, when it comes to humans, trying to pin one down is like trying to wrestle the moon, you just can't wrap your arms around it. I do have a simple way of identifying the people I interact with that helps me determine our relationship when it comes to my art. However, regardless of the identification, I interact with all of them equally.

Pretty Butterflies. They love art and flitter about from artist to artist. They are not loyal, but will buy expensive art if they love it. You may interact with them once, or sporadically.

Art Friends. These are people who buy art from you because they love both you and your art. They will invest the most in you and are extremely loyal, and I recommend investing in that relationship.

Static Cling. These are people that attach themselves to you because they think you are interesting. They also might believe they will get something from being around you and may try to take a lot of your time. They are extremely loyal, but may never actually buy your art.

Passersby. These are people who are completely uninterested in you and your art. They might glance over at it and grunt, but that's about it.

As you can see, it is the emotional connection and relationships that are most profitable. Not the selling technique or marketing plan, but the relationship is what ultimately matters.

Emotions also make sense of why people buy big ticket art for a lot of money in the mainstream art world. The problem is that a lot of us will stop at the dollar signs and not look a little deeper. Much of the motivation behind high dollar purchases has to do with either investment, prestige, or reputation. Going back to Elvis's guitar in an earlier chapter, it may not be the art itself but the bragging rights of who owned it before. Also, having a rare Warhol, Picasso, Dali, or Banksy will give the new owner prestige and additional bragging rights. It all comes down to what the art can do for them emotionally no matter how you look at it.

As artists, we already have an emotional reason why we make what we make. This puts us in an influential position when it comes to connecting with other humans. You may or may not be aware of the emotional scope and depth of what you produce, but it exists, and it is powerful.

Understanding the amount of power you have in shaping your narrative when putting yourself out there is essential. Don't take this lightly. There are too many creatives desperately trying to get noticed by any means necessary, even if it means causing controversy or drama.

What you do is powerful, and there is absolutely no need to be desperate. The only thing you need is patience, persistence, and a deeper understanding of human behavior and emotional needs.

Stop, look, listen and hear what your art is saying. It is the feeling evoked from your message that will connect. Pay attention to it. Listen to the art you create. What is it telling you? What does it make you feel? That feeling is why people buy art.

At the end of the day, humans buy what they buy to have their emotional needs met. They want to feel a certain way by having, using, watching, eating, wearing, hearing, and smelling whatever they just purchased. It is what they think the art can do for them and make them feel that ultimately matters. Luckily, as an artist, you just happen to be one of those incredible humans who bottles emotion in what they create.

THE COMPELLING NEED TO BUY ART

Now that we know our decisions are motivated by emotions, what exactly are we looking for when we are convinced to spend our hard-earned money on things? This is at the core of all marketing and sales and is honestly what matters most when you do ANY marketing. If you don't understand the actual motivation behind why people buy stuff, then your marketing might be useless. For example, life-size celebrity cardboard cutouts are popular, and that doesn't make any sense. Think about it, why would we buy a cardboard cutout of Bob Ross even though there is no practical reason for owning it? Bob Ross is a reminder of his message, and I would love to have him hanging out in my art studio.

For all intents and purposes Bob Ross's TV program was about learning how to paint, but that's not why people tuned in. There are countless people teaching painting techniques on the internet, but only a handful of them are popular. This is because they understand that the people that are tuning in want more than just painting techniques. They want to feel hope.

"The secret to doing anything is believing that you can do it. Anything that you believe you can do strong enough, you can do. Anything. As long as you believe." - Bob Ross

Now, just like Bob Ross building a personal relationship with his audience, what ultimately matters is putting yourself out there and sharing your voice. Bob was a painter, but his words, mannerisms, general attitude towards creativity, and what he had to say made him famous. It was what he offered emotionally that caused people to tune in.

We are all looking for something. We all have emotional needs. The question is, what emotional need does your art and message help to resolve? Bob gave some people reassurance of worth and a creative outlet in a world focused on a cutthroat 9 to 5 culture.

People all over the world discover and purchase hundreds of thousands of works of art every day. It can be challenging to determine why they buy what they buy. No two people are alike, and there is no way to point at something that works across the board. Anyone that says they have the secret to selling art is full of crap.

However, there are *some* things we can look at. Here are a few influences that will help you navigate some reasons why people buy what they buy.

Cultural factors.
Culture is the fundamental values, perceptions, wants, and behaviors learned by humans from their families and close friends. This could be an ethnic upbringing or just people in your neighborhood growing up.

These are friends, family, and neighbors with a shared value system based on shared life experiences and conditions. For example, when I was a teenager, I went to a store that sold religious candles and felt compelled to buy one because I grew up in a Hispanic household. The candles are hideous and not aesthetically pleasing to look at or smell.

So yeah, cultural influence. It was the safety that I felt having one of these religious candles lit in my house to cast bad spirits away that motivated me to buy it. So, my emotional reason for buying the hideous candle was the security that was passed down through my culture.

Social factors.
This is where a group of people share similar values and/or want to achieve individual or shared goals. This could be at work, favorite sports team, political party, or any other group of people a person identifies with. This is where the word-of-mouth influence plays a big part in buying behavior.

People will identify themselves as part of a group that associates to either a subculture, anticulture, or something else. For example, buying American-made, being a sci-fi nerd, a jock, environmentally conscious, or someone who works out, is all part of a social based culture.

I did an art show at a muscle car festival once and no one understood why I didn't have paintings of muscle cars. I obviously didn't sell anything because I wasn't sensitive to their car culture (social factor). Had I been, I probably wouldn't have signed up for the show and let another artist who created what they were looking for show their work.

Personal factors.
This describes a person's age, stage in life, occupation, economic situation, choices, attitudes, and personality. Coupled with both their cultural and social factors, this creates their unique identity and lifestyle that is both based on their upbringing and life experiences. Lifestyles are something that has been researched in depth by marketing companies.

160

This includes a person's hobbies, activities, interests, and opinions.

This is why a bottle of brown sugar water will be imbued with relatable social, cultural, and personal factors in its marketing. This is why story is so important. If you pay attention to most story elements in marketing you will find five qualities associated with lifestyle and personal factors: reliability, enthusiasm, capability, elegance, and ruggedness.

For example:

- *A Subaru is so reliable you might as well get a nap in while driving it (don't do that!)*
- *A Redbull is packed with so much enthusiasm that it will literally give you wings.*
- *Nike shoes will make you so capable you'll be marathon ready. (So put down that donut.)*
- *Chanel fragrance will make you so elegant that no one will notice that stain on your sweatpants.*
- *This bottle of whiskey (enjoyed atop a mountain) is just the thing for your rugged nature.*

Will a car make you reliable? Will an energy drink give you enthusiasm? Will shoes make you marathon ready? Will perfume make you elegant? Will a bottle of whiskey make you rugged? Probably not, but the story is compelling and gives hope to those who aspire to those emotional qualities.

THERE ARE SOME THINGS MONEY CAN'T BUY.
FOR EVERYTHING ELSE, THERE'S MASTERCARD.

Psychological factors.

Motivation research refers to studies designed to find hidden motivations. Maslow's hierarchy of needs classifies needs into a pyramid consisting of *psychological needs, safety needs, social needs, esteem needs, and self-actualization needs.* When you look at most clever marketing out there, it is directed at these emotional needs.

Everything fulfills some kind of emotional need. Whether it is a Bob Ross cutout, a banana costume you ordered at 3 in the morning, or a particular type of meal plan it is all fulfilling a need.

Altogether, it has been hypothesized that eight emotional needs may compel us to buy things. Marketing companies will target emotional needs in just about every marketing campaign you see. Because human emotions come in all shapes and sizes, unfortunately, much of that marketing targets insecurity and fear. However, as Rogue Artists, we can take this same knowledge and use it positively. Becoming familiar with how psychology is used in marketing will help you set yourself apart when putting yourself out there.

Emotional Need Number 1: *We Are Looking For Emotional Security.*
Due to not-so-great things like pandemics, disease, guilt, war, bad relationships, pollution, hackers, theft, bullies, abuse, and so on (the list is endless), people may not feel very safe or secure. So we are looking for comfort from it all. Sometimes, with everything going on, we can feel fragile and lose a sense of control over our world.

This is usually used in one of two ways: things that make you feel like everything will be alright, or something that lays out all of the world's dangers and why you should be worried. Either way, we tend to pay attention. The news media outlets tend to use the negative aspects of this emotional need to gain ratings and viewers.

As Rogue Artists, we can use our creative power to highlight what is going on in the world from an empowered point of view. Something that offers comfort within ourselves is very powerful and will set us apart.

What we have to share in the world as artists can make a huge impact. I am reminded of a special quote that keeps me going when things may seem dark. This reminds me why it is important to share our creations. When asked why he performed at a free concert just two days after getting shot, Bob Marley responded,

"The people who are trying to make this world worse aren't taking a day off. How can I?"

Emotional Need Number 2: *We Are Looking For Reassurance of Worth.* We live in a world that compares, discriminates, labels, and measures everything against unrealistic and arbitrary standards. Many people never come to understand that they are remarkable, beautiful, and precious.

People are expected to conform to the whims of society to be accepted. As a result, many humans feel unappreciated or unfulfilled at work, by society, in personal relationships, family, or higher social-economic classes.

It is pretty easy to feel insignificant in the world today and lose the sense of our own value.

This need is targeted in two ways. Either you are not good enough and need a product or service to be better, or you are already unique, wonderful, and worthy as long as you are part of "this" group.

This need is why there are so many sleazy schemes that will promise quick fame of some sort, money, weight loss, muscle gain, purpose, higher status, admiration, beauty, and more. As a result, we can find ourselves constantly chasing a carrot, trying to be more beautiful, successful, and perfect so we can be taken seriously.

As a Rogue Artist, we understand that every single human being is beautiful, precious, worthy and remarkable. We don't require them to purchase our art or even subscribe to what we're about in order to gain access to their own personal power. We treat everyone we encounter with respect, dignity, love, and appreciation they deserve with no prerequisite or hidden agenda.

Emotional Need Number 3: *We Are Looking For Ego Gratification.*
We live in a world of standardizing behaviors and lifestyles. In other words, it is easy to choose to conform to the particular lifestyle that you were born into but may wish for something more. Some people come from money, and some don't.

Some people consider themselves creative, sexy, eccentric, democrat, republican, planet conscious, vegetarian, meatatarian, religious, conservative, secular, weird, etc. Honestly, any label that a person can hope to identify with is marketable to someone.

This need is targeted in several ways. Either you need to keep up appearances by wearing, knowing, owning something exclusive, or by the promise that people will view you as "better than" if you use a particular product or service. This need also targets people who identify with specific causes or lifestyles.

The promise to make you more desired, more intelligent, more powerful, hipper, more successful, creative, greener, and better. This is usually touted as the right or smart choice, and you might actually feel superior because of it.

This is fueled by the narrative that no matter how "good" you are, you're never doing or being enough.

Your eyelashes look… fine, but they're not epic. Your body is fit, but not shredded. You're a smart cookie, but couldn't your IQ use just a little "boost?" Would you really subject your guests to this thread count of sheets? You're doing your part for the betterment of the planet, but are you doing EVERYTHING you can? This reusable tote can help you get there.

Companies back in the 60s and 70s realized that less consumers were buying their products because the hippie movement was anti consumerism. So, they started to promote products that seemed more anti consumerism and created a new niche that would satiate the new ego. Everything has a market that can be related to.

As long as you understand the emotional reasons why people buy things, you understand how to market. Ego needs will change and luckily, as artists, we don't have to chase trends. Our art will always touch on something emotional no matter how much it changes.

As Rogue Artists, we stand by our message understanding that someone out there will connect with what we have to say. It is not about stroking anyone's ego into thinking that we stand for the same things, it is about people finding us who are empowered by what we put out into the world.

Emotional Need Number 4: *We Are Looking For Creative Outlets.*
In this automated world where it's easy to binge on your favorite shows and most jobs are monotonous soul-sucking endeavors, people increasingly have little room for creativity.

For Rogue Artists who are compelled to create or die, it's easy to forget what it's like for people who don't have that outlet. The world is divided on whether or not artistic expression has value or meaning. So to make up for the lack of creativity, people find an alternative through products that enable them to be creative.

This need is targeted in two ways. Either you are hopeless unless you take the course and follow the specific rules, or you are already creative and just need to tap into that creativity.

Things like assembly kits, packaged meal ingredients, tutorials, classes, home improvement projects, wine shop paint classes, adult coloring books, and many hobby-related activities like video games, puzzles, and model kits can make you feel like a creative badass.

As Rogue Artists, we understand that there's nothing wrong with the above-mentioned outlets of creativity. We also understand that humans seeking a creative outlet are not wallets with legs. They are humans. So, we share our creativity and our magic openly in hopes to further inspire them to their own creative expression.

As Rogues, we create art in the world in order to give an example of what creative expression could look like.

Emotional Need Number 5: *We Are Looking For Love Objects.*
Just like children may have a favorite doll, blanket, pet, toy, or rock with googly eyes, adults have their emotional keepsakes as well. This is usually an object that represents much more than what the thing actually is. Usually, it represents a trait or preference that they admire about themselves, like collecting movie memorabilia or collecting merchandise from your favorite sports team. The wedding industry relies heavily on this need.

This need is usually targeted in two ways. Fulfilling representations of your existing preferences, lifestyle, and personality. OR, If you are going through a midlife crisis or a big life change, owning something new that may identify your new personality, likes, and lifestyle.

At the core of this is something beautiful. Humans love to love. We love to give love, and we love to feel love in return. This is why, as a child, we would have our favorite teddy bear (or in Klee's case, a really mangy looking stuffed cat). I think the thing that marketers miss in the equation is unconditional love.

Marketers are (sometimes, unfortunately) in the business of exploiting our desire to love and be loved with grandiose ideas about what love is, that miss the mark entirely.

Love objects are beautiful. You could love a crusty old blanket because it gives you a sense of security. You could love your grandfather's flannel because it makes you feel safe and warm. When it comes to art, we have no idea what the meaning will be to the person viewing it.

As Rogue Artists, we acknowledge the fact that if another person loves what you've created enough to take it home with them and see it every day, that is something inexplicably profound, and not to be exploited. This is why we pour everything into our art, because we know that what we put out there has meaning.

A creation that is born out of an artist's love and excitement will inevitably go on to spark love and excitement in another person, as long as you are creating from a genuine place.

Emotional Need Number 6: *We Are Looking For A Sense of Power.*
We live in what we believe is a power-driven culture. Financial success and power walk hand in hand. For the most part, many feel a sense of powerlessness and are looking for a solution.

Humans may feel the need to chase power (usually in the form of money) and are gratified by objects that symbolically represent it.

This need is targeted in two ways. Either you use their product or service to maintain power or to gain power and authority.

Advertisers will promise to move you up in the world. In moving up the social ladder, the need for power seems to increase in some people. Possessions get more expensive, the clothing gets fancier, and hobbies get weird. The promise of more power (like in a strong vehicle), more money, more time, more admirers, more control over others, and more control over your own life.

As Rogue Artists, we understand that real power doesn't come from hollow acquisitions or from selling another person on the idea of acquisitions as a means to greatness. Real power comes from inside of the individual.

It doesn't come from validation, it doesn't come from societal status, it comes from your own integrity and your own understanding that while you may not be able to control outside circumstances, you can ultimately control how you respond to anything that gets thrown your way. That is real power. As a working artist, you are a living example of this, as long as you remain true to your mission statement and values. Your work will reflect who you are, and thus make a powerful statement that people can connect with.

This emotional need is the reason many artists struggle with marketing themselves. If they undervalue their meaning and power in the world, they will find themselves chasing a carrot and being pulled by the whims of all the *SHOULDS* in marketing. Standing firm in who you are and what you stand for gives you the footing you need to carry yourself through the minefield of emotional challenges. Our biggest challenge in putting ourselves out there is not believing we are good enough to do so.

As artists, we have been historically symbolized as powerless, and the myth of the starving artist has dominated the minds and hearts of a culture. However, the truth is that we are the keepers of records, illustrators of the moment, we are the avatars of change, and we are the force that brings about innovation. We are powerful. When you remember that and remember that what you create can bring something exceptional to someone's life, you remember your important role in the world.

Emotional Need Number 7: *We Are Looking for Roots.*
We all want to feel a sense of home. The world seems to be moving so fast, and the things that felt familiar to our youth seem to be rapidly disappearing. This also represents familiarity and a sense of knowing what to expect.

This is why most chain stores feel and look the same no matter where they are. They feel safe and familiar, and you know how to interact in that space.

170

There's nothing wrong with that consistency, there's an entire section of this book dedicated to that very subject. The problem arises when a company's values get flushed down the crapper while the look of a place remains the same, giving the impression of "safety and familiarity" because they value appearances over integrity.

This need is targeted in two ways. Either there is no place like home or I need this product or service to make it feel like home again.

Advertisers' promise of all-natural, homemade, time honored tradition, connection to our childhood, strong family values, a callback to the greatest generation, make things great again, pride in the country, and pride in your culture are used to promote this need.

For a lot of us, roots are important, and wanting a familiar atmosphere or ideology to be comfortable in is understandable.

Here's the thing: people get all mixed up in their brain jars when it comes to the difference between roots and resistance to change. We have the tendency to remember "the old times" as better than now.

In case you are wondering, they were not. Our ancestors faced things that would make your twitter feed go silent for months. However, nostalgia is big business for marketing companies.

As Rogue Artists, we embrace change because we understand that it is inevitable. We also understand that change doesn't mean we throw away core values and foundations that made us what we are. The values we embrace will continue to guide us. You can honor your roots and embrace an ever-changing environment at the same time.

This is what propels us forward while not forgetting the wisdom we've gained along the way through struggle, joy, oppression, progress, failure, success, challenge, resilience, injustice, perseverance, separation, community, and all the myriad of events that make up the human story.

One important factor of putting yourself out there is flexibility and the understanding that things are in a constant state of change. Rogue Artists embrace change and look to the future because they know that sticking with an outdated ideology will leave them stagnant and not moving forward. There is nothing wrong with nostalgia and admiring the things of the past, there is beauty there. However, using it as a crutch to hinder change is simply a waste of time and eventually the world will pass you by.

Truly honoring our roots is not about going backwards or giving the impression of a snapshot in time. Truly honoring our roots is all about moving forward and bringing our earned wisdom and values with us into the now and into the future.

WHO YOU WERE, IS NOT A REFLECTION OF WHO YOU CAN BE.

Ultimately, the real sense of security we get from our roots has nothing to do with living in the past. It is the nurturing aspect of understanding that we will always bring our story forward into whatever new phase of life we are heading into. The world is changing, but if we are rooted in understanding that change *IS* part of our story, then we have nothing to fear.

Emotional Need Number 8: *We Are Looking For Immortality.*
Ok, admittedly, this section is difficult to write about. Undoubtedly, one of the most prominent fears a human being may face is *death*. People may fear that by kicking the bucket, they will be forgotten and/or will become a blank page in the book of life. This motivates some people to seek to create meaning in their lives. Others desperately seek to combat aging by any means necessary.

This need is targeted by companies by promoting constantly running from death, holding on to youth, or wanting to live on after death by leaving a legacy. There are all kinds of products that claim to help with this emotional need. The thing is, people are not actually buying aging creams, vitamins, life insurance, or diet programs. Instead, they are purchasing a chance to stay young and/or beat death. These campaigns will try to convince you that they are there for you in the fight to cheat old age, death, or being forgotten.

No matter how you look at it, the grim reaper is coming for us all. It is ultimately the ONE thing every single human on the planet has in common. It is a terrifying concept for most, and one of the fears that we all have to grapple with on our own. Some people grow old gracefully and enjoy their old age, while others see it as a reminder that their days are numbered.

The thing is that artists have an interesting role when it comes to death. Many of us are motivated by it and believe that the art we create will be our way to live on. Some of us immortalize others in our creations. I have personally done several memorial portraits of people and pets, and Klee has done several memorial and heirloom works of jewelry. It is an honor as an artist to bring some semblance of peace to such a difficult subject.

In this section, I'm not going to tell you how a Rogue Artist approaches this subject, but I will tell you how I approach this. I want you to keep in mind that these are my own personal thoughts on the subject and by no means a guide, this is something you would want to investigate yourself.

Personally, I don't run away from death, I embrace it. Let me explain. The truth is I have no idea how much time I have left. It could be a day, a few hours, or a hundred more years. The only thing I know for sure is that I am alive right now as I type this. The only thing I truly have any control over is what I am going to say in this sentence.

This is happening right now for me. Although you may be reading this several years after I have typed it, the fact remains that my moment in now and how I use it is all that matters.

Embracing the fact that I may croak at any moment allows me to fully appreciate what I have in front of me and do all I can now while I am here. I'm not waiting around for tomorrow to be happy, to say I love you, or to put myself and my art out there. I am going to do it now while I can. There is peace in that, because I am not chasing after the hope that I will live a little longer, I am making the most of the moments I have. So, whether it is a day or another hundred years, I will live each and every day to the fullest, and that is the gift of mortality.

Congratulations! You got to the other side of the eight compelling needs, and you are still here. I know this is a difficult section to put into a marketing book because essentially, we are just talking about our feelings. However, feelings and emotions are what drive the world so the more we talk about them the better. Products are rarely advertised as the product itself and all clever marketing is based on tapping into emotions.

In my experience, genuinely successful people help others authentically find their own success and don't try to put one over on someone.

This is why it is essential to figure out who you are, your story, and what motivates you to create. Unfortunately, many marketing campaigns use emotions to get what they want (mainly money) without any real benefit to the person purchasing the product.

This is why understanding the emotional needs that compel people to purchase things is important. Your reason for why you are putting yourself out there must be more than just making money. It must be more profound than that. It must connect and be meaningful to others. It must have a strong meaning to you.

"THE ONLY WAY TO DEAL WITH CRITICS IS TO GO OVER THEIR HEADS DIRECT TO THE PUBLIC." —JOHN LENNON

For example, let's say you do pet portraits, and you want to know a little more about why someone might buy a dog. Looking at each compelling need will give you insights into why someone may decide to bring a little furry beast into their lives.

Emotional Security: Having a dog makes them feel safe from threats and will make them feel less alone.

Reassurance of Worth: A dog makes them feel special every time they get home.

Ego Gratification: They consider themselves a dog person and own dog-centric things to show that they are part of this exclusive group.

Creative Outlets: Have dogs for therapy, go for walks, and take part in dog-centric social events.

Love Objects: They want something to love and take care of and want something that will love them.

Sense of Power: They own award-winning stock, elite guard dogs, or rare breeds. These dogs will be seen as prized possessions.

Roots: They've always had dogs growing up and want that sense of home.

Immortality: A gift from someone who passed away or a puppy from a previous dog.

What do you connect with the most?
What would your story be?
What would your content say that would appeal to each personality you connect with?
How can you benefit them?
Where would you find them?
What specific service or art would you offer each compelling need?

As a Rogue Artist, you investigate the deep emotional motives behind your art, and you try to put it in the awareness of humans who may benefit from it. However, if you don't think about how your work fulfills those compelling needs in your own life, you may not understand why anyone else would benefit from it.

I know some of you out there have a really hard time talking about your feelings or investigating this subject a little deeper. Many of us grow up believing that talking about our feelings makes us weak. However, in my experience, you can either bury your feelings and not understand most of what motivates you or choose to understand what actually motivates everyone.

There are stereotypes out there that can cause a lot of damage. Things like, "boys don't cry," "girls are too emotional," or "it's not good to show your emotions". The fact of the matter is that you are either emotionally intelligent, or you are not. When you take a look inside of yourself to identify what you are actually feeling and why, it gives you the space to think. From there you can make decisions and move forward. If not, there is no forward movement.

Unfortunately, many artists that quit don't know how to talk about their art in emotional tones. They talk about business and not feeling. They try to close the sale and hustle the work as if it were just any run of the mill product. They miss out on the powerful connection that the art brings. Feeling emotions is not a sign of weakness. On the contrary, you must be strong to be willing to go there. You must be willing to look deeper into the infinite onion that is you.

The truth is we all buy what we buy because we want to feel something powerful in our lives. Art is designed to tell a story and evoke an emotion. It is that story and emotion that will connect with someone. Pay attention to what needs your art and message may give some relief to and investigate that further.

YOUR STORY MAY BE THEIR STORY.

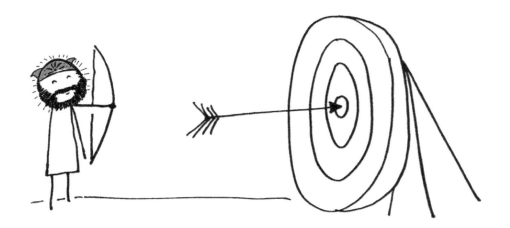

WHO IS YOUR TARGET MARKET?

If you've ever read or watched anything on marketing, you probably heard the term "target market." Typically your target market is the particular group of people at which your product or service is aimed. Your art is the flaming arrow, and your audience is the apple on someone's head. In other words, these are the primary type of people that buy the kinds of art you create. Everything you do is aimed at getting their attention. Your writing, social media posts, the events you do, the type of art you make, and anything else you put into the world.

Honestly, the whole idea of having a target market makes it sound a little weird to me. It's almost like hiding in the woods for an art collector to show up and fall into your trap. Luckily, it doesn't actually work that way as long as you remain honest about your motivations.

For example, if you have a burning desire to create pet portraits, your target audience is pet owners. So, you become infused into the world of pet-owner-hood. The blogs you write would be targeted at helping pet owners with tips on pet-owning, funny images, memes about pets' lives, and personal stories of the pet portrait commissions you have taken and why they meant so much to you. Basically, you are sharing how you feel about it all. Some of the ways I would go about this are simple.

- *I would contact local and online business resources for pet owners and find a way to collaborate and be part of any events they do for their public.*
- *I would also visit dog parks and do some outside painting of random pets with the owner's permission.*
- *I would become a member of online pet owner groups and not advertise my art, but casually talk about commissions I have done.*
- *I would make sure to travel to pet festivals and take part in pet-loving culture events.*
- *I would make fun videos of my art adventures with my pets and the funny life of being an artist with pets. Things like challenging my dog to create my portrait and other fun videos like that.*
- *I would write some guest articles for popular pet blogs, and every post on social media would be fun, pet-centric, and artistic.*

Most importantly, I would also have a pet. To really get into any culture, you must be recognized as a part of that culture. Don't get me wrong, you can create a pet portrait business and not own any pets, but that just sounds weird. I am always skeptical of someone who makes something they wouldn't want themselves.

Any culture club is readily marketable because you can easily find the places, services, and events where the members would congregate. This is called Target Marketing, where all your marketing efforts go towards one well-defined and specific section of the population that has a common interest.

It sounds complicated but it is not. In layman's terms, hang out where THOSE people hang out. These are clubs that already have their own culture and niche. Things like being into a sports team, dogs, cats, wine, motorcycles, cars, comics, plants, coffee, or anything popular that may have an existing market. If you create any art that appeals to that market, then you have found your niche.

I think this is an intelligent way to approach an existing market with something you create. However, as multi-faceted artists, I think you miss out on opportunities if you only focus on one niche.

I say this because many online marketing gurus try to get you to focus on marketing only one thing. They say that you will confuse the customer if you do too many different styles of art. In my opinion, people that say that don't understand art and have no business trying to teach artists how to market their creativity.

First off, people aren't stupid, and they don't get confused that easily, so just create whatever you want. Second, if you repeatedly make the same type of stuff, you may get burnt out on it.

As artists, we tend to experiment, play around, and try new things. I think we should put it all out there if we enjoy what we are doing. Why not? However, I do recommend that you separate things into series or categories to make it easier to find.

Every different niche you create could be seen as its own income stream. It may appeal to different people and thus you would market it differently to each. For example, I may market my pet portraits and wine paintings differently. Because of this, I will keep them in separate sections.

That way, the pet owner can easily find the section about pets. The wine enthusiast will easily find the wine art. The beauty of this is that there will always be a crossover that people can easily find.

If you have wine drinking pet owners, they may visit both sections and possibly buy from both series.

This is an example of an easy-to-follow strategy based on existing markets. However, for many of us, we have art that doesn't fit into ANY existing market. We all experience life differently and walk in our own shoes.

That being said, with billions of people in the world, nothing that exists is devoid of a market. That means everything that you create has a market out there that may have not been defined yet.

No matter what you create, EVERYTHING is marketable to someone.

When building a new market, you introduce a unique style of art that didn't exist until you came along. The good news is that with enough time and persistence, the art will grow an audience organically. The bad news is that in the beginning art takes on less significance in the absence of perceived competition. In other words, because no one has anything to compare it to, they may think it has no value.

This is a very strange phenomenon, but believe it or not, popular things get the most attention when compared to other popular things. If your art doesn't have anything to compare it to, then most people don't know how to relate to it or how to rate it. This is why certain revolutionary life changing things, upon their debut, have historically been ignored, downplayed, dismissed, and even vehemently disliked. They went over like lead balloons because in actuality, they flew right over most peoples' heads.

Hence real-life statements that have aged like milk.
Circa 2000 CE - "The internet is just a fad!"
Circa 1990 CE - "Skateboarding will NEVER be an Olympic sport.
Circa 2007 CE - "What is the point of having a camera on a cell phone?"
Circa 2010 CE - "Why does Steve Jobs think 'FACETIME' video calling would be great? No one video calls! iPhone fails!"

If you are wondering if the same thing happens to artists, the answer is a big fat YES. For example, Picasso's *Demoiselle D'avignon* is considered a revolutionary work that changed art forever. At the time of its release, his friends said it was hideous and he should hide it away. Which he did for years. Luckily for the world, he didn't hide it forever.

The truth is that just about every artist out there that paved their own way with their revolutionary art was rejected at first. People just can't wrap their minds around new things being any good unless they have a point of reference. Warhol, Monet, Vermeer, Cezanne, Toulouse-Lautrec, and many others had their art underappreciated for years until they grew in popularity. Honestly, the only reason we know them as revolutionary is because they persisted.

In my own art career, there were a lot of series that I created that just didn't make sense to people, and had I not persisted through the years, they wouldn't be out in the world. That being said, I didn't know what I know now about the emotional value of art. I had no mission statement, and I most definitely was not investigating or talking about my art. It was just the weird stuff I did.

However, if you are toiling away creating art that has never been seen before, you are not doing it for arbitrary reasons. No one would do that. There is only one thing that would drive you to create something that would probably fail to garner any attention... passion.

That's the powerful thing about passion. If you create from that place, and you put it out there, chances are it's going to make some people feel something. If something produces a strong emotional response in a person, it often doesn't matter if it's new or hard to understand. The feeling overrides the logic. It could be humor, beauty, awe, endearment, suspense, something primal, or something entirely undefined.

If you really want to reach people with new experiences, you need to bypass the labels and logic, and go straight for their emotional centers. Everything that exists, even brand-new things that don't fit into a genre or niche are built upon and tapped into something that came before.

Despite the fact that people may compare art to art, when you are tapping into the emotional side of what we do, art that does not have a genre or niche might be associated with something completely unrelated.

A painting might remind someone of their favorite song, a particular memory, a book they read and loved, a place of significance to them, or a person they adore. The way that connection happens is entirely through emotion.

It might take some time and persistence to get there.

When distinguishing yourself as a new art market, first, your audience has to find you. This means putting yourself out there a lot and probably for a long time. Second, they have to connect with your vision. This means you're going to have to put it out there with authenticity and courage. This is the most important part. You can create all the work you want, but if you're not actually putting it out there, no one is going to see it.

So, if you do not have a niche or a target yet, who do you target?

We have a history of stereotyping and categorizing people into groups, and we still do it today. Because of this, many of society's perceptions are based on stereotypical standards. It's almost expected and normal to over-generalize a group of people. We assume that everyone has a similar personality, preferences, appearance, or ability in said group. We live with stereotypes based on gender, race, ethnicity, economic status, age, the color of hair, and so much more.

LET'S TALK ABOUT V.A.L.s

For the most part, stereotypes are overgeneralized, inaccurate, absurd, and resistant to change. However, the information isn't completely useless. In essence, stereotypes are what marketing companies use to target their markets.

There has been a lot of research poured into values, attitudes, and lifestyles (VALs) by large corporations and marketing firms over the years.

To be honest, this is very generalized, and I wanted to toss this information in the garbage when I first read it, but there is some value here. Most of this is based on economic status, and the buying habits of said groups.

I'll cover this section quickly and try to make the dry research papers I read more tolerable for your enjoyment. Don't say I never did anything for you.

Need-Driven - *People Who Are Focused On Getting By*

The first group is called The Need-driven. These are typically impoverished people who are driven by necessities when they buy stuff. What they buy needs to be stuff they believe will help them survive day to day.

Things like food, rent, and necessities. This is the group that lower price points, discounts, and off-brand or value-brand products are targeted.

184

Now, all that being said, art is usually seen as a rich person's playground, but the truth is that art is universal. Some people out there that admire art simply can't afford some of it. When I was broke, I still bought art that I could afford, like postcards and other five-dollar items.

Being needs-driven doesn't mean someone is cheap or uncultured. It simply means that money is extremely tight. This is why I recommend having price points across the board. I have some affordable prints, postcards, and even some handmade pieces that I sell simply because I want everyone to afford my art if they wish to.

I cover all price points because I am not ever going to discriminate against a group that is tight on cash and assume that art doesn't matter to them.

Don't treat people like they are dumb or uncultured simply because they aren't ballin' out of control. I've been in booths at art shows where the artist only paid attention to the people who looked like they had money. That is disgraceful. Honestly, if you do that, you miss out on a fiercely loyal fan base of collectors... and you're a bit of a jerk.

Outer-Directed - *Middle Class to The Upper Crust In Society*

This is the most extensive and familiar part of the population. These are the personalities easiest to market to and most likely to give in to peer pressure. They are looking outside of themselves for answers. This group tends to find happiness in peer approval and the things they own. There are three types of outer directed people.

Belongers - They can be traditional, conventional, nostalgic, sentimental, puritanical, and conforming. They tend to be highly resistant to change and are the primary enforcers of the status quo.

Belongers like to follow trends, patterns, and popularity. They are the group that is most likely to worry about what the neighbors might think.

Their art purchases are meant to impress visitors with room decoration or a flowery story behind a work of art. They are not meant to stand out in any way as a method of self-expression.

This group is the reason the local artists recommended that I jump on the trend of beach art when I first started.

They are the largest group, so jumping on the wave would be an easy way to make money. The more they see your name and art out there, the more likely they are to collect your work, especially if it becomes popular.

Emulators - They are a step up from belongers in that they are not satisfied with simply belonging. They want to make it big. They tend to be ambitious, status-conscious, macho, competitive, and full of ideas.

They may be chasing a carrot and can feel looked down upon and unsupported. Emulators often have goals that revolve around money and have no real substance. These goals can keep them running in circles, and they may not realize it.

Since emulators are breaking out of the belonger stage, they tend to purchase art that is a little more self-expressive of where they want to be. Emulators will replace their fake big box store art with original local art to show they are cultured. They may be willing to pay a little more for the art than a belonger, but they will still try to haggle you down.

Achievers - They are competent, self-reliant, productive, object-oriented, hard-working, and successful. They enjoy comfort, beauty, and prestige. These are affluent people who are proud of their achievements and show them off with their surroundings.

Achievers are open to new kinds of art, but they resist radical change. So as long as they know that something is endorsed within their financial circles, they are more willing to purchase a risqué work of art.

All of the Outer-directed will follow some kind of trend. If you want to sell to them, I recommend entering contests and exhibitions where you build up your awards, accolades, reputation, and track record. Those kinds of things matter significantly to most of the group.

If you are "somebody", they will be more apt to buy your message and art. However, time also builds trust, so just putting yourself out there as much as possible and being patient will allow you to enter any and all segments of this group.

GO TO SCHOOL, GET A JOB. LIVE A NORMAL AND SAFE LIFE.

Inner-Directed - *All Economic Statuses but Guided By Their Own Inner Values And Not Society.*

These are individuals who have rejected the status quo of the world. These are the rogues, the misfits, the nonconformists, and the weirdos.

I-Am-Me - This is a short period where someone is leaving the world of the outer-directed. Typically, this person is fiercely individualistic and fighting to get out of their old life. They tend to be climactic, impulsive, and determined. Sometimes, they can be a bit self-absorbed with their new way of seeing the world. Any art or message that is about breaking free from bondage will speak to this person.

Experiential - After the eruption of I Am Me, the focus widens a bit. At this point, they tend to express themselves artistically and will passionately involve other humans in their thinking. Any art that is weird, exotic, strange, and natural will appeal to them. They also enjoy conversations of profound intellectual, human, and spiritual matters.

The Societally Conscious - This is where society as a whole comes into the person's thinking. They tend to have a profound sense of social responsibility and support conservation and environmentalism. Living off-grid, embracing a simple life, and the natural world really appeal to them. Their mission is to live frugal lives that conserve, protect, and heal.

Integrated - *This is the combination of inner and outer.*

Integrated people have a deep intelligence of how things seem to fit in the world. They tend to be ambitious, introspective, and forward-thinking while looking at many sides of an issue.

They are self-assured, self-actualizing, and self-expressive. They are great problem solvers and often have a worldview perspective.

All of these personalities don't care about accolades, trends, or what is popular. Self-expression is what matters. They care about your story and how you see the world. They value authenticity and creativity.

Once you establish a personal connection, this person may follow and support your creative career forever. Many outer-directed people have an experience that changed them to inner-directed, so keep that in mind when interacting with both tiers.

Obviously, these are just psychological and financial profiles studied by researchers for marketing purposes, and they do not reveal the ultimate truth of a person. People are way more complex. They will, however, give you a fun perspective on those funny-looking creatures called "humans".

It will provide you with an insight into the personality types that are accepting and rejecting your art. Just remember, most people grow and evolve through life, and 7 things should stay consistent in the way you put yourself out there to everyone.

Belief. If you believe in the art you make, then you have a story worth telling. You are making a contribution worth talking about. There is no need to persuade someone to buy when you believe in what you are doing and why. They will connect with you on a deeper level than any deceptive marketing tactics can achieve.

Meaningful Connections. Build, design, and create something that means something to you. Your masterpiece or opus is your life. It's not about getting mass media to like you. It's about connecting with a few like-minded people who will benefit and care. They will find you little by little. There are billions of people on the planet. Just a tiny fraction of that is more connection than you will ever need.

Be Authentic. You are not competing with anyone else. You are simply allowing like-minded people to find you.

Your story will match the narrative of your people, be honest about your intentions and build trust. In doing this, you become your own trusted brand. When this happens, more people will find you. Say what you mean, and mean what you say.

Mutual Excitement. In one simple word, marketing is all about word of mouth. On the internet, things go viral because people are sharing them. It is like digital word of mouth. You don't have to cause controversy or be edgy to get people talking. Excitement is contagious, be authentically excited about what you are up to.

Be Human. People who buy your art are intelligent and beautiful human beings. Do not allow yourself to fall into the "Me vs Them" trap, and don't look at people like wallets with legs. You cannot connect with people if you dehumanize them.

Most people approach marketing from a selfish perspective, "What can I get from the consumer?" vs. "What can I give?" Be giving and act with humanity. That will set you apart from the norm.

Be Persistent. Show up every day even if no one else comes to the party. Remain generous and enthusiastic about what you are doing for the rest of your artistic journey. Keep producing art, keep putting yourself out there, and keep striving to be genuine. Allow people time to build a relationship with you and what you are doing. Earn trust, don't assume you are entitled, and understand that trust takes time.

Be Flexible. Try not to be rigid in your approach to putting yourself out there. Be willing to try new things and take chances. Do incredible things and think outside of the box. If things aren't working, change it up and take a new approach. If they are working, don't coast. Always be experimenting and playing around with new ways of putting yourself out there. Most importantly, don't quit. Just change it up. At the end of the day, all this psychological and behavioral crap is just stuff that may help you understand more about your own motives. You can never honestly know what your art represents to the person interested in buying it. However, you can find out more about what it means to you. Find the heart of what you do.

Ultimately, the takeaway here is that people buy art for emotional and personal reasons, even if they are not fully aware of what that reason is. We all have a story, and our story is what connects emotionally. Art makes us all feel something.

- They could be wanting to complete the *feeling* of a room.
- They may be simply adding final pieces to a collection to *feel* complete.
- They may want other people to see them as fancy and *feel* good about themselves.
- The art may really speak to them and make them *feel* something powerful.
- The art may remind them of a special time in their life that makes them *feel* good.

The art is simply a vehicle that represents a means to an end. It means relief, a reminder, and a benefit to an emotional quandary that the person may be feeling. Art heals. Remember that when you investigate your own art and the personal reasons why you create it.

WE ALL HAVE A POWERFUL STORY TO SHARE AND RELATE TO.

So, believe in what you are doing, make connections, be authentic, get excited, be human, be persistent, and be flexible in your approach to other humans. Go out there and tell your story.

Once UPon A Time....

WHY PEOPLE PAY ATTENTION

If you have been putting yourself out there for a while, the one thing you learn is that no one is going to pay attention to you, until they do. Many artists reach out to me and ask if we would be willing to look at their social media pages in order to determine why they are not getting any traction. Often, upon review, we will see some pictures of art with text that reads, "Newest work, $50! Link in the description!" followed by a bunch of random hashtags.

If this is what your posts look like, I hate to break it to you, but this is a lame post. I think most people approach the internet or even putting themselves out there in person as an opportunity to sell. The problem is that although it is all an opportunity to sell something, if that is your only focus, then you are missing the point.

Unfortunately, when I say "*put yourself out there*" many people think it means putting any old crusty content out in the world. However, that doesn't work. There are plenty of artists, YouTubers, and humans who have been putting tons of content out there for years and are still scratching to get followers. Just because you're posting every day doesn't mean you're sharing anything of value.

If you are wondering what I mean by *value*, then chances are you might be one of the people that is missing the point. Don't feel bad, I missed the point for the first five years of posting my content out on the internet. I was doing well sharing value in person, but I was approaching the internet from a marketing and sales point of view. So, what was I doing wrong?

1. I was trying to be like other people who were popular.
I originally thought that popularity had to do with some algorithm that I didn't understand. Instead of posting who I was, I was trying to be the popular kid. I was competing with others who had the same schtick for attention by being fake. Why would anyone follow me, if they are just going to get the same antics as someone they already follow?

2. I had no real message.
I was posting vague motivational quotes and one liners, but not really saying anything. I wasn't sharing my story or anything about why I was sharing my art. I didn't have a unique voice.

3. I didn't know who I was talking to.
I was trying desperately to cast a wide net and everything I posted was general. I wasn't specific, I wasn't me. The fact is, I was that weird kid in class that never said anything, and when I did, you could tell I was trying too hard to please everyone. I wasn't reaching out to my peeps, I was just desperately trying to put stuff out there in hope that someone would take the bait.

4. I didn't bring any consistency.
I was one of those people who thought they could just start posting on social media and *"go viral"*.

The truth is, you have to be aware of what your consistent message is. What are you saying? and say it often. Whether it is in person or on the internet, it takes time to build relationships. I would post some random motivational quote simply because it sounded good, and wait for the likes.

When they wouldn't come, I would get discouraged and not post for weeks. Since I really had nothing to say, and was chasing likes, my message was not consistent. I was constantly pulled in different directions by what I thought the algorithm wanted. This experience sucked, and I am happy I left all that behind me.

5. Same crap, different day.

I was pretty much posting the same crap every day. Hey look at me! Hey look at this painting! Buy this painting! I didn't understand that consistency had less to do with repetition and everything to do with a clear message.

Every single day should be a challenge to entertain and delight people. They are not checking social media because they are interested in monotonous tripe. They want to take a break from their lives and share in someone's success. They want to see growth. They want to grow with you. They want to see you improve. They want to see you face struggles and come out ahead. They want to share in your journey.

6. I did not provide enough value.

This is the big one. I honestly wasn't posting anything that would be helpful to anyone else. It was just, "Look at this thing I made and here is the link to buy it."

The fact is that we all have value to bring to someone else. Every time we overcome a challenge, or have a thought that makes us feel better about life, it is of value. Every time you persevere and share that story, it is of immense value.

Every time you make someone laugh, cry, or think from a genuine and loving place, you are bringing gold.

7. I wasn't sharing what I learned.

We all learn in life. Whether it is about art, life, or something like cooking, we all learn something new at least every day. Back when I started, I wasn't sharing anything when it came to what I learned in my art career or life. Humans want to fill their lives with valuable information. If you aren't bringing something that you feel will enrich their lives, why would they pay attention?

It's not that people are ignoring you, it is that you are not giving them anything to pay attention to. Truth is, we pay attention to anything that triggers an emotion. Anything else becomes background noise.

Artsy Mcfartsy "Ghosts in snow." Acrylic on canvas. 11x14. $50.

#artist #acrylicpainting # acrylic on canvas #frameworthy

The brain is a phenomenal filtering system, but it is less of a supercomputer and more like a mood ring. That's why humans are still around. For generations, we have paid attention to things based on our basic needs. Things that bring us pleasure in life.

Eating, protection from the elements, wearing good clothes, being liked by others, and staying healthy are basic needs that make us feel good. It can be a very primitive thing. Our ancestors, who survived by paying attention, passed those traits down to us on a cellular level.

Next time you freak out because you hear a scary sound, you can thank your ancestors. Logical thinking goes out the window. That's a good thing too, because logical reasoning wouldn't help you scramble away from a crazed mammoth. We *feel* scared for a reason – because we need to pay attention.

Our ancestors survived by following their gut when necessary. Eventually, we set up our own emotional conditions to survive in the modern world. From what kind of toothpaste you buy to the car you drive, the most minor decisions are all measured according to the emotional standards you have set in place.

These conditions are hardwired in our brain jars, and some marketing people know precisely how to exploit these triggers. Even still, sometimes it works, other times it does not.

Recently, Klee and I bought a beautiful old house. One evening as we were relaxing, a bat appeared in our kitchen. After freezing in place followed by an excessive amount of chasing and flailing, we were able to capture and release it back outside where it belonged.

I don't know if you've ever encountered a bat in person, but they make a *very* distinctive sound. It's like a cross between a squeaky mouse and an exposed electrical current.

Immediately, not only did we hear bats everywhere, but we started to see all kinds of ads for various bat capturing and repelling devices.

Everywhere we looked, someone was trying to sell us a solution to our bat problem. For about two weeks, we were bombarded with ads, commercials, special deals, and limited time offers. This influx of ads and our awareness of them slowly died down after we found and sealed the opening where they were getting in.

Ultimately, the ads seemed to all but disappear, many were still there, we just didn't notice them as much. One ad however, did get our attention. We purchased an outdoor bat house. While we were able to self-solve our very compelling need to rid our home of bats, the *bat house ad* appealed to our emotional need to help protect those furry little winged buggers.

Even though the world has vastly changed, our emotional behavior hasn't changed much. Most of us will never be chased by a lion or have to take down a wooly mammoth with pointy sticks to eat. However, our brain still responds to all sorts of weird provocations. We experience fight or flight as a response to *ANY* stress, and it can be triggered by the most mundane things.

In my case with the bat sounds, for a while there, the refrigerator, dripping sink, floor creaking, and Klee's snoring caused me to jump out of my skin and pay attention. Like I said, it's primal.

Our choices are so subconscious that many times they don't make sense. Knowing the primal reasons you pay attention to things will help you come up with fun ways to capture someone's awareness.

Automatic Attention. It's a survival mechanism that helps us react faster than our brains can think and assess. Loud noises, bright colors, sudden movements, and *screplimenting* fall into this category. Bold trigger words in headlines and images as well as news anchor hairdos will obviously gain your automatic attention.

SCAREPLIMENT: To SURPRISE WITH SUDDEN INTENSE love Compliment.

Use this type of attention responsibly, our potential audience will not be much of an audience at all if we've startled them away altogether. Every time I do an art show, I make sure I have a brightly colored and bold work of art strategically placed in an area with the most visibility.

Many times, when I am posting on social media, I think about the story that the picture is telling by the colors, body language, and facial expressions I am using. Is it something that will grab someone, or will they scroll on by.

Perspective Attention. Our world's view is shaped by our family, friends, environment, personal experiences, and biases. As covered in an earlier chapter our cultural experience will have an impact on what we pay attention to. There are things that will be meaningful to us. For example, if you are a dog person, you are going to notice a cute puppy. Heck, even if you are not a dog person, but like dogs, you'll get a fuzzy feeling and pay attention. We also pay a good deal of attention to the things that threaten what we find meaningful.

If an image pops up of a puppy who survived being abandoned and left for dead, you may be feeling all kinds of emotions, but you are paying attention.

News media outlets tend to be biased to one general consensus or the other because they know that whether you agree or not, you will pay attention.

In my opinion, this is why your story matters. We have to remember that we connect with people, and they all have their own biases and beliefs. Folks tend to connect with like-minded people and try to ignore the rest as best they can. As an artist, sharing who we are is important. You want your audience to connect with you and what you are trying to say. This forms a solid bond between you and your collectors.

This trust needs to be established and may take a while, but it creates a lasting bond in the end. Your narrative might get someone to investigate what you are all about and want to support your point of view. That being said, not everyone will agree with you. Don't waste time fighting internet trolls, spreading hate, or pointing fingers at anyone else. Focus on what you can bring to the world and what you have to give.

"YOUR TIME IS LIMITED, SO DON'T WASTE IT LIVING SOMEONE ELSE'S LIFE."

— STEVE JOBS

Disruption Attention. I call this a pattern interrupt. We tend to pay extra attention to anything that defies our expectations. It is anything that seems out of the ordinary. These are contradictions to normal, like a pop-tart cat shooting a rainbow out of its butt.

The blob of cells in our head generalizes, deletes, and distorts the information you process. For example, it will generalize doorknobs so that you don't have to relearn how to open a door every time a doorknob looks or behaves slightly differently.

Imagine for a moment that you walk over to your bedroom door and find no doorknob. As you stand there in confusion, your brain uses all power to solve the problem. Suddenly you find yourself taking a closer look because that is not "supposed" to happen.

Your expectations are *how things work*, the things you think are supposed to happen. The more something disrupts the norm, the more it gets your attention. This also applies to human behavior and society norms.

You may do a double take when you see someone behaving or doing something you would never expect them to do. When something happens that is not supposed to happen in your version of the ordinary world, it is called expectancy violations theory.

Maybe you expect your kid's room to be a mess, and you walk in ready to enforce the cleaning of said room. Suddenly you find the room is spotless, and you freeze for a moment, looking around and taking in every detail. You stand speechless because suddenly, your world doesn't make sense, and your brain needs a moment to process information.

Artists are usually very good at this because we tend to be divergent thinkers that don't stick to many social norms. Because of this, we are great at getting attention with what we do.

It is when we try to *fit in* that we lose our creative advantage.

Many artists will take something ordinary and make it extraordinary. For example, imagine an ice cream truck melting like ice cream on a hot day. The life-sized sculpture "Melting Ice Cream Truck" by the Glue Society is a public work of art that fascinated and perplexed everyone who encountered it.

Maybe you are walking around a high-end gallery admiring the spectacular art when you approach a banana duct taped to the wall. It would be impossible to ignore at that moment. Your brain would go into overdrive trying to figure out what is happening.

This is a creative superpower that we have but only if we are willing to have fun and stand out. Going against the norms of the world could be surprisingly intimidating, but it is a great way to spread the word of your awesomeness.

Reward Attention. Feeling the reward vicariously makes us pay attention. Even the promise of obtaining these things can make us notice. This is why advertisers will show the satisfying end results of using what they are selling.

For example, *EVERY* get rich quick scam will have someone flaunting their mansion and expensive cars. It is more powerful to visually show the outcomes than to simply talk about them.

Don't just talk about the burger, show someone enjoying stuffing a burger in their face.

Don't just talk about the soft drink, show someone drinking it followed by a satisfying aaaaaaah.

Don't just talk about the luxury of the soap, show someone enveloped in its rich lather.

Don't just boast about the horsepower, show the car effortlessly taking on that terrain.

My only rule of thumb with reward attention is to keep it real. Our artwork *may* transport them to an exotic location, and even possibly make them rich, but we can't make that kind of promise.

What we can do is set the mood and give a genuine sense of what it would feel like to have it. We want those visuals and the feelings they evoke. We want to help people get in touch with how owning the thing will be rewarding in a genuine and powerful way.

Luckily for us, we sell emotion, locations, perspective, and beauty in the art we create. Give your art the respect it deserves by showcasing it the best you can. Get good at taking pictures of your art and give people examples of what it would feel like to own it.

You can do this in inventive ways, or you can use mock-ups. I use Canvy.com to create mockups of my art in different rooms so everyone can get a feel of what it will look like.

Many people need to see an example of how something will look and feel once they own it.

Reputation Attention. Experts are the most trusted spokespeople in the marketing world. This is why marketers will pay an actor to dress up like a doctor or professional in a commercial. A 2009 study found that the part of our brain that makes decisions will slow down or even shut down while getting advice from an expert we trust. This is why online courses will start with someone listing their credentials and accolades to establish themselves as an expert.

That being said, you are an expert when it comes to your opinion and the art you create. No one else is more qualified than you to share it. Be confident and bold in your approach.

Many times, artists approach sharing their art from a timid and disempowered place, unfortunately, this may bring skepticism from the person trying to enjoy what you share. If you are timid and doubtful, they will be timid and doubtful to respond. Be confident in what you create and share and someone will confidently follow you.

A warning to the wise, there is a big difference between being confident and arrogant. Stand by who you are and what you create, but do not ever put someone down in order to lift yourself up.

Mystery Attention. Ever wonder why we're unable to put down a good book or stop binge-watching a mystery series? That's because incomplete stories or tasks will stay active in our memory until they are solved or resolved. We are compelled to pay attention when something is a mystery or a cliffhanger.

It's called the Zeigarnik effect. As humans, we hate uncertainty and incompleteness, and will actively try to lessen it by any means imaginable. It doesn't even have to be that engaging or nuanced of a mystery. When a sock goes missing in our house, Klee practically goes mad with obsession. Sock is *everything*, and everything else must wait until the sock is found.

B-Movies have this dialed in. The movie doesn't even have to be super good to keep our attention, just as long as we're waiting to see what happens at the end.

You might even be watching and thinking to yourself "I know exactly how this is going to end." but do you stop the movie? NO. You watch to the end to see if your assumptions were correct.

As artists, we are masters at creating mystery because what we make can seem like a mystery to us, and definitely to others who didn't take part in the creation of it. This is why when you are creating a buzz for your art event, it's very effective to utilize some teasers leading up to some kind of mystery reveal.

Validation Attention. Most humans need some form of acknowledgment. We are looking for a sense of belonging to a community that cares and listens to us. We want validation and empathy from others. Create that feeling but remember to be genuine about it.

This is why I make sure I don't allow myself to get a big ego. It is easy to get lost in your own validation and lose sight of how meaningful it is to have *ANYONE* paying attention. I've seen artists completely ignore the few supportive people they have following their careers and focus on how many people are not following them.

One artist did a virtual live event and was upset that there weren't more people on the virtual live stream. Sitting there staring at the screen, I remember thinking, "What am I? Chopped liver?"

Just remember, no one needs to be following your art career, and their lives do not revolve around you and your events. If someone takes time out of their busy day to partake in something you are doing, appreciate that person for being there. Getting attention and shining a momentary spotlight on your art, ideas, projects, and marketing is easy. The magic happens when you establish a connection and turn a moment into a permanent experience.

A word of warning, don't chase attention. If you are craving attention, all of this may backfire on you.

1. Become Aware Of Your Actions And Motives.
Make sure that you are motivated by wanting to share and not getting a response. We tend to make foolish decisions when desperately seeking attention and not paying attention to our motives.

2. Your Self-Worth Should Not Be Based On The Response.
Don't allow yourself to get wrapped up in chasing the likes and followers to feel like you are important. This is a never ending cycle of despair. Instead, know you are loved, valuable, and worthy simply because you are you. Don't focus on what you think others think of you. Share because you want to look back at it as a reflection for yourself.

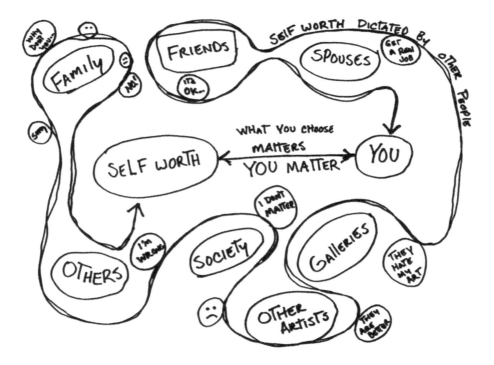

3. Accept Yourself For Who You Are.
Focus on what makes you happy. Self-confidence begins with the ability to accept yourself as you are.

4. Check Yourself Before You Wreck Yourself.

Ensure that what you are saying and doing is accurate to who you are and your mission and not just a desperate attempt to get attention or validation.

5. Understand Why You're Seeking Attention.

Are you seeking approval, validation, or self-worth? Understanding that your surface motivations may be masking what is really going on underneath is vital when putting yourself out there. This will keep you from saying or doing something you may regret.

This one is important because many people are afraid of putting themselves out there due to things like *cancel culture*, deepfakes, and the like. Trust me, I get it. It is all scary to begin with. Add a few conspiracy theories into the mix and it can feel downright terrifying.

Defining why you are putting yourself on a platform ultimately matters. If you are using it to start a controversy, seeking attention by hate mongering, or pointing fingers at someone else, then you reap what you sow. If you are simply sharing your story, art, and journey of art, then I highly doubt you have anything to worry about.

The truth is that if you are sharing in order to amass a GRAND following, then chances are that your motivation may be a bit skewed. I had to figure this out for myself along the way and realized that my motivation had to bring something positive into the world.

There are already too many people chasing what's popular and divisive on the internet in order to get more attention and followers.

For me personally I use platforms to communicate with the few that will find me and want to join me in my journey. I post because I use it to keep a public record of what I have done and refer back occasionally, like an online journal.

I post because I think that by sharing what I do and how I do it, I may inspire ONE person to do the same.

I post because it is part of my canvas of life and a record of what I have accomplished.

I post because sometimes people need a relief from all the bullcrap out there chasing after an algorithm, likes, or follows.

I think of it all like one of those art projects where someone takes a picture of their face from childhood to adulthood to keep a record of growth. If they share it with the world, others see it as mesmerizing and meaningful. I post because I would rather put something of value in the world and for myself than not post at all. No obsessing, no fear, and no chasing likes required.

6. Trust Your Own Way Of Doing Things.
There are people out there who are too timid to put themselves out there, and they may discourage you. Don't let anyone else tell you that your ideas are not good enough.

7. Do Not Compare Yourself To Others.
This slippery slope of *bird crap* is the most meaningless thing you can do to yourself when putting yourself out there. You are a Rogue Artist who is blazing your own trail. There is no comparison.

All in all, have fun and remain human. Remember that people out there are people. There are only two reasons why people are not paying attention to what you are putting out there. Either they are simply not interested, or you are blending into the background because you are not having fun with this.

5 Rules To Attention Getting

→ 1. DON'T DO WHAT EVERYONE ELSE DOES. BE DIFFERENT. BE YOU

→ 2. USE YOU SURROUNDINGS TO TELL A COMPELLING STORY. CONTEXT MATTERS. FIRST IMPRESSION IS CONTEXT.

→ 3. DON'T OVER COMPLICATE PEOPLE ARE SIMPLE, & THEY LIKE SIMPLE, SO KEEP IT SIMPLE.

→ 4. CONTRAST CALLS ATTENTION.

→ 5. ALWAYS LEAVE THEM WANTING MORE.

BECOME AN ARTROVERT

It's no secret that artists can be notoriously shy. Many artists have a hard time putting themselves out there because they consider themselves antisocial, awkward, or introverted. As a painfully shy person, I can relate. Klee and I are what you call artistic hermits. It's one of the things I love about being a full-time artist. We only head out into outside-land when required, so we keep socializing to a minimum. However, we have trained ourselves to enjoy interacting with other humans when we do put ourselves out there.

The worst thing that can happen to you as an artist or human is to go through life being unheard and invisible. I'll be honest, unless you face your fear and put yourself out there, nothing will happen with your art career. You can try and hide behind a keyboard, but you won't get very far. Even Banksy, who is notorious for his anonymity, puts himself out there across the board.

We all have our reasons for being introverted. I didn't have the best family dynamic. Alcoholism, domineering personalities, exclusion, and insecurity growing up, were all things I used to explain why I was so quiet and timid. I was picked on in school and didn't know how to speak up. When I wasn't getting picked on, I spent most of my time trying to please everyone around me to prevent friction.

As an adult, I had trained myself to avoid all conflict or social interactions. I rarely did anything outside of my comfort zone. I was like a nervous indoor cat who wanted nothing more than to go outside. I wanted to be more outgoing. Unfortunately, once out, I'd freak out and want to get back inside.

Society fosters that kind of behavior at school and the workplace. Keep your head down, be responsible, don't complain, don't ask for too much, and do what you are told. Do your job or lose your job. Get to work and just shut up.

My younger brother grew up in the same situation, yet he was way more outgoing. It would drive me crazy. Did he have something biological that caused him to be more outgoing? Was he born that way? I don't believe so.

This is one of the arguments where people love to bring up genetics, and I call bullcrap. I'm not a big fan of people throwing around labels as an excuse to justify emotional and learned behavior. This is one of those subjects that infuriate people because it is easier to use the shield of an introvert as an excuse to not face a fear than to admit that you can accomplish whatever you set your mind on.

You can open up and train yourself to be more outgoing, but you will have to face the fear. There is no other way around it. The only other option you have is to hide behind your shield and never show the world who you are.

The truth is that my brother simply coped with things differently. He started a band, played sports, and always spoke his mind. He pursued his dreams and what he wanted in his life. I, on the other hand, closed off, held things in, and expressed myself through my art. My brother opened up to new ways of expressing himself through taking action and pouring himself into his music. Honestly, he was as painfully shy as me, but he faced his fears instead of shying away like I did.

This is important because I had opportunities come up in my life that I sabotaged because of where my mindset was. Years ago, I suddenly found myself having the opportunity to show my art at an event sponsored by the Museum Of Contemporary Art in Chicago. I had magically applied for the show because my friends took it upon themselves to submit an application on my behalf. I wasn't happy about it but figured I would never get in.

Then I got in.

I received an acceptance letter a couple weeks later and immediately panicked. I then tried to sabotage the efforts and get out of the show.

During the month leading up to the exhibition, I pleaded that I wasn't emotionally ready and would most likely die from the stress. I "accidentally" damaged the work and protested that I wouldn't have it ready in time. I went as far as claiming to have food poisoning and insisting that I couldn't work on the art.

My friends didn't buy into any of it and thwarted all my brilliant attempts.

My final act of sabotage was to not show up for the opening. I let the air out of one of my tires and told them I had a flat tire. They were ready for that and picked me up and escorted me into the event kicking and screaming.

Yeah, this was not my finest moment, but fear sucks. Something happens in the brain jar when you allow your nerves to get the best of you. When fight or flight takes over, your "smart brain" shuts down and your "lizard brain," as Klee calls it, takes over. This causes you to make some foolish choices, and your focus gets warped.

This was one of the most incredible opportunities of my life. It had fallen right into my lap. I didn't even have to do anything to get there, and I fought it every step of the way.

Oh, just wait, it gets worse.

The show took place in a vast industrial warehouse that the museum owned for such events. By the time we arrived, there was a line of people wrapped around the block. To my relief, since I was a featured artist, I was allowed to enter through the back and avoid the crowd.

Upon entering, an amalgamation of music and hundreds of conversations washed over me. My nerves tightened around my throat. As we passed the high-end open bar sponsored by Smirnoff vodka, one of my friends got me a drink to settle my nerves. The place was packed, and I wanted to crawl into a hole.

I suddenly spotted some "big" Chicago art scene people by the hors d'oeuvres laughing and enjoying themselves. In the group was someone who I knew had the power to make or break artists.

His round glasses and bald head were unmistakable, although I had never seen him sporting a pink feather boa around his neck before.

"Interesting" I said to myself, almost forgetting where I was. My friend leaned in and asked, "What?"

I pretended I couldn't hear him. I knew he would get me to tell him who they were and then challenge me to introduce myself. I, on the other hand, planned on avoiding them at all costs.

I barely talked to anybody for the next 4 hours. It was excruciating. My family had shown up for a little while, and I spoke to them, but they made me feel worse. They scrunched their eyes at my work in confusion and said it was "different." Then went off and commented on how marvelous the art is on the other wall. Before they left, my dad tried to cheer me up by loudly saying one of my pieces reminded him of vomit. I was mortified.

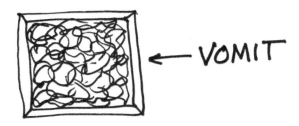

Later on, I was trying to blend into the brick wall. I noticed that the pink boa entourage was heading towards my art. I felt the blood drain from my face.

I wanted to run and hide but decided to drum up the courage to interact with them, so I stayed by my art.
"I love this so much! The texture and combination of color! I would just like to see this bigger. What do you think?" asked Pink Boa.

The crowd around him stared at the work and nodded in agreement. He lowered his glasses on his nose, looked closely at the texture, and stopped his hand right before touching the painting.

"Are you the artist?" he asked.
"Yes." I creaked. He looked back at the tag on the wall.
"Raafeee?" he asked.
I awkwardly half nodded and panicked.

Pink boa looked at the art carefully and asked, "So, what do you think? Can you do bigger? This is beautiful, but I would like to see it bigger in a gallery."

I paused. No, that's not accurate. I froze. I froze like a deer in headlights.

I'm not sure how long I just stared. Wide-eyed and lost for words, I just stood there. Pink Boa was nice, but it was apparent that I had made him uncomfortable. He decided to move on.

As he was walking away, he turned and said, "Stunning art Raafeee, if you decide to make them bigger, let me know."

I responded with a grunt and then crawled into myself.

As I said before, not my finest moment.

I look back at this moment in my life and can see exactly where I went wrong. I had no foundation to stand on. I was just there seeking approval and had zero confidence. I was trying to fit into a culture I didn't understand and had no culture of my own to share.

Because of this, I was petrified of doing or saying something wrong instead of standing in my own values.

At the time, I was so wrapped up in a narrative that I was an introvert that I allowed it to discourage me and cause me to panic. I was a timid character in my own story. As a character, you get pulled along by the narrative and the construct of the book you inhabit. As a character in your story, you sometimes can't see past the margins on the page.

We sometimes forget that we are also the author of that narrative. When you understand your power beyond the surface level, you get an insight into how you, as the author, are writing your own story. Without this insight, you have no sense of why things happen to you.

My own experience since then is why I don't believe that being an introvert or extrovert is set in stone. I think we are way more complex than that. I don't think there is anything wrong with identifying with either.

However, if you are using the label as a crutch in any way, then I suggest you rethink your self-identity. I used it as a reason to not put myself out there for years because I wrongly believed that I didn't have it in me to be courageous. However, we can do anything we set our mind to.

Personally, I believe being an introvert or extrovert is on a sliding scale, and we all sit closer to the middle somewhere. This is called an Ambivert. People may lean more to one side or the other, but it is extremely rare to be one-sided. We slide on the scale back and forth with every experience in and out of our comfort zones. When you are aware of this, you can proactively shift your place on the scale little by little.

For someone who is an extreme introvert, it means asking questions, commenting, and engaging with people more. It could be starting a conversation by complimenting someone. It could mean pointing at some art and talking about it. Yes, it will be awkward at first, and you'll have all kinds of negative self-talk come to the surface, but that is where the magic happens.

The more you do it, the better you get at it.

Introverts tend to think that they did something wrong in most social interactions, especially if they get a lot of attention, and they tend to blame and shame themselves. They may walk away from the conversation and second guess everything they said or did. This puts a lot of pressure on the introvert, and it can feel exhausting even before the interaction starts.

The only therapy for this is to face the negative self-talk and remind yourself that you don't have to impress anyone, you are who you are, and that is awesome. If someone is put off by it, it just means they are not like-minded, and you would have probably been put off by *them* anyhow.

For someone who identifies with being an extreme extrovert, there is still a lot of work to do. You may have to engage in active listening and talking way less. That means you are not simply pretending to listen while you are waiting for your turn to speak. Try to really listen and open your mind and perspective to let someone in.

Yes, it will be awkward at first, and you'll feel weird, but that is where the magic happens.

The more you listen, the more you will get from the interaction.

Extroverts tend to think that if they are not the center of attention that something is wrong. Basically, most extroverts dominate a conversation, not having gained any true insight into the other person in the room.

This is why extroverts may have many friends but often feel lonely and devoid of a truly intimate connection. The only therapy for this is just listening and getting out of your own head.

An ambivert is someone who sits right in the middle and can listen and speak their mind. Honestly, it is the most effective way to communicate and put yourself out there.

As a Rogue Artist, I like to refer to myself as an *ARTROVERT*. I take the whole of the sliding scale and slide back and forth, purposely pushing at comfort zones as part of my art.

I try to do it with everything, which is a big part of why I put myself out there so much. As an Artrovert, I can decide when I will talk and not listen, not speak and only listen, or get on stage with hundreds of people watching me paint, and all in the name of creative research.

Being an Artrovert means that you embrace the fun of facing fear. It also means that you go home if you want to. The choice is yours.

There is nothing you have to do or say to get people to like you. It is all about finding out who you are and being that in public. Some people will adore you, some people will not, and you push your boundaries to be ok with that.

Don't worry. You don't have to do it all at once. Being an Artrovert is a lifelong process, we never get it done, there's no pressure to get it right, and any way you approach it is the correct way. Take baby steps and face little comfort zones as you put yourself out there.

The myth is that being an extrovert is advantageous and being an introvert is a disadvantage, however, there is power in both. I think the thing I really want to get across here is that no matter what you identify as, you have the power to be whatever you want to be. Don't let labels dominate your life. However, if you have to label yourself, be an ARTROVERT, be a Rogue Artist, be awesome.

That being said, I want to make something obvious. If you are not ready to put yourself in the arena yet, remember that it is the act of doing it that will get you past the fear. You can wait, but no matter what, the challenges will be the same whether you do them now or at a later date.

You might have to be willing to sweat, bleed, and face your fears for what you believe in. You may have to take risks, deal with criticism, and deal with people telling you that you are stupid. This is ALL something you are capable of facing as long as you persist and keep going.

Being an Artrovert means that you become a creative warrior and take charge of your own creative destiny. You throw down the shield that kept you small and pick up the spear that will pierce through all your insecurities.

Genuinely being a Rogue Artrovert means:

- Allowing yourself to be extraordinary by facing the fears and roadblocks of coming out of your shell. You identify with the idea that you are extraordinary and have a voice.
- You are willing to put the time and energy into making something out of nothing.
- You are done looking for shortcuts because they are not viable and don't work long-term.
- You are willing to make mistakes and look dumb.
- You are starting where you are with what you have.
- You know that anything you do can be a head-turner, and you embrace it.
- You understand that your creativity will set you apart from any other marketing campaign ideas out there.
- You are done buying into your limitations.
- You are expanding your point of view beyond anything that can stand in your way.
- You are unstoppable and you own it.

You also understand that it is not about hustling, interrupting, or spamming. You are DONE begging people to buy your creations.

You are ready to take an active role in putting yourself out there and persist for as long as you have to. You are ready to make your dreams happen. Take the nervous energy that pops up when you speak to someone in public and slowly transform it from fear to excitement.

One day at a time, little by little. It is facing these fears that help us grow and evolve into living the dreams we never thought were possible.

The most terrifying part of putting yourself out there is feeling invisible, facing rejection, feeling like you will make a mistake, and feeling like you have nothing to say.

Just remember, you are not on trial, nor are you seeking validation. You are simply there to qualify whether or not people are a good fit for you and your art. So be an Artrovert, be a Rogue, be a badass.

If I could go back in time and change my interaction in the art show, I would not be an extrovert and try to talk pink boa's ear off, and obviously, I would not close up in terror, but I would stand in who I am and be myself. It's all about being empowered in your own skin and writing your own narrative. Maybe you are wondering how to do that. It's simple.

Mark Your Territory.
Artroverts create a space where they are comfortable. If you are doing an event, turn the space into your domain. Do this emotionally and physically if you can. You are the boss of your environment. Own it.

It's Ok To Smile, Or Not.
You don't have to be all smiles all day, every day. No one does that in real life. However, body language accounts for 70% of your communication. If you are sitting there terrified, it will show, and it may make you feel out of control. If you don't typically smile a lot, that's okay. Just find ways to calm yourself and greet people in a genuine and warm way.

If you want to smile and don't know how, just practice in the mirror – that way you don't look slightly disturbed trying to force a smile.

Practice Being Social.

I know it's terrifying to start a conversation, and chances are you will feel stupid doing it. So what? Force yourself to face the fear by talking with at least one person you interact with. This could be your grocer or someone random.

The more you do it, the more natural and comfortable you'll feel. Just something simple like, "How are you doing today?" will get the conversation started.

Recharge Your Batteries.

Allow yourself time to recharge. It is believed that extroverts recharge when they are interacting with people and introverts recharge during their alone time. Whether you want to recharge before, during, or after an event, give yourself the time to do so. You don't have to be on *all* the time, nor should you. Do what works for you.

Marianne Hasseldal

Join a Speaking Group Or Practice With Friends.
If you want to sell art, there will be occasions where you have to talk to people. You want to give yourself every opportunity to get comfortable doing that. Whether you need time to get used to listening, or speaking up, go ahead and practice. You can practice with friends, family, your pets, or in the mirror, however it is the moment of putting yourself out there that will make the most impact in your training. Just have fun with this. You are not on trial and you will not be tested later.

If You Are Invited To Speak, Just Say Yes.
This one may be very challenging and take you a while to get to, however, once you *THINK* you might be ready, just say yes before you can talk yourself out of it. Challenge yourself to say yes. By pushing yourself into new circumstances, you'll be making yourself practice facing the fears that make this hard in the first place. The therapy for fear of doing something like this is to do it.

Fa-Chunk Speaking.
Give yourself an out. Try to converse with someone for 5 minutes, and if it's not going well, you can end the conversation and try again later with someone else.

If it's going well, then you can continue. Many people add to the freak out because they believe they are going to be stuck in a dull conversation and not know what to say or how to escape. If you're like me, you just walk away. If you're like Klee, it's hard at first. You might start by standing there in agony and gradually get better at making your exit. Either way, just remember, this conversation can't possibly last forever.

Know What You Stand For.

This is why establishing your mission statement is so important. If you know where you stand, the concept of holding a conversation is less of a mysterious terror. Investigating who you are, why you do what you do, and a lot of the stuff that we talked about in previous chapters, will allow you to have a solid footing in how you interact. You'll be more comfortable in your own skin and might even find yourself undaunted by opposing viewpoints or challenging questions.

Call Yourself An Artrovert.

People love labeling themselves, but if you are going to do so, the label should be empowering. As an Artrovert, you understand that you can be introverted and extroverted in your own way. Maybe you like your quiet time, and that is ok. Perhaps you like the idea of meeting someone new who will inspire a great conversation or friendship. The only way to find out is to put yourself out there and determine who you are for yourself.

As an Artrovert, I spend a lot of time in my studio creating, but I also understand that it is up to me to tell my story and share my voice with the world. If I don't do it, no one will.

"ART IS TOO IMPORTANT NOT TO SHARE." - ROMERO BRITTO

BEING NORMAL IS OVERRATED

"Boy, that Freddie Mercury sure was ordinary. Love that guy." - No one, ever.

One of the challenges in putting yourself out there is dealing with the perception of fitting into the ordinary world. Let's face it, artists are weird. We pour countless hours of energy, blood, sweat, and tears into our creativity and still reject it. Some of us spend way too much time hunched over a canvas or computer, creating something that no one will ever see. We argue, fight, love, and wrestle with our creations, and no one is making us do it.

We can even get sad when we haven't toiled over creating for a while. There is nothing ordinary about this. However, we go out into the ordinary world and have regular conversations with people we think are normal. When we do, most of us don't talk about our secret life of creative struggle. It may feel next to impossible to explain our thinking process in a way that makes sense to anyone.

A quote that I ran across recently got me thinking about my life and whether or not I fit into what people call the "Normal" category.

"Normal is getting dressed in clothes that you buy for work. Driving through traffic in a car that you are still paying for to get to the job you need, to pay for the clothes, the car, and the house you leave vacant all day so you can afford to live in it." –Ellen Goodman.

I can't relate to that life anymore although I was that guy. I spent a long time trying desperately to be normal and to fit in. I hid the fact that I wanted to be an artist to avoid the looks of sympathy.

However, I also felt like someone was stepping on my throat while I slowly sunk into a vat of molasses. Is it normal to feel that way?

Listen, I'm not against having a job, a house, or clothes. I don't think those are the things that make you normal. They're just things that you do and have. How you interact with those things and how you live life is ultimately what matters.

Many of the things we all do in life don't make sense. We live in a culture where most believe that sacrifice and hardship are only worth it if they support you financially, and money is only truly earned through sacrifice and hardship. Most people go to work to make money.

Rarely does someone go to work to live, although we call it making a living. It's just weird.

Normal conversation usually consists of some drama that happened at work or at home. We talk about the weather, we talk about how bored we might be, or how we want a change. However, every once in a while there is something exciting to talk about.

Honestly, in my opinion, there is no such thing as usual, typical, or ordinary. We live in a society where we are surrounded by labels. People are accustomed to looking for, tagging, and categorizing similarities within one another. It allows people to have a sense of understanding if they can fit you into a standard.

When coming up with our story and putting ourselves out there, we may be tempted to try and relate to people, maybe everyone. We may try to fit in. We'll try to be what we think people are, or what we think will appeal to the most people. The problem is that no matter what you say or do, people are going to see what they think they see and hear what they hear. If you are going to call yourself an artist, be prepared, and don't shape your personality or content based on what you think other people may think. This will cause inconsistencies in who you are and, honestly, could lead to burnout.

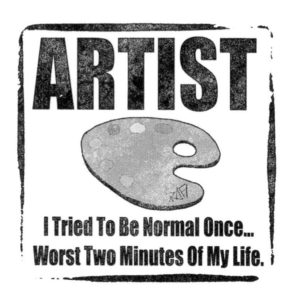

People are weird. One day, a friend of mine said that I'd probably get along with another friend of hers because I like superhero movies and he also likes superhero movies. I thought to myself, "I love all kinds of movies, not just superhero movies. That's a weird thing to say."

When Klee and I first started putting ourselves out there, a young man who noticeably had a crush on her exclaimed, "I see you are wearing a T-shirt, I like T-shirts too!"

We associate with one another based on the most random things. The truth is, we could never fully understand what shapes someone's thinking because we haven't walked in anyone else's shoes.

Even you, my beautiful and amazing readers. You are only capturing a short glimpse of my story and what I am trying to say. Ultimately you will file it somewhere that makes sense to you and your life. You are reading this book from your own perspective and filtering all the information through your life experiences. This is how *EVERYONE* takes in information.

When you share that you are an artist, or the things you are excited about, the person on the other side is only going to have part of the story. The other part of the story is what is going on with them. That's why someone might watch a 10 minute video of mine on YouTube and no matter what I say, they walk away with their own meaning.

The same thing happens with everything we create and put out there.

The fact is that not everyone is going to get you. People are going to misunderstand you, and that is ok. As long as you stay consistent and authentic to who you are, it'll all work out in the end. If you are trying desperately to connect on their terms, chances are you will be confused by your own message.

So many people try to fit in by chasing what is popular and trending so they can relate to others, but that is a constant race.

Don't try to be whatever you think *normal* is, because it will hurt your art brand. I have friends who run a small business, and they obsess over looking "professional". I'm always confused by this because what they think looks professional is dull. Their brand looks like everyone else's brand. Nothing sets them apart. It's boring, but it is also what is considered normal.

There is nothing exciting about *normal*. The truth is, normal is a myth. Normal is doing what everyone else is doing and thinking how everyone else thinks. None of us can fit easily and perfectly into a category.

We are ever-changing and evolving. We are becoming things and letting go of things. We are not the same person we were last week, nor will we be the same person we are now in a year. We are constantly in flux. We are weird and have our own weird thoughts.

We may not share them because we want to appear normal, but we are all beautifully weird right beneath the surface.

230

In my opinion, normal is not a natural state of being human. I refuse to be "normal" because it is torturous to deny my quirks and eccentricities to fit into a world that isn't sure what normal is anyway. I refuse to be labeled because, as a human being, I am too dynamic and ever-changing.

Over the past few years, I have learned to be proud of who I am and to not let anyone – no matter who they are, try to manipulate, change, or label me because I am not who they think I should be or they believe they have me pegged.

Yeah, life is too short to worry about all that jazz anyhow.

Go forth and be who you are – most of all, revel in your uniqueness and be proud of your qualities that make you innately you.

Show that off to the world in everything you put out there. Don't be afraid of being misunderstood. Embrace your weirdness and share it with the planet.

"Here's to the crazy ones, the misfits, the rebels, the troublemakers, the round pegs in the square holes... the ones who see things differently -- they're not fond of rules... You can quote them, disagree with them, glorify or vilify them, but the only thing you can't do is ignore them because they change things... they push the human race forward, and while some may see them as the crazy ones, we see genius, because the ones who are crazy enough to think that they can change the world, are the ones who do." - Steve Jobs

THE POWER OF MUTUAL EXCITEMENT

There is one rule that comes with being authentic in putting yourself out there. It is having a genuine interest in people. If you are not genuinely interested in other humans, then it is impossible to see things from any different perspective than your own. Without this, there is no positive engagement. There is no mutual ground to stand on.

Much of marketing today is focused on the bottom line and not having a genuine interest in people. Most marketers have to rely on less than honest approaches to putting themselves out there in their competition with one another. Their focus is not on building trust.

It is giving the illusion that they are more trustworthy than the other guy.

232

Some large companies provide the impression that they care, but they are rarely vulnerable and human. Everything is beautifully crafted to evoke a feeling that will be associated with these companies, but for the most part, it's all manufactured. If a company you love can make you feel a sense of mutual excitement for what they are doing or selling, you become their biggest advocate.

Things like "All-Natural, Clean, or Organic" on the label are an excellent example of this. According to the FDA, any company can call a product "natural" or "clean" and define that term any way it wants. In most cases, being "organic" doesn't make an ingredient better, safer, or justify the added costs. However, companies don't hesitate to slap on that label and watch the money cascade in, even if they are not completely honest. This is because they have an audience of people who are excited about living an all natural life.

It doesn't work that way for artists unless you decide to follow trends and create only what is popular. This is both difficult and nearly impossible. Art is not a trend. You can't add labels like "No MSG" or "Gluten-Free" to increase your art sales. Although, I think it could make for a great art series.

As Rogue Artists, we are the product, brand, and company. We are the trend that people will get excited about. Understanding that you are putting something extraordinary in an ordinary world is exciting. However, it starts with our own excitement for what we do and create.

We are not selling a toaster or a box of detergent. Many of us make the mistake of looking at our art as if it were just a product. We believe that our collectors look at it the same way, but they don't. You are giving other humans the exclusive right to a snapshot of creation that they will be able to enjoy for a lifetime.

We share in the excitement of that moment and that lives on in the interactions of everyone involved. It is the excitement of the collector that will cause them to point out your artwork to all of their guests.

"It's good...but is it glutton free?"

With the thousands of shows I have done, I never tried to sell my art. In fact, I knew that all I needed to do was be excited about the art I was showing.

Earlier in the book, we excitedly mentioned "Nana's lemon cake" and I'm sure you wanted some.

This is what it's all about. We are all excellent "sales people" when we eagerly list many reasons why we think someone should listen to a song, read a book, watch a movie, buy a product, or eat at a particular restaurant. We want to share good things with other humans. How many times have you eagerly recommended something because you were excited about it?

When we see something spectacular, our instinct is to immediately point it out to the people around us.

234

"Look, it's a rainbow!"
"That cloud looks like David Bowie!"
"Look, there's a dolphin!"

We get excited, and in turn, other people get excited as well. This is Mutual Excitement.

We are social creatures who communicate emotionally. If you are aloof and bored when you are talking about your art, how would you expect someone to feel about it? Believe it or not, our level of excitement has a significant impact on what we put out there.

Mutual excitement is one of the reasons that some sitcoms have a laugh track. Laughter is contagious. Looking at brain scans, researchers found that even in the absence of a funny prompt, just hearing laughter triggers the brain to respond by preparing our facial muscles to join in.

Think of a moment in your life where you and your friends had the giggles for so long that your face hurt afterwards.

It turns out, in social creatures like humans, all emotions operate this way. Researchers call this phenomenon *Emotional Contagion*.

The truth is that when we're excited, our emotions become so powerful that we are more likely to make a decision. Excitement leads to fast decision-making and cuts through the hemming and hawing that happens when you waste time weighing things out.

Strong emotions can cause you to be impulsive.

We tend to make decisions when we're feeling any kind of strong emotions. Whether it is negative or positive doesn't matter. Anxiety and financial stress may cause someone to sign up for a get rich quick program. Joy and excitement will cause people to buy something that will continue that feeling.

This is why I get excited about everything I am putting out there. Not only does it make me feel excited about my life, but that excitement is contagious and powerful.

Even when something is a struggle, I share it with excitement. We watch movies because of the emotions we feel, and we love happy endings. Life is exciting that way as well.

This is why your struggles in your art career or in life can make for an awesome story. However, you are either giving a resolution, or you are just complaining. I like to approach this like a storyteller. I set the scene, introduce the characters (usually me and Klee), and I outline the challenges, roadblocks, or obstacles. Then I share how the characters triumphed in the end.

Be excited about what you create and your story. People are excited to be on this journey with you. If you are simply trying to sell something and have no story and no excitement, then in my opinion, you're not doing your art justice.

People will ask me about my art at shows, and I am excited to share my thoughts. I'm there to show off my art, not to sell it. That being said, I have sold a lot of art and have never had to be salesy or persuade anyone into buying it.

Selling is NOT what most people think it is. It is not tactics and manipulation. The last thing anyone wants is to go somewhere and have someone try to sell them on something.

This is what will set you apart from the rest.

People are so used to typical sales tactics that they are ready to go in and fight. However, if you are just genuinely excited about what you create and are NOT trying to sell them something, it changes the dynamic right away.

So, you can either simply be excited about your work, or you can try and sell the art. If selling is what you are interested in, I will not disappoint. Here is a common selling tactic that you can try if that is what you fancy. This is taken directly from our experience purchasing a car, but this can be used to try and sell anything.

Start with psychological profiling by asking certain questions.

For example, things like, "How much are you looking to spend today?" Make sure you smile while asking about work, hobbies, and the like. The goal is to get as much information as you can to leverage the sale.

Speed up the clock.

Make sure there's a lot of waiting. Make a production of back and forth negotiating with managers, looking up information, looking busy, and having to get back to them on their questions. Wear down their patience to your advantage.

This or that.

This tactic will help you box them in. Ask questions that control the options by not allowing for yes or no answers. Things like, "Would you prefer the blue one or the purple one?" People who are stressed, will usually pick one and purchase it simply to get out of this situation.

If this, then that.

If *This or That* didn't work, then we bring in another tactic to box them in further. Ask this question while making it seem like you are doing them a favor. "If I could offer you a payment plan, would that be what it takes to get you to buy this artwork today at this incredible price?" Or offer them another option.

"If I can show you a work of art at the price you want but in a different size, would you be willing to buy it today?"

Basically, follow the "If I can blah blah blah, would you be willing to bla bla bla?" method.

The Ben Franklin Close.

If none of your brilliant attempts worked, and you feel the sale slipping out of your grasp, it's time to bring out the big guns. Let them wait for a moment to prime them for your next move. Come back with a piece of paper and present it to them. There will be a line down the middle of the sheet. On one side, you will have listed their reasons for buying the art. On the other side, you will have listed their reasons not to buy. Make sure to keep the list very unbalanced in favor of buying. This is an extremely common sales gimmick and one that should be a piece of cake for you. The idea is to show them in tangible form that they are better off purchasing the art.

Bring the pressure.

If your mark still hasn't signed on the dotted line, apply some pressure. "Man, I really want you to own this art, but someone already showed interest in it, and they are willing to pay full price. I could only go down this much." You can follow that with something like "If you don't get it today, it'll be gone tomorrow." If for some strange reason, they didn't jump on the offer by now, simply ask them "Alright, can we meet in the middle somewhere?" This affirms your altruistic intentions and reassures them that you have their best interests at heart.

You did it! You got them! But it's not over yet, we have more work to do.

The Upsell.

This is where you offer all the extras they're going to need if they really want to be good stewards of the art they now proudly own. Things like stain protection, a pro-bundle COA, a personal warranty for damage, as well as some lovely accent pieces that would really tie it all together.

Make sure all of this looks like standard procedure during check out. If they question it, say things like, "Well, people will get the stain protection because they value their investment." or "I've seen people walk out of here without it, and they inevitably come back regretting that decision."

Do you feel gross yet? Wouldn't you rather just be excited about your art and share in some mutual excitement? The process outlined above, as I said, is exactly what we experienced at the dealership when looking for our Jeep. However, I have seen artists employ these tactics at shows. It is sales 101, and while it sometimes works, it doesn't convey authenticity and it almost never leads to return customers or solid relationships.

What is interesting about these sales tactics is how well they cross over into all markets.

Many high-end galleries use these tactics to nitpick and exclude certain clientele to mark up the price of the art they sell. When this tactic is used on a timid person, you can easily come off as an expert who is trying to help them.

This is the only time you'll get a return customer because you will position yourself as the person that helped them make the right decision. This is because you need to trust the person you are purchasing anything of great value from.

Unfortunately, if you are using these tactics, chances are you will use the leverage to sell and not actually assist.

From a marketing perspective, every ounce of interaction you have with a person will determine whether or not they trust you. Art is very different from a car, people hate going to dealerships and dealing with less than honest tactics, but they should love going to you.

At the end of the day, the most potent form of marketing is word of mouth. In fact, all marketing is geared towards getting people to talk about something. The more people are talking about you, the better. At some point, word of mouth takes on its own energy. Every interaction, every piece of material, content, art, and everything else you put out there could be meant to start a conversation. If you are sharing your excitement, chances are that excitement will spread like wildfire.

That legacy begins with you putting your actions where your mouth is. It is you creating a sense of mutual excitement with the humans you connect with.

So many artists worry way too much about not knowing sales or marketing. The truth is, when you really take a close look at the tactics above, you're better off not knowing or using them.

Most of the information you'll discover regarding marketing and sales is just a bunch of tactics designed to persuade people into purchasing something they may regret buying. You are not selling a scam, you are selling something quite remarkable, and no one needs to be tricked into purchasing it.

Not following these overused tactics will set you apart. That means you have absolutely no limits to what you can do. Be scrappy, think outside of the box, take risks, and just put yourself out there however you can. What you don't know will be your biggest strength. Embrace being a Rogue Artist.

As a Rogue Artist, you can get excited about your art and all the new opportunities that you partake in. This excitement is contagious. You DON'T have to be a professional. In fact, if you try to come off as a professional, it might be hard to be contagious in a good way.

Embrace the quirkiness of being an artist. This morning I saw a picture from one of the wealthiest artists in the world. It wasn't a professional headshot or photograph of his art in a clean white space. It was a picture of a hairy, overweight man standing in his studio with nothing but red underpants, boots, and a paintbrush. Say what you will about Damien Hirst, but he knows how to get attention.

Artists are weird. Artists get excited over weird or mundane things. That head-scratching quirkiness is contagious. Your realness, your excitement, and your journey will give humans a reason to be excited, and they will thank you for it.

"Sharing your art is not about closing a sale, it's about opening a door."
-Klee Angelie

Art By RAFI

HOW TO GO ROGUE AS AN ARTIST

So many talented people are just waiting around for a chance. Some are waiting around for permission. We have all been told that there is a particular way we are supposed to approach an art career. It usually involves jumping through hoops and getting some form of validation. However, you can wait for all that to happen, or you can take your career as an artist into your own hands.

The way I *finally* got started in the art world was by just doing it. I had no accolades, no following, and no money. I had zero social media presence and no idea what I was doing. All I knew was that I needed to get my art in front of people and let them know that it exists.

As it turns out, that was the most effective marketing plan I had ever come up with.

I understood that I needed to get myself out there, and because nothing was happening for me on the internet, it was easier for me to put myself in front of people face to face. This ended up working to my benefit because it helped build my confidence, face my fears head on, and create an audience. This also gave me the time I needed to build up my online presence.

I am by no means saying that this is the only way to start or progress in an art career. This is just how I started. I jumped on every opportunity there was to display my art in my local market. When there weren't opportunities, I created them. In the first four years of my career as an artist, I did:

- **Flea Markets** - We rented a booth every weekend.
- **Farmers Markets:** We juried in and then showed art every Saturday.
- **Monthly Art Walks:** Two towns around us had monthly Friday Art Walks.
- **Gallery night Events:** We joined a monthly event in town.
- **Local Festivals** - We did about 12 festivals in the area every year.
- **Antique Malls:** We opened a spot that we would manage every week.
- **Businesses During Local Events** - I would get permission to live paint.
- **Gallery Events & Competitions** - We did a juried art show monthly.
- **Art Fairs:** We joined 3 art fairs in the area every year.

- **Conventions:** We did a comic book and horror convention yearly.
- **Holiday Markets:** We would do small holiday markets that would pop up.
- **National Art Festivals** - We joined 2 big national art fairs in the area.
- **Museum Member Show:** As members, we did a yearly show.
- **Art Association Shows** - I spoke and displayed my art yearly.
- **Local Businesses** - Several businesses around town showed my art.
- **Set Up In Front Of Local Businesses For Events** - When we couldn't show at an event, we would contact local businesses and set up. We would do a live painting, set up a booth, table, or wall with our art.
- **Local Galleries** - We've had stuff in all the local galleries.
- **Open Studio Visit Days** - Once a year, we did an open studio.
- **Yart (Yard and art) SALE** - When we'd do a yard sale we showed art.
- **Portfolio Visits** - I'd visit local business offices with a portfolio to show.
- **Art Scavenger Hunts** - I try to do one yearly to promote an event.
- **Live Painting At Concerts** - Several times, I would live paint at concerts and on stage.

We showed our art at about 100 events, businesses, and functions every year. When we weren't showing our art, we were attending art events in support of other artists. I was done talking about building an art career, I was doing it, brick by brick.

As aggressive as we were at putting ourselves out there, it still took time to build relationships with our collectors and audience. People slowly started to take notice of us and our creations around the third year. However, getting that validation wasn't what was driving us, it was the sheer determination to persist and do everything we could to put our message out there.

The more shows we did, the more we learned about other local opportunities and how to refine our story. We both grew and continue to grow as we take action and try new things. That is the most important lesson I have learned from all of this.

You are either a spectator in your own life, or you are making things happen by not allowing yourself to sit on the sidelines. You are either talking about doing, or you *ARE* doing.

The only way to learn how to put yourself out there and be ready is to put yourself out there. This is by far the most powerful way to show your work and market yourself. The key is to see every event, conversation, and interaction as an opportunity to market yourself. Success is based on how often you are willing to open your mouth and proclaim proudly that you are an artist. Success is creating art and putting it out there often. However, success is not based on how much money you make. It is about building a loyal audience.

Remember, everything is just a stepping stone. I highly recommend building your online market at the same time as putting yourself out there in person. These things work hand in hand. That way, you can easily expand globally when you are ready. If for whatever reason, you cannot put yourself out there in person, things may take a little longer, but you can still establish yourself online. The approach is exactly the same.

Ultimately, when I say put yourself out there, I mean do everything you can to get out in front of people. Face your fears and see it as an opportunity to expose the world to your awesomeness.

As Rogue Artists, we understand that it is all about building relationships. There is nothing more powerful than having a shared experience with another human.

This happens only when you share your craft, and you share who you are.

If you are hiding behind a marketing scheme, you diminish your power. To truly put yourself out there, you have to take risks.

The scariest part of putting yourself out there and promoting your art is facing insecurity. When you get in the arena, it can be terrifying. I think that is because we are afraid that we will get it wrong. Maybe we screwed it up in the past and went through the ever-consuming feelings of rejection because no one showed up to our event.

No matter how much promoting you do, it may feel like you are invisible, but it is nothing to be afraid of. I struggled with this fear for a long time, and honestly, it was counterproductive and got me nowhere. The more afraid I was, the less I was willing to put myself out there.

The other difficulty is the confusion that marketing lingo brings. If you ask a business owner to describe what they do for their marketing, they will usually list boring things they have invested in to get exposure. For example, they may list ads, have an email campaign, pay an influencer, billboard, and run discounts and sales. None of this is revolutionary.

In my mind, marketing is every interaction you have, whether it is in person, or someone comes in contact with something you created. Your art hanging on someone's wall is an opportunity to market you and your business.

It all depends on how excited the buyer was when they purchased it. Having a random conversation with someone on the street is marketing your business. Everything we do is an opportunity to market your art and who you are.

The mistake I see with many artists is that they separate the fact that they are artists from their identity. It's almost like they hide the fact that they create art. There is no mention of it on their email signature. They don't have it on their business card and don't mention it in conversation. They partially hide it or never communicate it at all.

The other side of that coin is treating your art career like a hum-drum business. When artists treat their art career like a boring job, they tend to treat their promotion like a tedious responsibility. People hardly talk about their job with any promotional enthusiasm, mostly, they are complaining about it.

However, art is not a job. This is a lifestyle. We have every reason in the world to share our enthusiasm about what we are doing. Being an artist is so unique that just about everyone you meet has an interest in finding out more about you.

As a Rogue Artist, I scream it from the mountain tops. I want everyone that I interact with to know that I create art. You never know what opportunities might come from some unexpected place unless you are willing to confidently stand in your identity as an artist.

You market yourself every day even if you are not trying. When you walk down the street, are you aware of what you are saying?

I look at everything as an opportunity to put myself out there in a genuine way. I keep who I am and what I am trying to say in mind with every interaction. I look at everything I do as an occasion to share my message. This includes anything from going to the grocery store to posting on social media.

When I am putting myself out there, I also make it a point to share my information in as many ways as possible. I like to call it the **Rogue Knockout**. It means that you focus on more than one way of putting yourself out there. To spread your messages powerfully, you want it to be multifaceted.

This can include newsletter emails, blogs, social media posts, posters, postcards, flyers, videos, podcasts, yard signs, press releases, business cards, mailed invites, listing on event sites, bulletin boards, guest appearances, interviews, publicity stunts, and anything else you can think of to promote one event.

It means leveraging multiple channels of promotion that will allow you to connect and interact with people across numerous touchpoints. In other words, don't do one thing to promote yourself and call it a day. Promote in person, online, on stage, in a parking lot, on your clothes, website, and anywhere else you can think of.

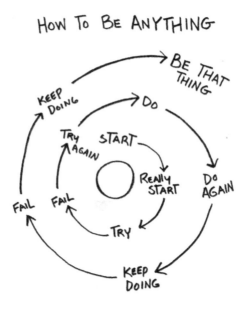

How To Be ANYTHING

Here is an important thing to add. You must be DOING something in order to promote it. For example, it is easier for me to promote an event I am doing because it is specific and time sensitive. I can give people the what, where, when, and why details they need. In fact, I do events all the time because it is a great way to put myself out there and promote it. Whether it is an existing event like an art festival, or one that I create doesn't matter.

What matters is that you are proactive and doing things that are noteworthy. This includes virtual events, small gatherings, or anything that is art centric and fun. If you are doing something, then you can create a buzz for it.

You can set up various ways of creating a buzz. Use small events to promote a more significant upcoming event. I promote myself heavily whenever I do any kind of event. Here are some of the things I might do to promote a significant event that I may have coming up.

- Do a free live painting at a public event.
- Paint or sketch in public just because and start a conversation.
- Hang something fun on community bulletin boards.
- Hang up fun street banners.
- Do a mini-art scavenger hunt promoting the show.
- Use social media daily leading up to the show.
- Hang window displays on your car and at local businesses.
- Print up a bunch of happy posters and put them around town.
- Set up a street team to walk around a festival or event and hand out small art gifts and promotional materials.
- Hang "You Are Awesome" door hangers on houses promoting your event.
- Go to art shows and talk about your upcoming event. (Just don't make that ALL you talk about.)
- Do fun and heartwarming stunts and let your antics land you on the local news, in the newspaper, on the radio, or in a magazine.
- Send press releases to your local newspapers.
- Do an open studio as a pre-show to your event.
- Design, give away, and wear t-shirts promoting your event.
- Start an online or in-person group and hold a pre-event Q&A.

- Leave post-it notes everywhere that say something fun with the event webpage link.
- Hold an online virtual art tour or concert as a promotion show.
- Collaborate with local artists or musicians to cross promote the event.
- Create and share a catalog of your art at the show and leave them with local businesses.
- Take some chalk out on the town and leave inspiring messages.
- Do an artist talk at a school or group and plug your event.
- Invite friends, co-workers, family, and ask them to bring a friend.
- Release a book or booklet of something fun for the show.
- Drive from point A to point B and think about how you can promote yourself and the show. Basically, look at your environment and come up with more ways to promote.
- Set up at an art show, booth, art walk, farmers market, festival, event, or even a table with a local business and talk about the event.
- Get involved in any community project and discuss your event.
- Give returning customers special Loyal Collector gifts for coming to the event.
- Make it possible to take different payment methods like credit cards. Do this no matter what.
- Get extra thank you materials and stuff to give with sold art, think about promotion for your next event.
- Work on a public mural and have materials next to you about your upcoming event.
- Host a fun photo, video, caption, or contest leading up to the show and tie it in somehow.

- Do a free live webinar or live event during or leading up to the event.
- Share your event when you teach creative workshops.
- Have conversations with random strangers about your art and your upcoming event.
- Offer layaway as an option for purchasing art.

As you can see, this list only scratches at the surface of possibilities. It is all about the way you interact with others.

That is because EVERYTHING YOU DO is an opportunity to talk about you, your message, your event, and your art. Just remember not to sit around hoping that someone will show up. You have to be innovative and brave. If you can grasp promoting your event, you can get what it takes to promote yourself and your art. It's not just throwing some money at getting ads online. That's boring.

You might have noticed that one of the suggestions on the list is *press releases*. This one intimidates a lot of people, either because they didn't know they could submit a press release to local publications, or because they don't know how to go about writing one. Basically, a press release is just an article that talks about what you're doing that is media worthy.

It follows a certain format, but there are press release templates available online and you can easily search for tips on how to write one. As a side note, be sure to spell check any press release you submit. Publications will not always do it for you, as we discovered by reading some of our own, complete with typos. This is just one of many ways to put yourself out there in the media. We have been interviewed several times because of our antics that we have done in public.

As a Rogue Artist, you train yourself to see the newsworthiness of what you are doing. Every stunt you do in public has the opportunity to make it into the news as long as you are bringing something spectacular. Something that will be a relief from most of the bad news that fills most news media. On average there are four things you want to think about that may be considered newsworthy.

1. Significance to many.
How many people will be affected by what you are doing. When I did one of my art scavenger hunts, I created about 400 tiny little pieces that had "feel good" sayings and put them all around the downtown area of Pensacola Florida. Because so many were affected, the local paper reached out. Eventually, when I had my first large solo exhibition, the same paper covered my show.

2. Proximity matters.
Things that happen near home and impact the community and the paper's readers will always make it into the news. This is why I will always have our local community and the surrounding areas in mind when thinking about an event or stunt.

Keep in mind that proximity only means the community. For example, when traveling to find our new home, we featured a small town in one of our videos. The community of that town shared our video with the world and a local paper picked up the story.

3. Prominence is a bonus.
Famous people get more coverage just because they are famous. If you have any friends that are famous or are able to mingle with a famous person at your exhibition, don't be afraid to approach them and ask if they will say a few words about the show. Most people that are in the limelight will be happy to help those that are helping themselves. They know what it is like to be in the arena.

4. Human Interest stories are powerful.

This is what most of our newsworthy stories will be about. Honestly, human interest stories defy the rules of newsworthiness. They appeal to emotion and aim to evoke amusement, joy, sadness, or caring. It's usually a quirky story that brings a feel-good feeling.

Newspapers often have a dedicated area for offbeat and interesting items, and News Media outlets usually try to end on an uplifting note.

"The noblest art is that of making others happy"
— P.T. Barnum

I find that the key to being newsworthy, is to do something selfless that will bring happiness to others. As artists, what we create can bring amusement, confusion, beauty, love, and or point a finger at something that needs attention. We have a great power within us to turn heads. However, if you are doing it *ONLY* to make the news, it may backfire. Be genuine. Too many of us are focused on making the sale and getting publicity because we think it will propel us to fame, it doesn't. Who you are and the reasons you do what you do is what will get you attention.

Look at any interaction as a social experiment to share your mutual excitement about what you are doing. I check to see what the reaction is and whether I'm getting my message across. I make sure that everything I do has a foundation that is based on a simple message.

It's all about getting the word out there. I make it a point not to look at any of my promotional interactions as an opportunity to make money for two reasons.

First, it screws up my measurement of results. If I am focused on money, then I am looking at how much money I made in the short term. I want to look at emotional reaction and engagement with what I am doing. Most importantly, I want to look for repeat engagement when I do my next thing. Money results are an imperfect measurement and motivator of the long-term.

Second, we tend to come off as desperate when we are chasing money, and it taints the entire project.

This is why you have to be honest with yourself about your motivation. If there is even a hint of desperation, it can put your head in a direction you don't want to go. Convey your message with confidence and not despair.

Social experiments are a powerful way to face fears, grow, and put yourself out there. It will also set you apart from the rest of the boring marketing that everyone is doing. A lot of the marketing today is like a suburban neighborhood where there are hundreds of identical houses. They all have the same size lawn, color scheme, driveway, and build. The only thing that sets them apart are the little personal touches that the owner might add, like some hanging potted plants and a welcome mat that reads, "We are probably pretending not to be home."

These little add ons will set the houses apart, but not that much. They could easily get lost in the sea of beige and white picket fences.

When you approach it as a Rogue Artist, it's like building your house from the ground up.

Your home would be made from taking risks, innovating, and trying new things. You may use existing methods and come up with new ones. Your house would stand out from miles away.

The key is understanding that, in essence, every interaction you have in society is a social experiment and one that you can learn from. So many people are desperately trying to get noticed that they lose sight of their own evolution and growth in the process. That growth is what will set you apart and make you unstoppable.

You can have several social experiments in the world at once, and every single one is going to teach you something about how people respond to your message. Most importantly, it is going to teach you more about yourself and what you are capable of.

Here are 10 easy Rogue social experiments to help push out of comfort zones and really put yourself out there in a fun way. Use these to inspire you to come up with your own. When you do any social experiment, remember your narrative. Don't just do it to seek attention, do it because you are facing a fear. That story is so much more compelling to anyone involved.

- **ROGUE IDEA #1** Conduct an art social experiment to see how people respond to your marketing style. Have a questionnaire on what they would like to see by setting up a table in public.
- **ROGUE IDEA #2** Put a piece of art on the outside of your car. Walk around with a work of art duct-taped to you. Let the world know you are an artist.
- **ROGUE IDEA #3** THE CRAZY ELEVATOR PITCH. Come up with an insane elevator pitch (30-second introduction of yourself and what you do) that will leave the person scratching their head.
- **ROGUE IDEA #4** Make large and/or tiny outside art signs that make people stop and laugh.
- **ROGUE IDEA #5** Have an art scavenger hunt where you leave a bunch of happy little creations around town.
- **ROGUE IDEA #6** Create a coloring book flyer or poster with a crayon attached and hand them out at carnivals or events.
- **ROGUE IDEA #7** Create a sign and do some terrible sign flipping on a corner.
- **ROGUE IDEA #8** This is your mission. Give away 100 business cards in 3 hours. If they are handmade, even better. For every 100 cards you give out, chances are that at least one person will respond.
- **ROGUE IDEA #9** Go to ALL the local businesses and ask if you can display your art there. Don't stop until you've been rejected 5 times. Then do it again, every other month, even if they said "no."
- **ROGUE IDEA #10** Send a special handmade note to people who purchased art from you just to let them know they are unique and awesome.

There are so many fun things you can do. Have a yard and art sale, grab some chalk, hit the town, paint in public, and just about anything else your brilliant mind can come up with. Think like a Rogue Artist and take the mundane and make it exciting. Once you start pushing out of fear and comfort zones, more ideas will come.

Turn everything you do into a social experiment and make it fun. We learn through trial and error and hands-on experience, so I hope you do more than just read this book. I hope you blaze your own way of putting yourself out there.

When I am putting together a social experiment, I keep certain things in mind. First is my mindset. A creative social experiment can detach you from the fear of failure. Everything is being analyzed and measured, including your reaction to the situation. It's not a failure if it doesn't work, it is an experiment.

For example, one social experiment I did was to go out and give small works of art to random people. The first woman was a waitress who was setting up the outdoor seating area. As I approached her, I could feel myself getting nervous.

I pushed through and awkwardly made my way up to her sheepishly. When I gave the art, she looked around suspiciously as if it all was part of some elaborate practical joke. It didn't help matters that I asked her if it was ok that I was filming.

Eventually, upon realizing it wasn't a joke, she was surprisingly excited. I was still nervous.

I still had four more pieces to give away that day. As I did, it got easier, but I was nervous and awkward the entire time. This experience taught me that next time, I would allow myself time to relax and enjoy the interaction.

Typically, whenever I have done any kind of creative social experiment, I find myself breaking through some sort of comfort zone.

Despite popular belief, I am painfully shy. I force myself to get on stage whenever I am speaking or whenever I am doing some kind of event in public. There's no way around it. If you want to be heard, you are going to have to take center stage.

The first time I did an art scavenger hunt around town, I scheduled it early so I wouldn't run into anyone. Little did I know the city would be waking up, and everyone noticed the weird guy hiding things around town. People approached me and asked what I was doing, and I explained my "Inspire A Smile" art campaign. It was an incredible experience, but every time I was approached, I faced a fear.

Art is a phenomenon of culture. It is a sensuous and beautiful form, which shows us the essence of being human. It turns the invisible into visible and the intellectual into perceptible. Everything creative is the perfect form of expression. That's why I think any creative project we share with the general public can be a powerful social experiment.

Every social experiment I do has to do with sharing a message or testing a hypothesis out. For example, I was curious to see how people would respond to happy messages on magnets around town in the art scavenger hunt. Would they be compelled to take them home? Would they be afraid to? Or would they ignore the art? What happens if I add a tag with my social media handle? Trying new ways of getting a response, will allow you to understand more about human behavior and why people respond to things.

Mostly though, these experiments are for me. I don't mean the benefits of getting exposure, but the benefits of facing fears and pushing past boundaries.

"DREAMS HAVE ALWAYS EXPANDED OUR UNDERSTANDING OF REALITY BY CHALLENGING OUR BOUNDARIES OF THE REAL, OF THE POSSIBLE." – HENRY REED

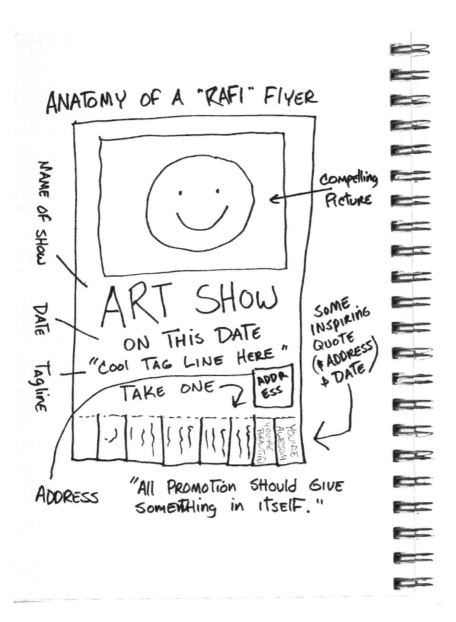

ANATOMY OF A "RAFI" FLYER

NAME OF SHOW

Compelling Picture

DATE

Tagline

ART SHOW
ON THIS DATE
"COOL TAG LINE HERE"

TAKE ONE

ADDRESS

SOME INSPIRING QUOTE (& ADDRESS & DATE)

YOU'RE AWESOME
YOU'RE BEAUTIFUL

ADDRESS

"All PROMOTION SHOULD GIVE SOMETHING in ITSELF."

259

Rejection. As artists, we tend to be overwhelmingly concerned with rejection. Yet rejection is necessary if you are going to grow past caring about what people think. The anxiety of not being accepted prevents us from taking steps to fly. The truth is that being denied is never as bad as we think.

- Ask a random person to critique art that you are carrying around town. Have a proper form with questions that you made up.
- Ask a group of strangers if you can show them your art portfolio because you are trying to decide which one to submit to a competition.
- Pretend to be an art missionary and spread the gospel of your art but dress up in a sandwich board that states, "The Art Is Nigh!"
- Challenge strangers to a chalk drawing contest and have people vote on whose is better.
- Ask a local business if you can set up a table with your art outside.

Will people say no to you? Of course, but probably not as many as you think. It's actually quite difficult to be rejected. The cool thing about this is that you face a fear, and you find out a little more about human nature.

Ask A Favor. Like rejection, asking a favor is one of those things that we all tend to avoid. We are not used to asking for what we want. However, this isn't about rejection. Ask for favors to show yourself how willing people are to support you.

According to the Ben Franklin effect, we cherish people more when we do them favors. We are testing this, but the fear we are facing is approaching someone with a favor to ask. Especially if you stack the favors from small to big.

A fun example of this is enlisting someone to do something they didn't sign up to do. Let's say you are doing a painting at a public event. Someone comes by, and they are watching you paint. You ask them if they will hold your wet brush for a moment while you make a call.

A few moments later, as you are busy with your call, you ask them if they don't mind making some minor marks on the canvas before the paint dries, and you show them where. Then a few moments later, you tell them you have to leave for five minutes.

Ask them if they wouldn't mind pretending to be the artist while you are gone. Chances are when you reveal the joke, the person will laugh and have a memorable experience that they will share with others.

You will be surprised how giving people are. People typically want to support one another. If you notice that people aren't willing to do favors, your demands may be too great. Please make sure that person walks away with a token of your appreciation and if you film it, ask them on camera if it is ok to use it in a video.

We have to face so many fears when putting ourselves out there, and most of them sit in our imagination. The only time we overcome fears is when we encounter them.

Why not overcome your fears and put yourself out there in a memorable way while you are at it?

Start small if you have to, one step at a time. Just remember that those who boldly share their message are the ones that get discovered.

Those of us who toil away in uncertainty are there because we fear the very things that will help us grow beyond obscurity.

Please make sure to keep safety and cultural politeness in mind. This is why I repeat time and time again, don't do social experiments because you are chasing attention. Do not humiliate or put people down to get likes. Keep it honest and fun. If you have something to say and learn from the experience, it will be a powerful way of putting yourself out there.

Don't Forget to Show Gratitude.

Always remember to thank people sincerely. They don't have to partake in your events, stunts, or harebrained ideas, and if they do, it means they connected with you somehow.

When the numbers are low, it is easy to get self-absorbed and feel sad and ignored, don't let this happen. If the numbers are low, it just means you need to tweak something or change it up a bit. That's why it's called an experiment, you are figuring it all out.

No matter what, show appreciation to everyone equally because they have the potential to stick with you forever. Whether it is attention or financial stats, appreciate everyone equally. I've had collectors tell me about their experience with other artists where they walked away unappreciated, and that will tarnish the relationship.

So, remember to always show appreciation to everyone you interact with, whether they are purchasing your art or not. Life is already one giant social experiment. You might as well use it to share your story and your art.

Have fun with all of this. As Rogue Artists, we approach every moment of putting ourselves out there like an opportunity to grow and challenge ourselves. To have fun and make the most of what we do. To connect and share in what it means to be alive and human.

HOW TO RUN A GOOD ROGUE CON

It is said that trust is hard to come by. However, as human beings, we are all wired to trust. We've got giant heads to house the fantastic and mushy machine between our ears. Because of this, we are born physically premature and useless to take care of ourselves and our big heads.

From the moment we take our first breath, our entire survival is based on trust. We automatically have to trust the people around us.
That doesn't mean that everyone is trustworthy. Some of us have a healthy

dose of skepticism when it comes to things sounding too good to be true, but people get conned all the time anyhow. We are all susceptible to compelling stories and fantastic promises.

For example, you are at the world's fair in the early 1900s. With great fanfare and showmanship, a man reaches into an old weather worn sack, pulls out a rattlesnake, slits it open, and plunges it into a boiling pot of water.

As you stand there in horror, he tells you the story of an ancient Hopi remedy learned by the cowboys of the wild west. The snake fat rises to the top of the pot as he continues his fantastic tale. He then skims it off, mixes it with a slew of secret ingredients, and pours it into glass vials embossed with the name CLARK STANLEY SNAKE OIL LINIMENT.

He apprises the growing crowd of the miracles his snake oil had performed and how Clark Stanley's Snake Oil Liniment was "Good for Everything a Liniment Ought to Be Good For."

Let's stop for a moment. There is so much more going on here than meets the eye. Clark Stanley is creating an emotional experience that is worth examining. First, this scene was at the World's Expo in Chicago, many people had never seen a real rattlesnake being murdered by a real cowboy. His presentation was a spectacle that caused word of mouth to spread and grow the crowd.

Second, he added to the allure by telling a story about the mysterious Hopi people teaching this ancient remedy to cowboys. Most people only knew about cowboys through fictional stories in penny dreadfuls, dime novels, and pulp magazines.

Clark Stanley had also published hundreds of pamphlets ahead of time. *True Life In The Far West By An American Cowboy Better Known As The Rattle Snake King*, is a book filled with amazing stories of the self-described cowboy from Texas.

It talks about how he spent years conquering the West. He detailed fantastic stories of his adventures, and they also happened to describe the magical powers of his Snake Oil Liniment.

Posters and flyers of the Rattle Snake King surrounded the fair containing images of Clark Stanley Surrounded by snakes. These also boasted the miracle cures of the "wonderful pain destroying compound."

According to his advertising, the liniment was for all pain and lameness. It was said to cure rheumatism, neuralgia, sciatica, lame back, lumbago, contracted muscles, toothache, sprains, swellings, frostbites, chilblains, bruises, sore throat, and more.

It also cured the bites of animals, insects, and reptiles. This was obviously the answer to everyone's health problems. Needless to say, we now know that this was an elaborate con. However, we want to believe. We want to trust.

If you scroll through social media, I'm sure you have come across a countless number of ads that promise some proven method that will make you rich, successful, admired, fulfilled, happier, or better in some way. These are gimmicks and scams that use emotional and behavioral needs to target someone who is looking for a quick fix.

Honestly, there is a little of that going on in most marketing. It has become common to use these tactics because most people are more concerned with the bottom line than remaining authentic. It is so normalized that marketing courses will teach these tactics as if they are ethical. We all accept it because it is just the way things are.

Some examples are:

- **Offering a free service although the price is rolled in** or there is a hidden fee. For example, the handmade online selling platform "Etsy" suggested we offer free shipping but roll the shipping cost into the actual price. That is being inauthentic no matter how you play it.
- **Puffery** means someone can exaggerate statements as long as they are vague and can't be verified objectively, like calling anything *the best*. It's basically false advertising but legal because it is nebulous and not presented as a factual statement.
- **Misleading implications** are where someone promises something that is a possibility, but they pose it as a fact. For example, "The food I will teach you to prepare will help you lose weight." They can never really know for sure.
- **Broken promises** are typical in marketing. For example, "Sign up now because this is a one-time deal, and there won't be a recording of the live event." Days later, they will announce, "So many people couldn't make it live, so the recording is now available for XX."

- **Price gouging** is a common one as well. We saw it happening during the recent Covid pandemic where online sellers were selling toilet paper at five times the value. We also see it in some traditional marketing. For example, someone offers an expensive product and promotes it aggressively.

  These usually have a sense of urgency attached to them, a "limited amount available." They have plenty, and once sales go down, they stop selling it and offer it as a free bonus for something new.
- **Crappy upsells** are big with some online coaches. For example, "This program teaches you all the steps you need and knowledge about [XXX] to achieve [XXX]. After buying the program, you end up on a page where you find out that not everything is included in the introductory rate. Instead, you have to pony up more money to get that critical part of the program.
- **Bloated promises** are a thing I'm always on the lookout for. For example, "I was just like you, and one day I discovered the secret to making millions fast. Sign up for the secret to riches and become a millionaire in less than a year."

The thing is that it has gotten so out of control that many more people are skeptical of everything. The marketing tactics themselves are not what make it a gimmick, scam, manipulation, or lie. It is the motive. The beauty of Clark Stanley and other conmen is what we can learn from them.

They know how to promote a show. Because of that, I am about to share how a good con gets people to throw away their money. Just remember, the motive is what matters. Tactics are just tactics, so use this responsibly, ethically, and authentically.

Ironically, one of the best ways I have seen of promoting an event or project you are working on is by doing what conmen do. For the most part, they sell a fictitious story using props and theater to get people to pay attention and invest vast amounts of money.

Something is compelling about that, and I find myself fascinated by the manipulation of human emotions. I also think it is way more common than people would like to admit because most people who are conned never come forward.

The question is, how do we use these very successful tactics as a Rogue Artist who is not trying to scam someone out of their money? We start at the beginning.

The first step of a con is to build the foundation.

This is where you put together the bones of the operation. You make preparations in advance for the release date and make sure no other events conflict. You plan out the event and design the different stages of marketing materials which are: the teaser, the lead-up, and the big reveal. These will be hand-made or ordered flyers, door hangers, yard signs, posters, t-shirts, and postcards.

I suggest three months of foundation building and planning of the event. Contact local newspapers, event calendars, and cooperating businesses and let them in on your occasion with a confidential press release.

Build a website, design and order materials, hire assistants if required. You do your due diligence, market research, and data gathering by analyzing the response to the information you will make available. Set up a landing page for the event so you can check how many average visitors you get every time you release information. Spend time getting a general idea of who your buyers are, their habits, and what they like.

Later in this stage, you may release a teaser while you finish preparations. Something that creates a sense of mystery, is unique, and grabs attention.

For example, there could be flyers and yard signs around town that say, "The Truth Is Coming Soon To Downtown" with a link to the website. The website should have a newsletter sign-up and a countdown on the landing page with a mysterious picture or logo.

In the weeks that follow, put up more nondescript flyers, posters, door hangers and start posting on social media. Also, build a street team to help put things up around town, give away t-shirts, and create a buzz.

For most conmen, a paid ad, a free gift that requires an email, cold calling, or any other deceptive approach is typical. As Rogue Artists, we don't need to do any of that because we do everything as if it is the most significant event anyone has ever seen.

The second step of a con is the fantastic promise.

Although you have already made a fantastic cryptic promise with your buzz material stating, "The Truth Is Coming Soon To Downtown," it is time to add to the allure the closer you get to the countdown. Most conmen will promise extreme wealth, security, power, or any of the other emotional needs.

This is where claims of "You don't have to work for someone else, you can be your own boss and make millions" are the norm. In our case, we are just teasing so far. This is the lead-up where we share that something will be revealed and resolve the mystery.

For example, we release some more materials as the week of the end of the countdown approaches, "The Truth Will Be Unveiled."

THE TRUTH UNVEILED

Around this time, I may also do an art scavenger hunt and leave little waterproof works of art around town promoting the website and the show. By giving a little back, you build trust and add to the excitement.

The third step of a con is to use a targeted approach.
At this point, you have done your due diligence and collected several emails for your newsletter and some followers on social media. The day before the countdown ends, you send out an email reminder to everyone via newsletter and social media.

Now that we have everyone's attention, it's time for a good story with a cliffhanger. Contact the local media with your press release of the compelling story, so you control the narrative.

The fourth step of a con is a compelling story.
At this point, most conmen will tell you their story of rags to riches after they discovered some proven or secret method.

They will show visual cues of success like standing by an expensive car or a big house as they describe their story. It is what those things would make us feel that causes us to pay attention.

They are also establishing themselves as an expert. This part of the con also contains a lot of puffery, so they tend to use vague power words like tremendous, best, and unmatched.

In many cases, the victim is promised to profit from participating.

Greed is encouraged, such that rational judgment of the situation might be impaired. Therefore, most victims won't come forward because they would reveal their own greed in the process. Luckily, we are not about that. This day we reveal just enough to entice them to feel like they need to come to the event to find answers to all this fun craziness. This is also where you introduce the promise.

For example, on the website, a video pops up as soon as the countdown stops. Dressed in a ridiculous outfit that fits the theme of mystery, I say,

"Welcome to The Truth. Some of you may know who I am, some of you may not. I have practiced art in this town for five years and have experienced something quite remarkable. A truth about humans, nature, and the world.

Extraordinary depictions of the human spirit and secrets can hardly be explained using the limitation of words. That is why I will reveal it all in my next limited-time exhibition in the downtown area. This is no ordinary art show. This is an experience that no one will forget. The first hundred people to arrive will receive a token of my appreciation.

So, mark your calendars and save the epic opening date. We will have delicious hors d'oeuvres, an open bar, and legendary photo ops. The event is free to enter, but only the people who enter their names below will get V.I.P. access. There are only 50 spots available. Hope to see you there. This message will now self-destruct. Not really, but I do hope to see you at this special event."

Then it ends with live testimonials from patrons having fun at my last show, and finally the words "The Truth Exhibition" with the date.

272

The fifth step of a con is to show social proof/pay off.

So, conmen usually do this in several different ways. If they have already been lured, the victim may receive a small payout or convincing result. This builds trust in the scheme.

Testimonials are always great as a convincer. If the conman can get an expert or celebrity to promote their product, even better.

"MY EYEBROW GREW BACK AND IT LOOKS LIKE A GIANT FUZZY CATERPILLAR ON MY FACE. I LOVE IT !!!!" – SUZY FOREHEAD

In my case, the website would have testimonials, and the payoff has been promised to the first 100 people who show up and the 50 V.I.P.s. The payoff has been promised, along with free t-shirts, scavenger hunts, and the fun of a mystery.

Now here is where it gets a little more difficult for me than it is for a conman. I need to make sure the show is extraordinary. I have spent months preparing, and honestly, if it wasn't, then I am not doing a good job.

The show has to be something that people will talk about after they leave. That means photo ops, interactive art sections of the gallery, unexpected and immersive art, good music, good food, alcohol, and an epic reveal.

It cannot be just another boring art show with white walls and a stuffy disposition. The experience needs to be memorable. I am going to keep my promise of more than an ordinary art show.

On the other hand, the conman will be leaving town at some point, so there's really no pressure for them. The whole point of the con is to not deliver on the promise. As Rogue Artists, our goal is to over-deliver.

Now, at this point, people are talking about the reveal on my website. Some are upset because they were expecting more than some stupid art show. Others are excited and sharing. Either way, people are talking about it, and that is good.

The sixth step in a con is creating a sense of urgency.

A conman may manufacture a sudden crisis, a higher tier price, or change of events. This forces the victim to decide immediately because the clock is ticking down or there is limited space.

This is the pinnacle of the con and marks whether it succeeds or fails.

Because we are not actually scamming anyone, we built a sense of urgency from the beginning. The information gained from how many people sign up for V.I.P. and the newsletter will indicate the show's success and if anything needs tweaking.

The main goal is to get many people to the exhibition and show them a good time. The sales of the art will happen as a side effect of the experience they are having. So don't try to sell them on anything. You are building a legacy. This means that if the show is incredible, they are more likely to attend any event I do in the future.

The seventh step of a con is to introduce an accomplice.

For a conman, they will have someone in on the con that plays the part of an interested bystander. This person then gives money to the conman, and it builds legitimacy and reassures the victim. This provides the conman with more significant control over the situation.

We also want accomplices to give us more control over the event. However, we will not be using them to con anyone. For example, on the opening day of the art show, friends and possibly family will be working the free bar, the food, music, and will mingle with the guests.

The idea is to make sure that everyone looks like they are having fun. Some will just look closer at the art and have friendly conversations about the art and artist.

As the artist, your job is to mingle and make sure you greet everyone.

Make sure someone is handling the sales, filming, taking pictures, and ensuring everything runs smoothly. That way, you are not bogged down with anything other than mingling.

Whether you are doing a pop-up event, gallery show, yart sale (Yard and Art Sale), or open studio, you can use any and all tactics in a way that doesn't harm people.

As Rogue Artists, we look at it all, develop creative ways to have fun, and put ourselves out there in epic ways using all the available tools. Even if they are tools that are usually used in nefarious ways. Make it worth it to the people you are inviting to your event or shindig.

Finally, because this isn't a con, at some point, you are going to thank everyone for being there, and then you will do your big reveal. Have fun with this and make it part of your grand creative social experiment. For example, at my last exhibition, my big reveal was an invisible sculpture.

The reveal happened with a whoosh of a curtain and dust flying through the air. It was epic. People were utterly confused and then burst into laughter. Obviously, your big reveal could be tangible. Just make it awesome.

At one of my exhibitions, I had an interactive sculpture that hung from the ceiling and giant wings with a dark side and light side, where people could take pictures. It doesn't have to be super elaborate, just something different from what they expect from you.

I know this is an elaborate example of putting yourself out there. But listen: in my opinion, contrary to popular belief in marketing, we have no right to go into someone's home or life without benefiting them in some way.

The marketing should offer some value or entertainment. I feel like it is insulting to do otherwise and just a waste of time.

Something that is important that can easily get overlooked is something you will hear me say repeatedly in this book, and that is to make it easy. When thinking of putting on an in-person or virtual event, keep the experience of the collector in mind.

You want to make it easy for them to get to where they need to get to. If you are setting up an in-person event, this means thinking about things like, "Where are they going to park? How easy is it for them to find us? Is it a direct path or are there obstacles? Is it enjoyable? How can I make it all part of the experience?"

By appreciating the time a person may spend following your antics, you build genuine trust. Building trust is so important. Being fake and only trying to benefit yourself robs you of that creative family that will support you and your art.

In my mind, the event in itself and the way it is promoted is a giant work of art. It is expressive of me and what I want to bring into the world.

Turn all your marketing into a big creative social experiment and have fun with it. Do it your way and create what you want to see.

Most importantly, I laid out the wacky way to do some fun events, but you can take any theme and message that means something to you and bring it to life. Make it yours and reflect your values.

It's not about tricking people into liking you or your art. It is about giving them an experience they will never want to forget.

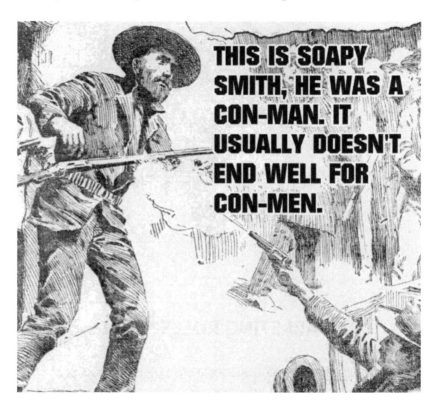

At the end of the day, a conman is remembered as a swindler and a charlatan. You on the other hand will be remembered as a legend. Every time you promote yourself, you are saying something about yourself to the world. Have fun with this.

MARKETING RULES I STOLE

Many artists will ask me which artists from the past inspire me. Usually, they mean who inspires my art work. The interesting thing is that I find inspiration for art everywhere. A better question would be who fascinates me. I am fascinated by artists who succeeded in persisting and putting themselves out there. Whether you look at Picasso, Dali, Klimt, or anyone one else known, the fact is, they had to persist through a lot of suck times to get to where they were.

This is what inspires me to *keep going.* Self-help or achieving success courses will recommend that you model someone you want to be like. I am not a fan of this method and feel like it will always lead to disappointment and an identity crisis.

We are all unique and will find our success in unique ways. The modeling technique requires choosing someone with the skills or personality you would like to explore and improve in yourself. Then you do like they do. It's a little more involved but in my opinion, if you try to be like someone else, you may miss out on the magic that is you. Besides, it's already been done.

When it comes to putting yourself out there, I look at all the different approaches from several other humans doing what I would like to do. I look for patterns in their actions that match with one another. For example, I see many similarities between Picasso and Vincent Van Gogh in areas where they struggled with personal life and relied on a strong work ethic towards their art.

I also learned that you don't need to struggle to be prolific. I see similarities in marketing philosophies with every mega-popular artist I study. Here are five things I have learned from watching other artists succeed.

Be Memorable By Being You.
- Andy Warhol sounded shy, bored, and aloof in public interviews.
- Salvador Dali was zany, strange, and unpredictable in discussions.
- Banksy is disguised, laidback, and snarky in interviews.
- Picasso was bold, mysterious, and opinionated in interviews.

These artists are all different, yet they were all memorable in just about any public forum. They seemed to play into their own strengths and weaknesses in personality and magnified it on the public scene. Be yourself when putting yourself out there. Things that you consider disadvantages may be your most significant strengths.

Another artist that inspires me greatly is Steve Martin. I am incredibly inspired by comedians because their job is to literally fail in public over and over again until their comedy act is where they want it to be. In an interview, Steve Martin listed some questions that he found helpful in discovering his unique persona and voice. He also made sure to point out that ALL of these can be used to discover your strengths, including the ones that seem negative.

What am I?
What easily describes me?
What is my best quality?
What is my worst quality?
What kinds of humor do I like?
What is my manifesto?
Who or what is my nemesis?
What vacuum can I naturally fill?

Sit with these questions often, because they will give you a powerful insight into who you are and where you may want to go with your art and what you do.

Don't Try to Please Everyone Because You Can't.

Every artist I have come across has had people love what they create or absolutely hate everything about them. The artists that I admire embraced this. In fact, they encouraged it. Salvador Dali realized that his eccentric nature seemed to attract attention. At the same time, others only felt repulsed by his personality. He seemed to understand whether people spoke good or bad about him, he was part of the conversation.

"It is not necessary for the public to know whether I am joking or whether I am serious, just as it is not necessary for me to know it myself." - Salvador Dali.

280

Don't Be Afraid to Create What You Want, And Create a Lot Of It.

I've said it before, and I'll repeat it, create what you want to create and stop worrying about whether people will like it or not. Young artists approach me every single day with statements like, "I'm known for painting flowers, but I love painting some darker images, and I'd love to share it. However, I know that's a big no-no, and I should stick to what I'm known for."

I would love to know which marketing or art person started this stupid myth. Look closer at Banksy, Warhol, Dali, Picasso, Jeff Koons, Gerhard Richter, Damien Hirst, and almost every artist out there who is known, and you will see diversity in works. Most people think that artists are only creating in the medium that they are most known for. So, you end up with young artists following the advice of some idiot who thinks that you have to focus on one thing to become famous. That couldn't be further from the truth.

Many artists crisscross mediums, styles, techniques and experiment all the time. You never know who will come out of the woodwork to support one of your crazy creative projects. However, you will never find out if you hide or avoid working on it because you are forcing yourself to only focus on one thing.

"A jack of all trades is a master of none but oftentimes better than a master of one." This is the full quote, and it is intended as a compliment. Diversifying what you do with the eagerness to delve into new creative areas will build your versatility and make you adept at many things.

If You Want to Be Known, You Have to Put Yourself Out There.

Every single artist that I investigated deeply that became famous started somewhere. They all seem to have taken different roads to get there. The one thing they all have in common is that they took the risk of putting themselves out there over and over in unique and creative ways. They fell on their faces several times and just kept going. Your journey will evolve and grow, but *ONLY* if you persist.

If You Want to Succeed, You Have To Keep Going And Be Patient.

What sets these artists apart from the prolific and sad myth of the starving artist is that they didn't quit. They fell on their face, ran into roadblocks, got rejected, got criticized, got ignored, were broke, dealt with unsupportive people, and probably felt it was impossible, yet they persisted. They figured out different ways of putting themselves out there and got creative with what they had available to them.

So many artists today sign up for artists marketing programs and courses thinking that if they throw a little money at the problem, they'll find the secret formula. They want a quick fix and a fast solution. I hate to break it to you, but there is no secret formula. None of these artists became famous overnight. Some worked for 10-20 years before they could support themselves with their art. It's not easy. Every part of being an artist is a series of opportunities to face fears.

- *Fear of being invisible.*
- *Fear of rejection.*
- *Fear of criticism.*
- *Fear of exposure.*
- *Fear of first impressions.*
- *Fear of failure.*
- *Fear of disappointment.*
- *Imposter syndrome.*
- *Fear of negotiating.*
- *Fear of being taken advantage of.*
- *Fear that you are not good enough.*

This is just scratching at the surface. When you decide to pursue an art career and put yourself out in the world, that is when you will find fears within you that you didn't even know existed. This is something that Rogue Artists understand deeply.

The only way to truly grow your career as an artist is to grow by facing your fears head-on and taking risks. We take every opportunity to put ourselves out there and learn from every experience and build for the next.

Putting yourself out there is all about facing fears and growing stronger with every experience. The more you do it, the more you will figure out who you are and how exactly you want to be remembered.

Make your amazing art. Put yourself out there. Create your own culture. Blaze your own trail. Develop your own art world. Persist and never give up.

"PEOPLE TELL YOU THE WORLD LOOKS A CERTAIN WAY. PARENTS TELL YOU HOW TO THINK. SCHOOLS TELL YOU HOW TO THINK. TV. RELIGION. AND THEN AT A CERTAIN POINT, IF YOU'RE LUCKY, YOU REALIZE YOU CAN MAKE UP YOUR OWN MIND. NOBODY SETS THE RULES BUT YOU. YOU CAN DESIGN YOUR OWN LIFE."
- CARRIE- ANNE MOSS

BREAKING LAWS LIKE A ROGUE

In marketing, there are a lot of different approaches and philosophies. In fact, there are so many rules in marketing that it is impossible to keep up. Therefore, I think it is important to make up your own. In my research for this book, I ran across a book called "The 22 Immutable Laws of Marketing." This book was filled with a bunch of dry information for product marketing, and it doesn't perfectly apply to us as artists. However, I think it is important to look at this and get an understanding of how it could apply to us. So I tweaked them to make them work for us. Some, I just threw away because I felt they were garbage. Here are nine laws that I deemed helpful.

The first law is The Law of Leadership.

In a competitive market, the idea is that it is better to be first on the market than to be a better product. As a Rogue Artist, I think a better way to look at this is to realize your uniqueness. If you have a new creative way of putting yourself out there that is unproven or unpracticed, and it works, you will always be remembered for doing that. You will have been the first. Anyone else who copies your method is playing a game of following the leader. This is where innovation with your art and how you put yourself out there comes in.

Challenge yourself to think outside of the box. For example, Banksy is the first artist to create a miserable theme park installation. Any other artist who follows will build on his idea and always be compared to Banksy in their efforts.

The problem is that when something is unproven and new, we are afraid that most people will reject it. When Picasso started his weird, distorted faces style, his paintings were rejected and considered ugly by just about everyone he knew, but he persisted. Those same ugly paintings are now seen as revolutionary. Just go for it. The best-case scenario is that you are the first to do something new and innovative. Worst case scenario is that no one likes it but eventually everyone will come around.

The second law is The Law of Category.

A competitive market states that If you can't be first in a category, set up your own category, you can be first in. As a Rogue Artist, I think we are already in a class of our own. Unless you are trying to be or create like someone else, you are already in a unique art category.

I call my art style *"Rafi Art"* because it's the only category I feel comfortable fitting in.

I am not a big fan of labels and titles because they can be constricting. Labels also inspire comparison, which I think is bull-crap.

For example, if you call yourself a portrait artist as your main label, people will compare you to every other portrait artist out there even though your styles may be totally different.

I market myself as having Rafi-style art where I create Rafi-portraits, Rafi-abstracts, and Rafi-figurative. Create your own categories or use existing labels as a reference, but don't let them define you and control your work.

The third law is The Law of Mind.

It is better to be first in a person's mind in a competitive market than to be first in the marketplace. As a Rogue Artist, I use this as a reminder to stay relevant and put myself out there in new and exciting ways. It is easy to get lazy with putting yourself out there and stick only with what you know already works. The problem with this is that people get bored quickly.

This is why I think approaching the act of putting yourself out there as an art form in itself is so powerful. If we see it as art, we will constantly approach our marketing to build and keep evolving. This will keep your presence fresh and exciting.

The fourth law is The Law of Perception.

In a competitive market, it is understood that the battle is over perception and not about the actual quality of the products. As a Rogue Artist, I both agree and disagree with this. Perception does matter but so does the quality of your art.

The story you tell needs to be authentic and confident. This is why it's important not to criticize or nitpick your art publicly. Your art skills will always be improving, that's a given. How you talk about your art in the public arena builds the perception.

This is why mutual excitement is so important. My rule of thumb here is to always over deliver on the emotional aspect of the experience because this is what builds trust over time.

The fifth law is The Law of Exclusivity.

In a competitive market, two companies cannot own the same tagline or feeling in the prospect's mind. For example, if two companies sell the same exact product and claim to be healthy, one will win out over the other in that person's mind. The person can only choose one as the healthier one. That's why companies are very strategic about what they say.

As a Rogue Artist, I think this is the perfect example of the statement "Real artists steal, wannabe artists copy." This means that when we look at something that inspires us, we may take the idea and make it our own by tweaking it and making it more us, but we don't copy it line for line.

When an artist copies a work of art, they are diluting their reputation and being unoriginal. I know that young artists trying to find their voice will copy several different artworks as they practice, and honestly, I don't have a problem with that at all.

However, I have seen some artists blatantly copy works and build a reputation on those works and eventually fall flat on their faces. When you put yourself out there, be original, be yourself. Even if you haven't found your voice yet, people will follow you on your journey as long as you are you.

The sixth law is The Law of Perspective.

In a competitive market, it is crucial to keep in mind that most marketing effects take place over an extended period. As a Rogue Artist, I believe this is one of the most crucial concepts regarding marketing.

TAKE THE LONG ROAD!

When I am contacted by artists who launch a website, show at an art festival, or start posting to social media, they express their frustration at the lack of attention they are getting. When I ask them how long they have been at it, usually it is less than a month.

Many of these artists scoff at the idea of sharing their story and building their narrative. This is because they are not looking at the long term of building their empire brick by brick. They want quick results that require very little work, not much risk, and things to fall in their lap. Unfortunately, that method rarely works out.

However, suppose you understand that every single appearance, show, festival, market, conversation, online post, and interaction you have is only the laying of one brick of the foundation that will be your creative empire. In that case, you have a better grasp of reality.

Every tiny thing we do in the public eye tells our story, and our empire is built on that story. That is why it is vital to recognize what yours is. It will take time to share that story, so look at the long road and don't chase quick results.

The seventh law is The Law of Success.

The law basically states that success often leads to arrogance and arrogance to failure.

As a Rogue Artist, it is crucial to recognize that we can quickly become full of ourselves once we gain some clout. I keep a close eye on this because I know how small your world can get once you forget your humbleness.

It's important to note that feeling like you are fantastic is not being arrogant. Reminding yourself that you are more awesome by comparing yourself to others is. If you must put anyone or their art down to feel better about yourself, then you are an arrogant jerk. When you start doing that, you put everything you built in jeopardy.

The eighth law is The Law of Failure.

This law states that in marketing and business strategies, failure is to be expected and accepted.

As a Rogue Artist, I understand that failure is simply part of the formula. If you try something and it doesn't work, you are better equipped for the next time.

Many artists are afraid to fail. The irony is that failure is a necessary ingredient for success. If you are running away from or avoiding failure, then you are avoiding success as well. By embracing failure, you gain a powerful edge in moving forward in your art career.

The ninth law is The Law of Hype.

This law states that the situation, event, or news is often less exciting or even different from how it appears in the press. As a Rogue Artist, we understand that most of the things we think are bold and big have more to do with the story that was told about it.

Most people overhype their marketing and don't deliver. Rogues set themselves apart by always overdelivering. If you are going to claim to have "The Greatest Show On Earth!" then the experience should delight the people attending. It doesn't have to ACTUALLY be the greatest show on earth, that would be impossible to determine, but you want to deliver on what you promise. Don't be afraid to claim that your event will be great. Look at how excited (and murderous) this kid is about baked beans.... and yes, this is real advertising.

(Why is he making direct eye contact while eating?!)

Whenever I do an event, I love blowing up and having fun with my marketing material. One show I did, I called:

"The ART-STRAVIGANSA of the century! Be mystified and amazed by the colorful creations of an awkward artist!"

In a later section, we will cover power words. These are words that capture attention. The idea is to have fun with this. Blow it up, but always make it a memorable party. You can hype it up, but if it ends up being just another run of the mill boring art show, then you are not delivering. Make it an experience.

Also, whenever I do an event, I will announce something extraordinary but keep part of it a secret so they are blown away when they attend.

Use these laws when thinking about your marketing and how to approach it, but break the rules. In fact, if you run across any advice from marketing people, tweak it to work for you. Don't simply follow what they tell you to do. Blaze your own trail in putting yourself out there.

If you have ever researched marketing, chances are you've heard about the four P's. Place, Price, Product, and Promotion are the cornerstone of most marketing courses and programs. This was something else that I had to make sense of from the perspective of a Rogue Artist. To make it simple, here's what they mean.

Place: Where do you promote? Where do your peeps go to find information?

Price: This is how much you charge and how people see you because of what you charge.

Product: This is what you sell. This can be tangible goods, services, ideas, thoughts, perspectives, and so on.

Promotion: How are you putting it out there? How often are you talking about it? What are you doing to let people know you exist?

We've all heard the sayings,
"Location, location, location."
"Price matters."
"It's all about the product."
"It's all about the promotion."

This is all part of the story you are telling. Are you posh, scrappy, low budget, eccentric, weird, modern, traditional, high-end? How you position yourself, show your art, how much you charge, and promote will be part of your story.

Rogue Perspective on Place.

When I first started my art career, I showed art at a flea market due to the lack of galleries and opportunities in my area. I am pretty scrappy, so it fits my personality. However, what set me apart is that I was selling original weird art and other artists at the location were selling quickly made novelty and touristy art.

Eventually, I couldn't picture myself at the flea market anymore because I felt I had outgrown it, and I moved on to a high-end farmers market, art walks, art festivals, and gallery shows.

Eventually, my "place" was where I live because we showed art at multiple venues every month. As a Rogue Artist, it is essential to remember that your origin story is whatever you decide it will be.

I am not at all embarrassed by starting at the flea market. In fact, I am proud of my ingenuity, unwillingness to give up, and ability to set myself apart no matter where I am.

You have to start somewhere, choose your place, begin where you are. Remember that every opportunity is simply a stepping stone. Just make sure you are controlling the narrative of your own story.

Remember that place can mean many things in many different situations. It can indicate how you display your art in person to how your website looks. It can be the quality of the pictures you are posting on social media, how you dress, or where you are. Ultimately *PLACE* is the context of your story.

The Rogue Perspective on Price.
What is most important to us as Rogue Artists is what story the price is telling us. I'm not going into pricing your art because I cover that in-depth in my "making money" book, but I will say that art is subjective when pricing. We all have some weird money mentalities and definitions of wealth that we picked up through life. What ultimately matters is that the story you are telling yourself and the potential buyer is an empowering one for everyone involved. Keep in mind that the story of price is also very much tied into the place or your context.

Think of it this way. Imagine you wanted to buy a painting, and you find yourself in front of three shops right next to each other.

The first looks very high-end and is advertising an art print for $25.
The second is very hip-looking and promotes an art print for $15.
The third looks kinda gross and is advertising an art print for $12.

Which one would you pick? The exciting thing about this question is that no answer is the same for everyone. I could ask three different people and get three different answers. Most people, however, would choose the first or second place.

What you charge for your art or service not only determines how much money you can make, but more importantly, how you're perceived and how you view yourself. This is ultimately an internal journey. If you are just getting started in your art career and have no reputation, you may put people off with high-end pricing. Going too low may say your art is cheap. However, what is too cheap? You may be tempted to use someone else's art as a comparison, but that can complicate things. Price it for yourself, but not as a competition with someone else. Your art is unique.

Ultimately, when it comes to price just remember that it will evolve and change as you grow in your art career. You have to start somewhere, and your prices will go up as the demand increases. As long as I am being fair to myself and the person purchasing the art, I am happy with my price.

The Rogue Perspective On Product.
Of course by product, I mean art, and I mean anything you create, think, or put out there. Your art is one of the most critical ingredients in your marketing campaign because, without it, you don't have a place in the art market, and you unquestionably can't sell or advertise something that doesn't exist.

Well actually, you can. At my last art event, I sold invisible sculptures to raise money as a fundraiser for a local art school. Your product could be an idea, a story, a service, and a perspective as well. As a Rogue Artist, everything you put out there is your art. This is the essence and lifeblood of your unique message.

At the end of the day, your product is who you are, what you create, and what you communicate with the world. From the short social media post to the epic art installation. It is *ALL* your creation.

The Rogue Perspective On Promotion.
This is everything you do when putting yourself out there. This includes events, shows, ads, blogs, posters, flyers, business cards, live paintings, collaborations, social media, sponsorships, and basically any interaction with humans regarding your art or message.

Every single interaction you have with any human will become part of the story in that human's mind. Do you want them to think of you as trustworthy, playful, eccentric, weird, fun, or offbeat?

Or would you rather be known as rude, cold, mean, uncaring, arrogant, or greedy? You are your brand, your product, your message, and you can stand in that power or run from it.

Your voice should be reflected in every communication you have on every platform and everything you do, whether in person or online. We remember great artists not only for their art, but because of the impact they made in the world. They are the ones who persisted, they were the ones who kept creating, and they were the ones who kept striving for more. Their art is just a wonderful gift that these exceptional humans left us.

Ultimately, the four P's are meant to be an easy reminder that everything you do, the places you show, the prices you are charging, the stuff you make, and who you are is part of the narrative. Everything you do is marketing.

You don't have to follow a standard that marketing history has set up. Follow your own means of what you want your art career to be.

At the end of the day, you choose what place, what art, what price, and how you will put yourself out there. It's not a scheme or tactic, it is just life. You are either remaining small and quiet or you are standing up, taking charge, and speaking your message to the world through EVERYTHING you create, do, and say. Take the reins of your life and be bold and unforgettable.

THE POWER OF WORDS

You have probably heard the phrase "Words have power". Well considering that this book is full of them, I hope so. Words have power because anything you are using to tell your story has the potential to shift perspectives and reality. Certain words are really good at triggering certain emotions. Words have the power to fascinate or alarm the public.

In my opinion, as long as you are entertaining and delighting people, you could get away with exaggerating your headlines. In marketing this is called "puffery," which means claiming that what you sell is the "best in the world", or something completely unbelievable or unmeasurable like claiming the "Peoples' Favorite".

Speechwriters for politicians know the power of words all too well. If you ever break down a speech and look for the most repeated words, you will find what I call power words. These words are evocative and make you feel something on a deeper level. Needless to say, these are used as newspaper headlines and in marketing all the time because they tend to be attention grabbers.

Words used in promotion or persuasion will be words meant to paint a picture. Words have power because they tap into your imagination and tell a story before you even know what is said.

For example, what comes to mind when I say, "The Lord." Do you think religion, medieval times, lord of the house, or do you picture someone in particular? Now, what happens if I say, "The Lord of The Rings." Do you have an entire narrative running through your mind? Maybe you didn't watch or read it, and the narrative is your annoying friends saying that you should. Either way, words in and of themselves tell a story – and when you combine them, they can tell an epic.

Certain words on their own will trigger certain emotions. Putting these trigger words together in a purposefully crafted sentence or paragraph will steer the emotional direction of the message to an extreme.

This is why companies spend so much money and effort developing their tag lines for their business. Now remember, language changes all the time and so do words, so take the following lists as examples. Do not be afraid to explore this concept on your own and play around with words that evoke an emotion within yourself.

"RAISE YOUR WORDS, NOT YOUR VOICE, IT IS RAIN THAT GROWS FLOWERS, NOT THUNDER." -RUMI

Attention Grabbers.

Here are some tremendous attention-grabbing words that you can use to describe something. These words tend to stand out when used in a title, tagline, or name.

OBSESSION.

SURGING.

PIONEERING.

UNSURPASSED.

CONFIDENTIAL.

BOLD.

TEMPTING.

UNCONVENTIONAL.

DARING.

ASTONISHING.

EPIC.

EXPLOSIVE.

For example, *"Watch the astonishing approach of Rafi Perez as he daringly puts himself on stage using unconventional and bold techniques to tempt audiences with his unsurpassed style of creating art!"*

Fear Words.

Some words trigger fear. It could be the fear of missing out, the fear of making a mistake, the fear of losing money, or just anything the person wants to avoid. This is typically used to incite fear and drive people to protect themselves by buying, voting for, or adapting whatever the other person is selling. I tend to stay away from these unless I am trying to warn people about a scam.

FOOLED.

BEWARE.

BLINDED.

ALARMING.

DEVASTATING.

HEARTBREAKING.

HOAX.

RISKY.

SCARY.

COSTLY.

FRANTIC.

HAZARDOUS.

UNTESTED.

TERROR.

For example, *"Don't be fooled, beware the marketing guru who may have blinded you to the devastating and heartbreaking effects of following untested and costly methods."*

Trust Words.

Some words trigger a feeling of safety. Marketers will use these words in their advertising to evoke a sense of trustworthiness and dependability. These words typically bypass our defenses and red flags.

AUTHENTIC.

NO-STRINGS ATTACHED.

SECURE.

BACKED.

TESTED.

NO-OBLIGATION.

PROVEN.

APPROVED.

MONEYBACK.

PROTECTED.

VERIFIED.

CERTIFIED.

For example, *"I am certified in the art of Making Art and Making Money. If you follow my tested and proven methods that are backed by successful and thriving artists all around the world you will secure the means to success. No strings attached. No obligation. To get started just sign up for my free eBook."*

Urgency Words.

Some words cause a sense of urgency. Primarily this is used in ads, speeches, and marketing where they want the audience to take action right away. People are more likely to engage if they think they'll miss out otherwise.

NOW.

EXCLUSIVE.

SCARCE.

RARE.

IMMEDIATELY.

INSTANTLY.

HURRY.

ONLY.

LIMITED.

LIMITED-TIME.

LIMITED-EDITION.

TEMPORARY.

For example, *"Hurry now! Don't miss this limited time offer to instantly gain access to this rare opportunity to own your very own limited edition copy of this weird 'Rafi Phone Doodle' This exclusive offer is only available for those who act immediately! Hurry NOW!"*

Convincing Words.

Some words are used as convincers of value. This is where someone is trying to convince you that you are getting a good deal on something or it is worth it in another way. These are the words most marketers use to entice the public to engage with them.

FREE.   TESTED.
UNBELIEVABLE. BONUS.
BARGAIN.   EASY.
AFFORDABLE.   EFFECTIVE.
DETAILED.
BETTER.
NEW.
REMARKABLE.
PROFESSIONAL.
BEST-SELLING.
GUARANTEED.
UNIQUE.
APPROVED.

For example, *"It's easy to get started with our new, more detailed version of this best-selling classic. Achieve remarkable and professional results at an unbelievable bargain price with our unique system. Tested, approved, and guaranteed to perform. The first 50 orders will receive a free bonus gift."*

Infomercial Words.

Here are words that have been overused by marketing. This is due to infomercials and other types of marketing out there. I use them all the time because honestly, they are the most fun to use.. There is a reason why these are all so popular in infomercials.

GROUNDBREAKING.   OPTIMIZE.
ONCE-IN-A-LIFETIME. PROMISE.
REVOLUTIONARY.   SATISFACTION-
PERFECT.   GUARANTEED.
IMPOSSIBLE.   CUTTING-EDGE.
MIRACLE.   HIDDEN GEM.
ONCE-ONLY.   LEVERAGE.
VISIONARY.   WIN-WIN.
TRANSFORMATIVE.   VIRAL.
JAW-DROPPING.   HOLISTIC.
SPELL-BINDING.   INNOVATIVE.
GAME-CHANGER.
OUTSIDE THE BOX.
SYNERGY.

For example, *"This cutting-edge technology is truly a hidden-gem and a game-changer. You'll be able to leverage your time like never before and optimize your workflow with this innovative development from visionary pioneer John Smith." What's the secret? His holistic approach and outside the box thinking, bring a once impossible synergy into reality and into your home for the first time ever."*

Lazy Words.

I am guilty of using lazy words in my marketing. These are lazy because they are overused and honestly unoriginal. Many of these words are too vague to make any real impact.

CLICK HERE.

SUBMIT.

BUY.

BUY NOW.

GREAT.

VERY.

STUFF.

THINGS.

AMAZING.

HUGE.

AWESOME.

DEAL.

SPECIAL.

BEST.

For example, *"Huge awesome deal! Very special amazing things! Really great stuff! Best time to buy now! Click here to submit!"*

At the end of the day, these are just examples that are popular in marketing. They can be used in shady ways, or they can be used in the way of the Jedi. If you use it for clickbait ads, deceptive products, or things that will actually harm people, then you have gone to the dark side of the force. We all have the power to amaze and delight, and it starts with our words and the willingness to have fun.

Claim that you are putting together the greatest art exhibition on Earth! Why not? Or if you don't want to go so big, claim that it will intrigue and amaze! I want you to carefully choose your words and think a little more about what you are saying and how you are saying it. Is it making someone feel something unforgettable? Is it demonstrating your excitement for what you are putting out there?

Take some time and make a list of words that really grab your attention. Make sure they resonate with you and what you are trying to say. Play around with these words in phrases and create powerful mantras that you can use when talking about yourself and your art. The more memorable the mantra is, the more people will use it and think of you. Have fun with this and go big! Reach for the stars. The bigger you present your next event, the more you will strive to make it exceptional. Just remember to not overcomplicate your words. Try to keep it simple and memorable.

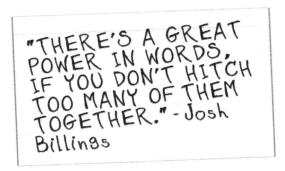

"THERE'S A GREAT POWER IN WORDS, IF YOU DON'T HITCH TOO MANY OF THEM TOGETHER." - Josh Billings

ADD SOME ROGUE WITH SOME ROUGE

As artists, many of us work with color every day. We have our favorite colors, and many of us use color to tell a story. We mix our pigments until we get the right hue and proceed only when it feels right. Like sound, the different colors we use set the tone of what we are trying to say. Anyone who is putting themselves out in the world should understand what feeling a color could evoke.

The reactions to color may not apply to everyone. This is because we are all different humans who see the world in our own unique ways. In fact, Red and green, which are two complementary colors, can't be distinguished by people with certain color blindness. So yeah, different paint strokes for different folks. However, there is tons of research done on the emotional reactions humans have to color. As a painter, I find this fascinating. This applies to my art but also to all the material I use to put myself out there and tell my story.

The ideas and research behind color in marketing state that color profoundly influences the message being communicated. It also has a physical effect on humans.

In fact, companies will often color their interiors depending on how they want their employees to perform or their customers to respond. For example, red, orange, and yellow are believed to stimulate and excite. Other colors such as pale greens, light yellows, and off-whites are supposed to be more soothing. Think about that when you are designing your creative space, your website, and your marketing materials.

Red is an intense color. It can have a profound and powerful impact on a person's personality and emotions. It is the universal color symbol for passion, anger, and excitement. It can be a loud and playful color. If you are looking for an understated or conservative look, red is probably not the color for you. Red can also be used to symbolize celebration, purity, strength, energy, fire, sex, love, speed, heat, arrogance, ambition, leadership, masculinity, power, danger, blood, war, and revolution.

The color of products also matters in how people respond to them. I mean look at how excited these two are over a glass of red V8 juice.

Blue is considered to be a relaxed and non-threatening color. It seems to have a tranquilizing effect on the mind. It is typically used to symbolize water, depression, tranquility, trust, confidence, conservatism, dependability, wisdom, wealth, royalty, truthfulness, creativity, and religious beliefs and ceremonies. Blue inspires a sense of calm and spiritual awareness along with feelings of trust.

Green typically symbolizes a balanced and a reinvigorated mind. It can also symbolize growth, rebirth, renewal, nature, fertility, youth, good luck, generosity, health, abundance, stability, and creative intelligence. Green is one of the more restful colors. It doesn't force the eye to make any adjustments, thus you are able to relax. It gives a sense of balance and calm as well as connection to the natural world.

Yellow is usually associated with a happy and cheerful disposition of the mind. It can also symbolize things like sunlight, joy, earth, optimism, intelligence, hope, wealth, femininity, gladness, and friendship. If you want to draw in a human with a comforting, warm embrace and youthful energy, then yellow is a great choice.

White typically represents purity, peace, neutrality, and tranquility in the mind and body. It is commonly used as a backdrop to give a neutral effect. White can also symbolize youth, sterility, light, reverence, truth, snow, air, cleanliness, coldness, efficiency, luxury, and humility.

Black can symbolize absence, rebellion, modernism, power, sophistication, formality, elegance, mystery, style, evil, emptiness, darkness, substance, power, authority, respectability, seriousness, conventionality, unity, sorrow, professionalism, sleekness, and mourning.

Gray is one of the most neutral shades available. It can portray elegance, respect, practicality, efficiency, timelessness, urban, reverence, wisdom, balance, mourning, and neutrality.

Orange is yellow's louder and more playful counterpart. It can signify a happy, balanced, and enthusiastic mind. It typically portrays energy, heat, fire, youthfulness, playfulness, desire. Its aggressive friendliness presents a great color for any calls to action you may have.

Brown typically communicates an earthy and environmental quality that is regularly coupled with green. Brown tends to symbolize calmness, boldness, depth, natural organisms, richness, tradition, heaviness, roughness, steadfastness, simplicity, dependability, and friendliness. If you are looking to portray a sense of quiet supportiveness and reliability, you could do well with brown.

Pink is a lighter shade of red and is typically considered to have a soothing effect on the mind. It is often considered the most feminine of colors. As a lighter shade of red, it retains a sense of energy and cheer blended with a soothing calm. Pink can be associated with sex and sexuality, but also symbolizes gratitude, appreciation, admiration, sympathy, health, femininity, love, marriage, joy, innocence, flirtiness, childlike behavior, and sweet taste.

Purple has been considered to be the color of royalty, wisdom, and creativity for generations. It typically symbolizes nobility, humility, spirituality, luxury, authenticity, high quality, introspection, ceremony, mystery, wisdom, enlightenment, flamboyance, exaggeration, sensuality, pride, and essence.

I recommend playing around and experimenting with color combinations and how they represent what you are saying. Take a close look at color, how it is used on most products and what the company is trying to say with the color. It will give you an insight into using color in what you put out there.

Do social experiments, and most importantly, have fun with this. Use this list as a loose guide and not a set of rigid rules. This is meant to inspire you to add color to your marketing and be as deliberate with it as you are with your art.

The color you use on every part of what you put into the world is saying something. Make sure you are saying what you want to say with the color schemes on your website, marketing material, graphics, and everything else.

Become a ROGUE.

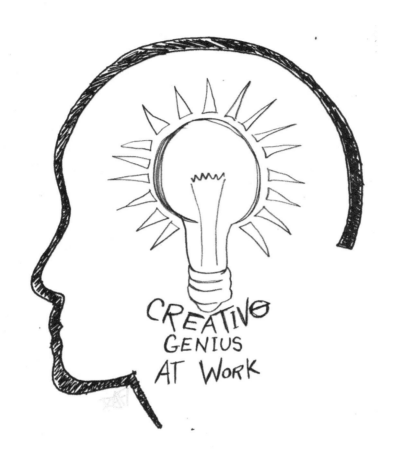

GOING ROGUE ON THE INTERWEBS

The INTERNET can be a loud and daunting place, filled with the social noise of a billion different voices. It is easy to feel overwhelmed and lost when you are thinking of approaching the online market with your art. Luckily there is a way to evade the social turbulence like a ninja and effectively put yourself out there in the virtual world.

The truth is that whether you are putting yourself out there online, or in person, it's all the same thing. Being a Rogue Artist on the internet is all about being yourself and sharing that with the world. One thing to remember is that the internet, like any other form of communication, is simply a tool to connect with other humans.

It's no different than running into someone at the grocery store and having a conversation. The only thing that sets it apart from the live experience is that you don't even need to put on pants or leave the house to interact with one another.

Whether it is the internet, the telegraph, the telephone, text messaging, radio, television, or postal mail, it is all about getting a message from one person to another. Because of the diversity and reach of the internet, it tends to be seen as something much more complex. Most people approach it mainly as a marketing platform instead of a tool for communication. I think that's where things get confusing.

Although every form of communication has been used for marketing throughout history, their true intent was always much simpler. Junk mail, spam telegrams, telemarketing calls, commercials, and radio ads must interrupt the conversation in order to be heard.

People didn't tune in or sign up for the ads. In fact, they tuned in despite the ads. The internet is no different, yet most people trying to sell online think of it as just a tool for marketing.

"Hey, look at me! I have this thing you need! Buy it now, and I'll give you a good deal!" seems to be the dominant theme everywhere you look.

The irony is that most forms of communication that have been invented, really took off in the mainstream once they became a platform for creatives. Whether it is sitcoms, movies, music, books, photography, art, documentaries, or audio programs, the reason people engaged was because they wanted to be educated, entertained, or mystified. People connect with things that enrich their lives in some way.

(In case you were wondering, YES spam telegrams were a thing. This gentleman was VERY unhappy about dealing with SPAM.)

TO THE EDITOR OF THE TIMES.

Sir,—On my arrival home late yesterday evening a "telegram," by "London District Telegraph," addressed in full to me, was put into my hands. It was as follows :—

"Messrs. Gabriel, dentists, 27, Harley-street, Cavendish-square. Until October Messrs. Gabriel's professional attendance at 27, Harley-street, will be 10 till 5."

I have never had any dealings with Messrs. Gabriel, and beg to ask by what right do they disturb me by a telegram which is evidently simply the medium of advertisement ? A word from you would, I feel sure, put a stop to this intolerable nuisance. I enclose the telegram, and am,
                                    Your faithful servant,
Upper Grosvenor-street, May 30.   M. P.

Marketing companies understand that if you want to get your product in front of a large audience, follow the creative artists. It is writers, directors, musicians, artists, performers, actors, and other creatives that will draw the crowd. Therefore I say that as artists, we have unlimited power. No one is going to only stream commercials and ads when they sit down to relax for the evening.

That being said, the commercials and ads that find a way to entertain and surprise are the ones that we don't seem to mind, and in fact remember and talk about. It's not dry, played out, crusty old tactics that create memorable marketing. It's creatives behind the scenes, thinking about new ways to make it entertaining and compelling, that engage our attention.

Every platform that is meant for communication is a creative platform, this includes the internet.

Each day we have a tiny window to grab someone's attention and make an impact with our message and art.

Yet so many of us waste that time and energy only trying to sell.

Many artists are searching for that one elusive thing that'll go viral and get them rolling on the path to success. They get entirely self-absorbed in the marketing rhetoric and lose sight of why they share their art and create it in the first place. It can be easy to forget that genuine connection takes time, persistence, and authenticity.

In 2015, the band They Might Be Giants posted a new song and music video every week online for a year. This was a modern take on their Dial-A-Song campaign that was originally launched in 1983 from their kitchen via an old answering machine. People literally *dialed a song* and listened in on the latest and greatest from the band.

They found fun and innovative ways to use the technology available to share their art. This was *years* before their career took off on a global scale. Over the years, TMBG have consistently used new platforms available to communicate and share their music directly with their fans and are now legends for it.

Artists are the innovators. The band offered this service for free and it was later copied by major labels who tried to monetize it and failed. They just didn't get it. You don't build a loyal audience by trying to squeeze everything you can from them. You build it by giving value in what you put out there.

There's no shortcut to establishing an audience for your art online. It's a long, winding road with a lot of obstacles. Because of this, some artists avoid it like the plague. However, if you want to grow globally, having an online presence is the way to do it.

A lot of artists will say they don't have the time, money, or skillset to approach the internet, and I think that's a shame. Never before have we been able to connect with and get our work out in front of so many people. You can do it at virtually no cost, with hardly any gatekeepers obstructing the way.

As long as you have a way to get online and a healthy dose of imagination, a global following is out there waiting to find you. It will take time to connect, but they're out there.

Maybe you've wanted to do more online but think that it's somehow "too late." We constantly hear people saying that online is not worth it anymore. There will always be rumors and myths around timing, don't listen to the naysayers.

When I started putting myself and my art online, people told me that it was too late, that the market was saturated. That's just garbage. The world is saturated with all kinds of creative people, whether you are online or not. You can use that as an excuse, or you can come to the conclusion that the only ones that get noticed are the ones that persist and don't buy into myths and rumors.

"Those guys got in at the right time. That's why so many people are following them. I just got in too late." This is bullcrap and one of the most prominent excuses on the internet to not even try. Stop it. Stop comparing yourself to where someone else is. You don't know what it took for them to get there. Write your own story, stop being a critic of someone else's life and successes.

I say this because I was saying the same thing. I ignored my online presence because it just wasn't growing. The irony is that it wasn't growing because I was ignoring it. Loyalty and trust take time to build, and it doesn't happen overnight.

Whether it is online or offline, an art career doesn't just fall in your lap. You have to go for it. Even then, chances are you will feel like nothing is happening.

It might sound cliche, but your presence on the internet is like planting a tree. If you plant a tree, the least productive thing you could do is sit around and complain because you can't see it growing yet.

314

"How long is this going to take?? I want to sit under its shade, and it's been three days, and nothing is happening yet!"

When you plant a tree, you tend to it, water it, and trust that it will grow because you are sustaining it. If you care for it, in 20 years, you won't still be wishing you had planted a tree. Instead, you'll be sitting in its shade. It takes time to get there, but it is worth it.

The problem is that everyone wants things to happen fast. Slow down, take your time, and enjoy the journey. Just because it's virtual and technology is fast-moving doesn't mean that human nature changes simply because you are online. The internet is a place to make connections.

It is a place where the gatekeepers come to you instead of you jumping through their hoops. It is all based on what you are willing to build, but it all starts with a seed.

The world is advancing and more and more people in the art world understand that. A local gallery owner told me, "The worst exhibitions have been those where the artist isn't on social media or doesn't use it to engage. I now take an artist's social media presence into consideration when deciding whose work I will show."

So how do we get our message out there, connect, and begin building our online presence?

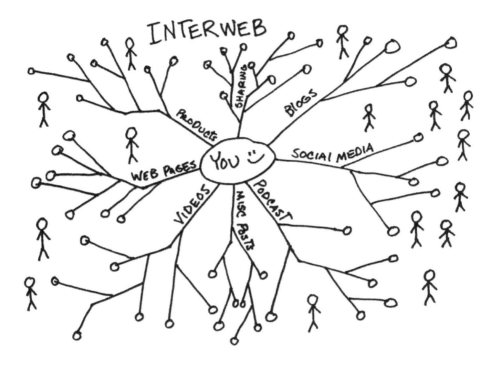

Think of the internet as a giant virtual landscape. Within this landscape are massive, bustling cities that you may have never been to before. When you search for something online, you take a road to one of these cities, or a specific place within the virtual landscape. As someone who wants to share their art, you decide you want to have a piece of property in this landscape, and there are plenty to choose from.

You can rent an apartment, a place at the mall, flea market, or strip mall in *Search Engine City*. You can also buy a building to renovate on a patch of virtual dirt.

A community selling platform like Etsy, Amazon, or eBay is like having a place at the mall or a flea market. You can run your business there, and these platforms make it very easy for you. However, the platform has full authority and control over the location. They can change policies and rules on a whim that will impact how you run your store.

Having an eCommerce website that runs on a service like Shopify or Teespring is like having a store in a strip mall. You have a little more control of your business and policies. However, you are still renting a spot, and ultimately, they are your landlords.

Having your own website is like purchasing an old building on undeveloped land that needs renovation. There is a lot more work and investment involved, but you oversee your own policies and rules. However, you have to take care of *everything*. This is the one I prefer because I don't like anyone to tell me how to run my business. That being said, every opportunity online is an opportunity to show your work.

Everything we do can be a stepping stone to the next. In real life, I started at the flea market, then at shows, then galleries, and eventually my own home studio. On the internet, I started on selling platforms and eventually ended up selling my art predominantly on my own website. Whatever choice you make will be up to you. Just remember, that you will want to keep growing and evolving.

Honestly it doesn't matter where you start, it is understanding that no matter what, you are ultimately responsible for how many people see what you are sharing.

Let's say you start with your own website. That is like getting a building on undeveloped land in Search Engine City. As you stand in the middle of an empty floor, it dawns on you that no one knows you exist.

There are no roads leading to you, and although you have something to say you have no one to say it to.

This is precisely what it feels like when you first get a website. You are in what I like to call *Internet Antarctica.* Honestly, when you first get started ANYWHERE on the internet, it will feel like you are in a frozen tundra of isolation.

Looking over the virtual landscape there are thousands of buildings. Some buildings have bright neon signs with large arrows proclaiming loudly, "I am here. Look at what I am saying!" Some large complex buildings have large emblems that say Facebook, Instagram, TikTok, Twitter, Myspace, or any other social media platform.

They are large complexes where you can claim a small studio and share pictures and messages on a wall that other people have access to.

A good way to get people to visit your far-off building is to create some roads that lead to it. This is when you get on social media. It's like obtaining a free studio in one of these social media complexes.

Maybe the first thing you do is post a funny picture on the wall and wait eagerly. After a few minutes, someone walks by, looks at it, and gives you a thumbs up.

Then your grandmother shows up. She writes some disapproving words on a post-it note and sticks them under the picture. Before she leaves, she tells you to be her friend by connecting a virtual road from her room to yours. This is like a string that allows her to just show up whenever she wants. It also allows you to visit her room as well.

Bewildered as to why your grandmother is at a social media complex, you decide to also open studios in other complexes. You make sure to connect each studio to your building so people can visit and see what you have to offer. Every time you share something from your building, it creates another virtual road.

Over the course of several months, you have been renovating your building and sharing it in the social media complexes. With every picture of your life, creations, and inspiring messages on the wall, you create more roads back to your building. People pop up occasionally, but no one really sticks around for long.

You start writing some blogs which are like bulletin boards within the Search Engine City.

Anytime you write a blog, add a page or a merch page on your website, it is like renovating a new space in your building. For each blog you send, you build another virtual road back to one of your rooms and down to the main floor.

When something goes viral in the different complexes, it gets shared all over the place. Suddenly you see new virtual roads forming everywhere as people frantically share them. You realize that your grandmother shared the infamous cat on your wall with a post-it note that states, "Now this is funny."

After seeing how many roads lit up, you realize that the best thing to share is something other people will share as well. You start to focus on offering valuable information. The value comes from being helpful, entertaining, or thought-provoking. Also, you realize that if you are going to build roads back to yourself, you might as well be as authentic as possible. That way when people show up, they will be *YOUR* people.

It's been a year, and you have expanded your floors and are building up. Your building has several rooms, including an about me room, a merch room, and more. You've also expanded your blog rooms to include several different subjects. So far, you have built many virtual roads leading back to your main floor. People pop in and out more frequently and you have much more interest, but you're not really selling much yet.

You decide to expand your reach by going to the audio and visual social media complexes to build more roads back to your building. With each video and podcast, you can add links in your description that lead back to your website. Thus, every time you post, you build a road. Every time someone shares your video or podcast, they build a road back to you. In fact, since everything you put out there leads back to your website, anytime ANYONE shares any of the valuable information you put out there, it builds a road that leads right back to your building.

As you look out the window that night and see the spider web of virtual roads leading from buildings, complexes, bulletins, walls, and rooms, you smile. The glow from the neon signs illuminates the night sky as you realize the future will look bright as long as you persist. You may only have a few virtual roads leading to you, but the more you expand your reach, the larger your empire will become. Eventually, it will be in the thousands.

With every single post, blog, creation, platform, social media event, video, podcast, email, comment, or link, you have the opportunity to build a road to your website. The more people are encouraged to visit, the more comfortable and familiar they will become. The more compelling your story is, the more they will share.

As you can see, all roads must lead back to home when it comes to your website. Think of it like a spiderweb of virtual roads leading from place to place. Whoever has the most roads will have the most traffic.

The more consistent your message is, and the more places you share it, the more chances someone else will share it. Every time they do that, then they are building a road back to you as well. There are certain things I keep in mind when building my roads.

Make it easy for people to find you. Don't make people take a million turns before reaching your website. There should be a maximum of two steps for people to get from a shared link to the destination you want to send them.

Share your web address everywhere. Build roads that will take them directly where you want them to go. Be direct, don't beat around the bush, let them know where to go and why.

Be consistent with your brand. Try to get the same social media handles and stay away from having a billion different names. For example, wherever you go, I am @rafiwashere.

Be consistent with your message. Consistency is what will bring people to you. Don't confuse people by saying something that has nothing to do with who you are. This is what happens when people chase trends of popularity. Just be you. Be a trend maker and not a trend chaser.

Focus on the connections. Roads build relationships and allow us to find each other easily. The more links that lead straight back to you, the more opportunity you have to build a connection with someone. The more you create and share, the more you are virtually putting yourself out there.

Think long-term. It takes time to build your empire. You may need to adapt and evolve as things change. Ultimately, online platforms change and some go the way of the dodo. This is why I recommend you spend your time building up your website and building a foundation that is yours. Get people used to connecting with you on your website by being authentic, dynamic, and valuable. Your website has the potential to be one of those places that stand the test of time, even if all else is gone.

At the end of the day, no matter how overwhelming or saturated the internet might seem, it is still all about the human connection to one another.

This is how I market myself online. It's all about building roads and building a connection. The way most people promote themselves online is more like showing up to a virtual party and holding up a product, followed by begging people to buy it.

Would you do this in real life? Most likely not. You would talk to people and make a connection on mutual perspectives and interests. Yet people have this weird notion that it's not like that on the internet. They think we have to act like robots, but we are not. We are human. So be human. Be yourself.

Some people are afraid that if they are too human online, they will expose their private lives. One person actually told me, "God forbid I want to sell my art! Maybe I just want to sell my stuff and not tell my story! AKA, MY PRIVACY!"

To which I replied, "You just told me part of your story with this comment. Your approach to treating the online connection as just a method to "sell" also tells a story. Everything you say or do online tells your story. The question isn't whether you are telling a story, but whether you are controlling the narrative."

I am not saying – nor do I recommend – airing your dirty laundry, private details you wouldn't tell your grandmother, every single play by play, info that would compromise your security, venom about how messed up Uncle Steve acted at family dinner, or any kind of TMI exposing yourself online. I'm just saying to act with humanity.

I get it. The internet can seem scary and confusing, but we define ourselves every time we face something that we are afraid to do. We also define ourselves when we avoid something because we are scared. One is empowering. The other is disempowering. Either way it is ALL telling a story about you.

Maybe you are not sure of what to share online. Here are a few ideas, just off the top of my head. The important thing is to remember the narrative. What are you saying about you?

Original Story.

This could be a story about the art you are working on and why. It could also be a story on why you want to be an artist. Honestly, it could be a story about anything. It doesn't have to be deep or even personal, just something that says why you do what you do. "I saw a flower that was just beautiful, and I wanted to capture it" is a story. Don't overthink it.

Finished Art.

People love seeing finished art, but they love reading the captions the most. If a work of art is posted and the caption has nothing to say, it will disappoint. Post a mock-up picture or complete picture of your art, and say a little something about it. Get creative and have fun with this.

You Interacting With Your Art.

Maybe a picture of you holding it up or looking at it at an art show. What's the story there?

Closeups Of Finished Art.

A closeup on texture or a specific part of the piece that you are really proud of. Why are you proud of it?

Works In Progress.

A picture of you working on your art. Talk about your creative process with that particular piece. People are intrigued by this kind of stuff.

Your Artworks.

You could do a collage of your various artworks and talk about them.

Walkthrough Of Your Studio.

Talk about your studio. People are fascinated by artists and their spaces.

Your Exhibitions.

Announce, show, and talk about your experience at an art show, exhibition, or virtual show. Talk about the fact that you are nervous to show your art if you are, people will relate to that.

Collector With Art.

Interview or get a picture of one of your art collectors with you and the art they purchased. Tell the story.

How-to's or Tutorials.

Give some art tips, best practices, lessons, or something you learned.

Share New Available Items.

Share something that you just listed in your online store. Talk about why you created it.

Mutual Excitement.

Talk about stuff you are excited about and want to share with your online family.

Shoutouts To Artists And Humans.

Share some work, quotes, or things you love. Give someone a shout-out. Tell people why you dig them or it.

Art-Related Blog Or Content You Enjoy.

If you read something that resonates with you, share it with your online peeps. Why does it resonate with you?

Creative Updates.

Update people on a project you are working on. How are you feeling about the project? What are your challenges? How do you plan on overcoming them?

Art Industry News You Find Interesting.

Talk about something going on in the art world that you have an opinion on or are excited about.

Local Exhibitions And Events.

Share some local exhibitions you liked or are excited to see. Tell people why.

Don't Push Your Product, Just Show It.

One thing that I learned from marketing companies that I find powerful is how they will promote their product in the background. For example, they will engage in product placement in a movie or sponsor an event. This means that any good feeling you have associated with the movie or event will be projected onto the product.

This is one of the reasons that I will share my message and not worry too much about selling my art. The simple truth is that your positive message will project onto ANYTHING you create. So, don't try to sell, just be real and share what you are about.

To make it simple, share anything that you want to connect with the world about. I have one rule for myself when it comes to sharing anything online. My life revolves around being creative and focusing on the empowering aspects of life, so I will not say it if I have nothing empowering to say.

I may be struggling with something important that I think will give some kind of benefit to someone, but I'm not going to complain and call that end of story. I'm going to share once I have found a resolution for myself.

It has become a trend to complain, blame, and hatemonger on the internet. I think I can safely say that most people don't find that appealing or authentic. Most of us want to connect, inspire, and be inspired. We want to remain authentic, and we crave authenticity in others.

So how do I know if I am authentic? Easy.

Ask yourself, "How do I treat those people who can do absolutely nothing for me, will never buy my art, and may never follow me?"

Your answer will tell you everything you need to know about your ultimate motivation behind why you are doing what you do. It is an online community. Remember the word *community*. Focus on your genuine connection with humans and treat people like people. If you are looking at people as nothing more than potential likes, follows, and sales, then you may need to rethink your motives.

Royal Precision LGP-30 Electronic Computer

COMPACT...
MOBILE...
LOW IN COST...

high-speed computation right at your desk

HOW DO I BUILD ROADS?

If you are just getting started approaching the internet, or you've been doing it for a while but not seeing much traffic, it might be time to build some virtual roads.

There is one important thing I want you to remember here: the things I am listing here are merely suggestions. I am not saying that you have to do this or that. These are simply the things that I have done to connect with more and more people over time.

Start A Blog. It's a great way to talk about yourself and your art. It allows people to know a little more about who you are. The truth is that most people buy art from people they are comfortable and familiar with. I find that there is no better place to start connecting with your art's potential future collector than on your blog.

The blog should be hosted on your site. As mentioned before, each blog that you write is an outstretched road on the sea of the internet that leads right back to your website. People can also subscribe to your blog and thus be reminded of the awesomeness that is you.

Although your website might have the most excellent information in the world on it, it might also be in its own distant universe if no roads are leading back to it. Share your blogs on social media so that people go to your website to read new stuff.

Many people spend a lot of time working on their social media presence and little time on their websites. They just let it sit there like an old business card.

Unless you are writing blogs or doing something that makes your site more dynamic, nobody will have a reason to revisit. If they are not visiting often, then they will not have the chance to become comfortable navigating your website.

You may think, "But I post new art all the time, and my website is cool."

Sure, but how often do you visit static sites just because? Rarely. The fact is that everyone is busy and their time online will be dominated by what is pulling their attention. If your website is not visible to them, it will be out of sight out of mind. Honestly, some of the websites I visit the most stay fresh on my radar because I am prompted by a blog that offers some value.

If you are struggling with what to write, then you are overthinking it. Pretend you are writing a letter to a pen pal who is curious or asking questions about your art, career, and life. Ultimately, when it comes to writing a blog, it is just another way for you to creatively express yourself. Also, if you do guest blogs, they will link back to your website.

Have Social Media Presence. Some despise social media and complain that everything is saturated. Others think it is a breeding ground for forgery and getting your art stolen.

Some run their entire art business on them and feel they do quite well. Some love the sense of community they get from the people that follow them. Everyone has a different opinion, and I'm not here to argue with anyone, but this is my book, so I will tell you what I think… If you are going to post, don't be lame.

LAME INSTAGRAM POST

Social media sites have become a game changer for all manner of creatives. It has allowed us a chance to put ourselves out there and be shared by others.

To build ourselves and our art and draw a collection of people that appreciate it. I'm not saying that social media doesn't have its downsides because it definitely does, but as long as you avoid drama and have fun, you should be fine.

Also, don't take on too much, or put all your eggs in one basket. Your website should be where you do all of your business. Your website belongs to you. Your social media account is somewhere you can be evicted from.

As I said before, social media is about being social and putting yourself and your art out there. It's like sharing your art around the world for a brief second. Sure, maybe one or two people may see it at first, but that's more than not having it on there.

Every platform is different, so you'll have to experiment and play around with how to best use them for you. I take the lazy approach in which I post the same information across all my social media profiles. I only use it to keep a record for myself.

That way, I'm excited about posting daily and not chasing likes. It's like keeping a public journal or photo album that I can refer back to.

There are ways to make it easy and automate your posting with different services online if that is what you fancy. It is an option, but you can also just snap a picture and post when you have something to share.

YOU GLOW WHEN YOU ARE YOU!

My Thoughts on Paying For Ads On The Internet.

Social media ads have the power to reach thousands of people out there, but honestly, they may not do much for you. Sure, you'll get a little hit on the analytics, but unless you are selling a niche product, it is hit or miss. I get so annoyed with overpriced "Artist Marketing Mentor" courses that tell you to buy ads on social media as if that is new revolutionary intel that's going to save you. It's bullcrap. Listen, I'm not against purchasing ads, in fact I am planning an ad campaign for my books. The key is remembering that the traditional ways most ads are used are unimaginative and interruptive. In my opinion, you have no right to interrupt someone in their home unless you are bringing them value. Even if that value is simply to give them a laugh.

The ads that entertain us are the ones we remember. Even if we don't buy the product, we remember the ad and that is the power of marketing. Many people putting ads out there rely on repetition, but unless you are spending 6k a month, you may not have enough ads to make a difference. As you have read in this book, there is a lot more going on with why people buy stuff. Flaunting an ad in front of their face may not work. Commercials and ads are everywhere, surrounding us at all times. It has become a landfill in the landscape of our world. The saturation of ads has resulted in a phenomenon I called "Bull-Garbage Blindness." For the most part, we have learned to ignore and overlook the ads.

That's why if you are going to do ads, think outside of the box and try to entertain, enlighten, or enrich with the ad itself. If people are engaged, they'll want to find out more, but it will get lost in the mix if you are just promoting the same typical minutia.

6 Tips ☺ HOW TO BE AWESOME ON SOCIAL MEDIA!

1. POST AS A REMINDER TO YOURSELF THAT YOU ARE AWESOME.
2. DO AWESOME STUFF IN REAL LIFE $ SHARE iT.
3. TAKE COMPELLING $ FUN PICTURES $ VIDEOS.
4. DON'T CHASE likes OR VALIDATION.
5. BE HUMAN, NOT A MARKET ROBOT.
6. HAVE FUN SHARING YOUR VOICE $ BE "SOCIAL."

CREATE VIDEOS OR PODCASTS LIKE A ROGUE

For all intents and purposes, Bob Ross was the first art vlogger. Love it, hate it, or are terrified of it, videos (and audios) are a powerful medium of expression. In reading this book, you rely on your imagination to fill in the blanks of my voice and expressions based on the text. Yet only 7% of the whole meaning is communicated in the written word. If you listen to the audiobook, you receive an additional 38% of the entire communication through my tonality.

If I were standing in front of you or in a video, I would communicate the additional 55%. The fact is that 93% of meaning is shared non-verbally. That's one reason why writers have to paint a picture using descriptive words to give you a real sense of what is going on. That is also one of the reasons people use emojis. Sarcasm gets lost without body language.

With audio and video, you can communicate clearly to your audience. Whether you only use videos on your website or start sharing podcasts or videos on online platforms, it can feel scary if you've never done it before. One of the biggest fears I faced when I decided to add video to what we do is the faceless mob of haters that might spring up.

The anonymity of the internet, in particular haters, trolls, and naysayers, were terrifying. Over the years, I have learned to ignore them. Honestly, they don't matter, and it never really has anything to do with you. You will always have someone pointing a finger from the sidelines when you are in the arena. An artist I know that goes by the name Multi-Media Susan says it perfectly, *"If you are an introvert like myself and are afraid of putting your face and/or voice out there in front of huge numbers, you may be afraid of the haters. You might want to start off speaking behind the camera as if you are only speaking to one or a few friendly people that may be interested in your art. As time goes by, you will care less and less about the haters. While constructive criticism can be beneficial, the opinions of haters hold no real value."*

Whether it is writing a blog, posting on social media, posting a podcast, or posting a video, the only way to get comfortable with it is to do it. That goes for anything in life. If you are afraid of talking to people, but you want to put your art out at the local market, the only way to get past the fear is to do it.

I highly recommend doing videos and podcasts, although I know it can be scary to get it started. For most of us, it is the equivalent of standing on a stage and having stage fright. However, as an artist, putting yourself out there, it is the perfect way to take center stage.

You may have some great reasons why you don't want to, such as:

- I don't know what I'm doing.

None of us know what we are doing when we first get started on something new. It is effortless to get stuck in a research loop and convince yourself that you are not ready. The only way you are going to really learn how to do something is to do it.

-I don't have the equipment. I have a crappy camera.

When I first started doing videos, I had a cheap $50 camera with a horrible microphone. When the iPhone came out with a video camera, I started using it. Just about all my videos were recorded with my phone. Little by little over a decade, I've bought some equipment, but my videos are not high quality. One important thing that I have noticed on YouTube is that there is no correlation between views and good camera quality.

-I'm not comfortable on camera.

Neither am I sometimes. When I first started, I would panic before, during, and after filming. It was a struggle to convince myself to even post the video. The biggest insecurity I faced in the beginning was the fear of looking stupid. Honestly, that fear dominated my life for a long time and was why I stayed small.

This goes deeper than just posting a video, and I have entire chapters about this in my survival guide book, so I'll just say: The only way to get past this is to take one step at a time.

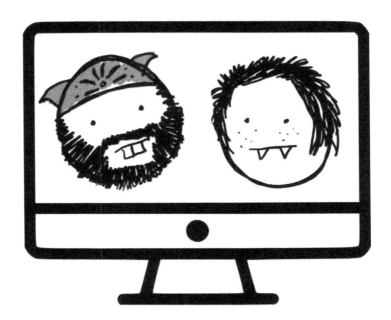

-I don't know how to edit the video.
I hear this one a lot. People will often ask me what program I use. When I first started, I used some apps on my phone, and whatever free movie editing program came on my computer. Later on, I found deals on other editing stuff. The best way to learn a program, in my opinion, is to film something, then edit it and look up tutorials online when you get stuck. By the way, I use Vegas Pro as my movie editing software.

-I have no audience.
No one does when they first get started. You have to start somewhere. I'm going to be honest with you, whether you are posting videos or on social media, your audience takes a long time to build. I've posted consistently on YouTube for years and have a medium audience compared to some people that started around the same time.

Some have less. It can take 12 to 48 months of consistent posting to build a decent-sized audience, so don't do it for a large audience.

Big subscriber counts look great on paper, but honestly, I would instead rather manage a smaller channel with a dedicated and loyal following. Over time, the following will grow little by little, giving a chance for organic growth.

-I have no time.
Although a brilliant and common excuse... It's just an excuse. I know artists who have a full-time job, manage an art career, do exhibitions, have kids, and still manage to put out some videos here or there. Don't fall for the hype of having to post weekly, post at your own pace. If you want to do anything in life, make time for it. If you don't, you'll wish you had. Trust me, I used this excuse on many things, and as the grim reaper approaches, I realize I would much rather do something badly and grow than never have done it at all. Honestly, most of these excuses are just a fear of breaking out of a comfort zone and are universal to just about anything we do that is new.

I'm not in the business of giving specific "do this" advice when it comes to how you should approach anything you do, but I will tell you what I've learned DOESN'T work over the years.

Things To Avoid Doing With Video or Audio.
Avoid the death stare or business voice. A statue pose and robotic delivery are not natural. Unless, of course, you are a robot, the Statue of Liberty, or a speak-n-spell. 93% of your communication is your body language and tonality. Don't be afraid to move your body. Talk as if it's a typical conversation between yourself and a friend. Relax and have fun.

Avoid talking shit. There are some people who have made a career of being argumentative and confrontational on TV and the internet. If this is your thing, then go for it – but honestly, although you might have a good run, it never ends well.

Avoid doing things just for fame. There are a few online personalities that have done some really stupid things in order to get more traffic. Some of this has been offensive, mean, disgusting, and harmful. Some have gone to jail, others had their reputations fall apart. Think about what you are saying with your actions and what kind of attention you will attract.

Don't be a remote island. A big part of this whole pie is engagement, and so many people mistakenly concern themselves only with how much engagement they are *getting*. Roads flow two ways, so make sure you are making efforts to connect and engage with your audience. If they take the time to comment on your video or podcast, show some love. If they have a channel or podcast, check it out. We can't be everywhere all the time, but we can make efforts and show some reciprocation.

Video provides a new creative dimension for art and lets people convey beauty through sight, sound, and motion.

The key is to remember that the internet is simply a reflection of how you are living your life. If you are not giving yourself engaging projects to work on and pushing out of your comfort zones, there won't be much of a compelling story. The best way to create irresistible stuff that people will want to follow on the internet is to live life and put yourself out there as much as possible.

If you hide behind a screen buying ads and don't enter the world it just won't be as compelling. It's all about sharing the adventure and journey that is the life of a creative.

KEEP GOING! YOU'VE GOT THIS!

Klee Angelie

SHORT SECTION ON SEO AND ALGORITHMS

I'm sure everyone reading this has heard about SEO and algorithms. You've probably received emails or phone calls from people trying to sell you their service for search engine ranking. Don't pay anyone for that crap. It's not that complicated, and you don't need a master's degree or expensive service to show up on search rankings. Here is a quick way you can make sure your site, blogs, and other things are optimized.

-Name your pictures and fill in the data in the properties of the image. This is called metadata.

-Use the exact words of an image in the title of a blog or page in your content. Use similar words throughout the writing of the page, especially the first paragraph. This will help the search engine identify what it is about. If you want to pick a "searchable title" then you can do so, but I usually just have fun with power words to make it catchy.

-Add Your Meta Descriptions. This always sounds complicated, but it's not. Your meta description is the little blurb of text below your link when people receive their search results. There will always be a place to enter this. If not, think about the first sentence of content in your writing.

-Add Your Website To All Social Media Networks. More links leading back to your site, the better. Build many roads. This is what let's search engines know you are legit.

-Create shareable stuff on your site and be consistent. Build as many roads as you can.

-Submit your site to search engines. You can look up how online.

-Think about how you search for things online, and use that to title your blogs, pages, items, pictures, or anything you put out there. "The Nuanced Pigmentation Of Strands Of Me" might not rank first in any search results. "How I created a unique blue pigment" probably will. Another example, taken directly from my learning experience in listing my art titles is "The Wild Blue Flame" (awesome, but less searchable than) "Blue Horse Original Art". You can always delight them with your existential meaning in the description.

-A word about the "Newest blah blah blah." A lot of folks get frustrated because as soon as they understand how a platform works, the geniuses behind the platform release a new feature. They will give priority and visibility to those who jump on board right away. My approach to this is simple. I'll try it out if it seems like fun, but I don't stress out trying to jump on the trend just because it's popular.

Don't get too wrapped up in SEO's and algorithms. They are constantly changing and what works this week isn't guaranteed to work next week if you're simply trying to keep up. It comes down to two things with searchability. Unique content (i.e., you didn't copy it from somewhere else) and consistency within the content (i.e., the search engine can easily recognize what it's about and put it in front of humans it might be relevant to.)

Honestly, it's all very simple. The almighty search engines will only go by the content and descriptions that you post. If you are keeping things consistent, for example, if you post a blog about "How I Dominated My Last Art Show", you are going to want your images to have the same title because 'IMG1098' doesn't say ANYTHING about what you are writing and will confuse the almighty algorithm. The truth is, algorithms are just programming that is trying to make things easier for the person searching for information. So if you keep in mind making it easy for people to find you, you will be unstoppable.

THE MEANING OF GOING VIRAL

A lot of people are inquisitive about what kind of things go viral online. Honestly, it's not any different than gossip in a neighborhood. The worst gossip spreads really fast, but so does the inspirational stuff. There is no exact formula about what kind of things are sharable, but I know that emotional intelligence plays a big part. Whether it is a blog, social media post, podcast, or video, you can see a pattern of popularity with specific posts.

Happiness = More Shares.
Positive content seems to spread faster on social media than any other type of content. I know what you're thinking: "Whoa Rafi, WTF. That can't be true. I see the controversial hype trolls getting quite a bit of traction." That might be true, but when you look at the things that are *most* viral, you will find a common theme of joy, hope, and fun.

Despite how it may seem, people want to share things that make them feel good. At the time of writing this, the most viral video of ALL TIME is *BABY SHARK*. If you're reading this 100 years from now, apologies, back on track. Here's my personal experience: I find that whenever I am sharing an anniversary or some epic good news in my life, it tends to get a lot of engagement.

Sadness = More Clicks.

As the somewhat depressing adage goes, if it bleeds, it leads. Things that elicit an emotional reaction of sadness usually garner more clicks and engagement. Humans naturally want to learn more about it. I would caution here, I don't recommend sharing anything sad unless it comes from a real place. If you are using it as a tactic, then your authenticity will come into question.

Whenever I have a moment where I might be struggling with something, I may share. However, I always look to some positive outcome that will come in the future. We will all experience sadness in our lives, and it is one of the things that helps us grow.

When it comes to sadness, people want to know that there are better days ahead, share your story, but most importantly share your story of overcoming, there is something powerful in that.

Fear/Surprise = More Loyalty.

Experiencing negative feelings, such as fear or shock, we naturally look for warmth and reassurance. Offering reassurance during difficult times is powerful in many ways but using fear mongering or shock to promote yourself and get attention is a jerk-bag move.

I may talk about difficult or scary things, but I focus on the solution and not the problem. Obviously, news media outlets are big on presenting news that causes us to tune in because we need to know what's happening and if we are safe. Life can be scary, but there is no reason to live in a place of constant fear.

Surprise, the more congenial cousin of shock, is also a state of heightened emotion. We can use the unexpected to surprise and delight, incite awe, and also create a sense of togetherness in the experience.

The startle mechanism has always been an effective one. How you use it is up to you.

Anger/Disgust = Seemingly Viral Content.

This one is big in politics, news media marketing tactics, and the pervasive angry hairdo you might see on your TV or computer screen.

Anger and disgust can elicit intense emotional reactions, which can often turn into arguing. Anger is something we feel, and when we feel it (especially if we perceive wrongdoings), there is nothing inherently wrong with that.

However, let me state my position clearly: It is not to be exploited for ratings or hollow gains. Unfortunately, this is all too common. The more people argue, the more attention the subject will get. This includes sharing, gathering, forwarding, or commenting on the subject of attention.

I find this tactic most abhorrent and the one that runs most under people's radar. Since people are so busy fighting with each other, they rarely question the source or find themselves able to have productive discussion.

Potential solutions are often lost to the inescapable pull of the argument itself. The result usually involves incendiary comments, controversial reactions, polarized perspectives, and a lot of finger-pointing to be spread.

No matter what you do on the online landscape, remember to remain genuine and make an effort to connect with people. That's what matters here, we want to connect, not polarize.

In my opinion, it's not about going viral by any means possible, it's about doing something so awesome that people want to share it. Honestly, it is *EASY* to get attention with this stuff, but it is not sustainable in the long run.

As much attention as Anger/Disgust may bring someone, they will have to continue to chase polarizing topics to stay relevant because eventually resolutions will prevail.

Ultimately, it's all about forming a long-lasting positive relationship with your audience. A strong friendship is something that will last the ages, become a friend to the world. Although most marketing gears around doing whatever it takes to get the most attention, be selective about what you will talk about, especially if you are angry and spitting fire.

The truth is that opinions change, people evolve, and we all get to choose for ourselves how we feel and how we will take action to *ACTUALLY* make a difference.

Whether you are online or offline, what ultimately matters is how you approach the world and what you have to give. This is more important than becoming famous, this is your legacy.

If you are timidly approaching the world and hiding behind a screen, the world will timidly approach you. If you are fake, the world will be fake and shallow with you. If you are authentic, bold, and genuinely care about people, the world will follow your journey and care about you. If you are just trying to make a quick buck, the world will trade you in at the first opportunity.

We've all had friendships, some good, some bad, some shallow, and some deep. The key is understanding that your audience and art collectors will become your loyal friends if you allow them to. There is no marketing tactic in the world that can compensate for that. Your actions will ALWAYS speak louder than words.

This next part is vital, so I want you to pay close attention to my words. Your website is your home, and the person visiting is your guest. You are there to entertain them, enrich them, and make them feel at home.

Even though most marketing and salespeople love referring to humans as "leads," the fact remains that the people that buy your art are human. These humans could love your art, but they are not obligated to buy it simply because they love it.

Yet, I have seen artists treat other people like a "*bad lead*." This is what salespeople call a lead that is unlikely to become a paying customer. They feel like it is wasting their time, and they ignore the person.

I have had many *"bad leads"* in my career that loved my art but couldn't afford it. I still gave them the same time and attention I would give someone who had the means to buy my art. As it turns out, many of these *"bad leads"* have become some of my most loyal collectors over the years.

The main thing that drives me crazy in this world of consumer marketing is that people are seen as herds of cattle with price tags attached to them based on a plan for fast money. It's all about persuasion, and the connection gets lost.

I personally think that the impact on our society is terrible. Using fear, scarcity, manipulation, and propaganda has us at each other's throats, believing a reality fabricated by financial gains and agendas.

If you want to set yourself apart on the internet, remember that the internet is simply a tool to connect with other humans. Allow people to find you, one person at a time.

Just like in real life, some will be interested, some will not, and some will hate it, but at least you are sharing who you are with the world through your art. You are connecting with like-minded humans, and that is important for so many reasons.

Not only are you connecting with people that may collect your art, but you are connecting with other creatives that can live on the other side of the world. This gets lost in the current formula of competitive marketing, and I think it works against us.

Artists are so influential and can accomplish amazing feats, yet many of us are surrounded by people who don't challenge or inspire us.

We can spend a lot of time feeling lost and alone in facing the world because art can be such a solitary practice.

Suppose your focus is just on collecting buyers and what you can get out of people. In that case, you are approaching the internet just like everybody else and will have to rely on scheming tactics to survive the competitive market. When you do this, you miss out on the long-term financial and emotional benefits of connection.

An artist and friend, Christopher J Rhoads, illustrates this perfectly in this statement:

"I STRUGGLED TO REMEMBER HOW TO LIGHT MY FLAME, BUT A SIMPLE CONVERSATION WITH ANOTHER PASSIONATE PERSON WAS ENOUGH FOR THEM TO LEAN IN AND TOUCH MY EXTINGUISHED TORCH TO THEIRS AND VOILA!

THAT IS THE JOY OF OUR PASSION. IT IS CONTAGIOUS. IT CAN BE SHARED. AND SO LONG AS THERE IS ART AND ARTISTS IN THE WORLD...NO ONE'S FLAME EVER NEEDS TO FIZZLE OUT FOREVER."

SO NOW WHAT?

When arriving at the point that is the end of writing this book, if I were a solely reach-driven, financially motivated, savvy marketer, I would submit this edit to public opinion via focus groups, surveys, working editions and so on. That would help me determine if the content I wrote here is digestible and consumable.

I didn't do that. Instead, Klee and I edited and re-edited this book for over a year. While I could have used market research to craft a version of this book that is more palatable to the masses, it would likely have lost something in the process.

It would not be my truth, not in whole, but a diluted, easily digestible, maybe consumable, and possibly distorted version of what started as raw and authentic.

If I were selling you on marketing, this is also the stage where I would include a call for action that would require you to sign up for the next step in my marketing course. I hate to disappoint, but there isn't one. If you've made it this far, you know that is not what I have ever set out to do, and that is not the intention of this book. So, without further ado, welcome to the "What do I do now stage."

It's simple. Right now is the time to *PUT YOURSELF OUT THERE* and face the fear of ACTUALLY doing it. No more hiding behind ads or complaining that you don't know how. If you want something to happen, you must take action.

I'm not going to lie, it's not going to be easy. I get it. There's going to be that terrifying moment that comes after you hit publish, post, send, face a crowd, or pick up the microphone. A split second of realization that you are vulnerable and exposed.

You've volunteered yourself and your thoughts upon the world. You've poured your heart and soul into the work that will now be revealed, rejected, criticized, judged, loved, or ignored. You have taken the leap and put yourself out in the arena. There's no going back. It's time to either run and hide or face the music. It is both invigorating and panic-inducing.

Everything in your life as a creative has led up to this point. You are pushing out of your comfort zones and putting yourself out there.

Unfortunately, many creatives spend much of their life avoiding this particular scenario. Yet, it is essential to be in the arena to share your art and voice. There is no way around it. We have to face the terror.

Living your life within your comfort zone means passing up on these moments. If you never finish writing a book, you need never receive a review. If you never sign up for an art festival, you won't get rejected. If you never apply for a competition, you'll never know if you could have won. If you never promote yourself, you'll be invisible for a reason.

When it came to putting myself out there as an artist, I was painfully quiet, I struggled to interact with people, and I feared rejection more than anything. I was terrified of making any mistakes, and I believed that nothing I did was ever good enough. I felt small and helpless. Galleries, art competitions, and businesses rejected me. When I did manage to share my art, no one seemed to be interested at all. My debt kept growing, and I wasn't sure how to keep going. I had every excuse in the world to give up, but I persisted through all the bull.

This doesn't mean that I didn't come close to quitting several times. I struggled greatly for the first five years, and honestly, it all seemed impossible. However, with every experience and every disappointment, I learned something powerful. Because of this experience, I made several promises to myself. These are promises I repeat when I forget my own power as an artist.

- I promise that I will no longer be quiet and small.
- I promise I will not feel responsible for other people's fickle emotions.
- I promise that I will speak up if I disagree or am being mistreated.
- I promise that I will ask for what I want without expectation, but I will ask, Damn it.
- I promise to remember that people may have expectations of me, but I am not those expectations.
- I promise to not blindly do what I am told.
- I promise to be willing to make mistakes and grow from them.
- I promise to never allow anyone to be abusive, rude, or manipulative. I don't have time for that crap.
- I promise I will not feel bad when rejected. It is NOT a reflection of me.
- I promise I will be kind to myself and others, but I don't have time for jerks.
- I promise to be my biggest cheerleader and remember that I don't have to seek approval from anyone else.
- I promise to remind myself daily that I am good enough.

- I promise that when I make mistakes, I'm not going to dwell. I'm going to learn and move on. I will remember that each mistake is a step closer to success.
- I promise to remind myself that I am big, bold, and empowered in every situation that life may throw at me.
- I promise to remember that I get to choose. I get to decide what I think and feel about myself and my art.
- I promise to be done hiding who I am or seeing my kind nature as a weakness.
- I promise to love hard and glow as bright as I can in the world. If somebody doesn't like it, they can eat a bag.
- I promise to stop focusing on money and letting it make choices for me. I will do what I want because I want, not because I will make easy money. Chasing money will not rule my options.
- I promise to not let people label me or tell me who I am. I am whatever I decide to be.
- I promise that no matter what anyone says, no matter what things look like, no matter how much I have failed, I will not quit. I will be flexible, change direction, and persist through all the bull-crap.
- I promise to remember that even if it seems like I'm not ready for the next step, I am always capable and will figure it out as I go.
- I promise my measure of success will not be based on what other people assume is successful. I choose what success means to me.

When I finally decided to make the leap to becoming a full-time artist, I knew that I would have to get my art in front of other humans to support myself. I started what would become my decade-long study of a creative marketing social experiment.

The first three or four years, I was utterly lost in a void of marketing information that was either useless or incomprehensible. It was like staring off into a black hole. All the information went in, but none of it came back out. No one seemed to understand this large and overwhelming force, and the closer you got, the more terrifying and confusing the experience became.

I followed step-by-step guides, took art marketing courses on what I should do, and nothing seemed to work long term. Fancy acronyms and marketing lingo just made me feel dumb and like the answer was just out of my grasp. Three years' worth of tactics, and I was still no closer to understanding how and why I was marketing myself. Eventually, I threw out the rhetoric and decided to view it all as part of my journey as an artist. That's when marketing became an opportunity to creatively put myself out in the world.

Putting yourself out there is the term I use because it encompasses everything. Everything you do that interacts with any number of individuals is considered marketing. If you post something, print a flier, display a painting, have a conversation, or pay for an ad, these are ALL part of putting yourself out there. It is also one giant social experiment, and you are the creative researcher who is constantly experimenting and measuring the results.

Listen, I'm just saying, marketing is taken so darn seriously and is always used to try and persuade people to buy something, sign up, or trick someone into caring.

The truth is, it is just a performance. Either you are performing like all the other people who are marketing themselves, or you are being yourself. You are either the star, or a background character in a chorus line. To set yourself apart, keep certain things in mind when you are putting yourself out there.

- **Have Fun And Be Creative.** The most striking and noteworthy marketing I have seen is from creative people having fun. Turn your marketing into another creative craft and enjoy what you make. Think out of the box and have fun!

- **Authenticity.** Whether it is marketing or anything else you do, make sure that you are honest with yourself and the people who will receive any message you put out there.

- **Social Timing Awareness.** Things will get associated with you because of timing. Know what is going on in the world before posting. You don't have to be hog-tied to the news. In fact, I rarely watch the news. Scroll for a moment before posting anything or announcing an event.

- **It Only Takes One.** Whether it is one or one million followers, show appreciation for the people giving you their attention. Way too many times, I've seen people desperately trying to grow their audience or build their email list and ignore the following they already have. Extensive followings on the internet or in person may be sought after, but the quality of the relationship will always beat out the numbers.

- **Be A Tease.** A love for teasing people with the things you are excited about (mostly because you can't keep a secret when you're excited).

- **Mutual Excitement.** If you are genuinely excited about something and share that excitement, like-minded people will share in it.

- **Be A Human.** Put yourself out there and let the world know the creator behind the creations. This is usually a terrifying step and can tug on insecurities, but honestly, the only way to get past them is to just do it and keep going.

- **Be Unpredictable.** The more you view marketing as a social experiment and just a different medium of creation, the more it becomes distinct. This only works if you are genuinely approaching it as an artform and not chasing likes.

- **Constantly Try New Things.** Experiment with different ways of putting yourself out there and put them into action. Stop talking about it and do it.

- **Fa-Chunk It.** Break everything into small chunks and give yourself five to fifteen minutes to work on it. After the time has passed, you can stop, but chances are you'll keep going. Do this whenever you are procrastinating.

- **Don't Wait For Approval.** Don't wait around for validation, approval, or acceptance. No one changed the world by waiting around for approval. We are either blazing our own trail or we are jumping through someone's hoops hoping to be accepted. Do it now, don't wait.

"You owe the companies nothing. You especially don't owe them any courtesy. They have rearranged the world to put themselves in front of you. They never asked for your permission, don't even start asking for theirs." - Banksy, "Wall and Piece."

- **Not About Selling.** The focus is on saying what we want to say, doing what we want to do, and living how we want to live. You want people to discover you and build a relationship of trust. If they like your message, they will like you and your art.

- **Break Some Rules.** Be willing to push the boundaries. Be a Rogue. In my opinion, as long as there is no property damage, and you are not breaking the law or hurting anyone, some Rogue antics and shenanigans should be fine.

- **Take A Stand.** Believe in something and make it part of your message. My stand is personal empowerment, equality, and happiness for all humans, so everything I create, whether art, video, music, or marketing, has that theme at its core.

- **Put Your Name On It.** Whether it is your name, signature, logo, or whatever, make sure it is somewhere on your creation that you are putting out there. This also goes hand in hand with your unique style. Create what YOU create.

- **Take Matters Into Your Own Hands.** Start where you are with what you have and do it your way. There will be many "make it work" moments where you might have to take care of stuff outside your comfort zone or knowledge level. There is no better time to learn.

- **Content In Context.** Whatever you are doing, remember to keep in mind the proper context. The circumstances that form the setting for anything you do, think, or create should communicate what you want.

- **Create A Buzz.** Let people know what you are doing, and don't resort to just one method of communication. Put yourself out there. Shamelessly promote yourself to the world and let them know what you are doing on multiple platforms and in numerous ways.

As a Rogue Artist participating in Rogue anti-marketing, your most powerful weapon is your creative mind and perspective. Your perspective and mindset can make or break your efforts of putting yourself out there.

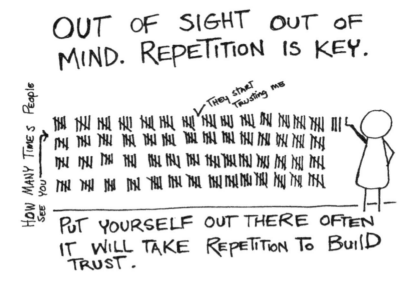

There are so many ways of putting yourself out there that haven't been discovered yet. It is up to you to innovate and claim your greatness. Get creative with what you have available to you, and go for it. What really matters is that you are putting yourself out there.

If you don't, you remain invisible. No one is coming. No one is going to save you. No one is going to discover you unless you allow them to find you.

As a Rogue Artist, everything you put out there is your art. This includes anything you do that you might consider marketing. It should all be creative, it should all say something about you, and it should be authentic. It's art. It is emotional, it has a story, and it is human. This can come with a mountain of baggage. It is also a tremendous opportunity to become unstoppable.

How much you can manage your self-doubt makes all the difference in how you put yourself out there. If you face risk, failure, doubt, mistakes, and criticism head on, they become your teachers. If you run away from them, they become your jailers. Many of us think that our limiting thoughts and emotions are in control. We may believe that the act of putting ourselves out there or doing something scary is beyond us, but we each get to choose how we respond to these feelings and thoughts. The best way to overcome them is to face them by putting yourself out there.

You can put yourself out there and experience what you might think is a failure and use the experience to train your brain on how to rise above the noise. You can talk to yourself better and make your mind work for you. You can also choose to beat yourself up about your own ability and competence. It's up to you, but only one of those is a surefire way to fall on your face. The other will allow you to get to places you haven't even dreamed of yet.

BE ONE OF THE HEARD, NOT ONE OF THE HERD.

It's exhausting to be competing all the time and honestly doesn't do much for scaling up your art career and life. Typical marketing approaches and tactics don't allow you to think bigger. You get trapped in a world of measurements and standards, but art doesn't sell because of analytics. It sells because it touches someone's heart and mind.

Essentially, people are just looking for something that will make them feel better. Your art can do that for them. Whether adding beauty, self-expression, status, empowerment, or a thought-provoking experience, the power is in your hands.

I hope that you glean and recognize the immense power in connecting with people on an emotional level when you put yourself and your art out there. I feel this is what most of us miss when we are just blindly following some marketing tactic that has been overused.

We are NOT big companies selling a product that is emotionless. We bottle emotion in everything we create. We are emotional beings who create unique works that mean something. Those individual works are seen by other emotional creatures who buy them. Every human out there has laughed, cried, felt happy, felt down, wanted more, or wanted less. We are all experiencing this crazy thing called life together. We can all relate.

Every person out there who is breathing has gone through some crap in life. Some of it was good, some of it bad. We've *all* gone through it, and those experiences are what connect us. In my experience, it doesn't matter how much money you have, where you live, what ethnicity you are, or what political leanings you choose. Our fears, courage, love, and insecurities are *ALL* relatable.

What is your story?
What are you saying?
What are your promises?
Are you genuine?

If you are an artist, chances are you feel completely alive when creating something authentic. That is where the disconnect happens with marketing. That is why as artists, it seems boring, tedious, and challenging. It doesn't have to be. It can be part of your authentic creativity. It can be part of your art and public expression of self.

In my opinion, in every action you take, you are either empowering people and yourself or disempowering people to give yourself an advantage. That's why people lie in marketing. We don't need to lie to someone to sell art, the art sells itself. We just have to make sure we are not standing between the art and the person that connects with it by *TRYING* to sell it.

The road to putting yourself out there is a continuing journey that doesn't have an end goal. We never get it done because it is simply part of this adventure that we call life. How much you give and take will determine your actual quality of life. It will also determine what people are saying about you.

In the end, that's all marketing is. It is word of mouth, and your actions will speak the loudest in your narrative and story that is being shared. Since putting yourself out there is all about taking action, it is essential to remember this question.

WHAT STORY ARE YOUR ACTIONS ACTUALLY TELLING?

Think About Who You Are And What You Have To Say.
Whether it is your art, the way you dress, what you do or don't do, it is all part of your story. If you complain and don't take action, what are you saying with that? If you want things to happen fast, what are you saying with that? What are you saying with how you put yourself out there? How do you talk to people?

Create Art. First And Foremost, You Are An Artist.
Without the creation of art, there is no art career. Don't get tied up by tedious marketing tactics. Your art is communicating something already. Tap into that. Use that message to create the most powerful way of putting yourself out there. How you do that, should be a work of art in itself.

Put Your Art Out There In As Many Places As You Can Within Reason.
Share it. Communicate it. Approach the world boldly and show off what you have to say. Yes, you will face rejections and hardships, but that is all part of the creative journey. Every success story is the result of a journey of roadblocks and failures.

PERSISTENCE IS KEY

A person only becomes a success after falling in the muck several times yet standing back up and entering the arena. This narrative is way more compelling than having it fall in your lap.

Expand Your Market (Think About The Future But Enjoy The Present).
Enjoy the ride and understand that everything you experience is merely a stepping stone. Look at what you want, but enjoy where you are and make the most of it. That is how you move forward.

Creatives Are The Most Innovative Marketing Peeps.
Trust yourself to know what you need to know about yourself and your art to put it out there. Only you know how you can shine, but you may have to dig deep. You may need to push past your imposter syndrome. Be willing to go there.

Don't Be Desperate And Try To Trick People. It Shines Through.
Stay real. Don't chase money, subscribers, and likes because it will make you look desperate when putting yourself out there. We don't create art to become famous. We create art and put it out there because we want to be heard. This takes time, so don't chase the quick fix.

Get Social (In-person & Online) And Accept Credit Cards.
Get on social media, put yourself out there, break some comfort zones. If you want people to know you exist, you will have to go where people are and introduce yourself. If you accept credit cards you open a whole new area of opportunity. You want to keep up with new forms of payment methods as they become available, to make it easy for people to purchase from you. The more payment methods you accept, the more accessible you are and the chances of missing a sale go out the window.

Stop Complaining, Blaming, And Stagnating.
If you are going to sit around and say that life is unfair and the cards are stacked against you, then "welcome to the club." This is life. None of us get a free pass. When you look at someone who succeeded in their art, it is because they didn't waste their time complaining and spent their time *ACTUALLY* doing something about it. I love artists, but man, are there some of you out there that spend a lot of time stagnating and ruminating on what doesn't work. Get moving and head in any direction. Don't get stuck in your own quicksand of lament.

Don't Do What Everyone Else Is Doing, And If You Do Make It Yours.
Plenty of people are out there using typical marketing tactics. Everyone is doing it, and it will not set you apart. Take those tactics and make them an art form that fits your narrative. Then create your own and blaze your own trail.

Build Your Own Tribe, Quit Trying To Find Them.
Create your own culture and let your people find you. There is no special place where you magically find your collectors and followers. Artists get discovered because they put themselves out there to be discovered.

Persist Through The Bullshit.
The creative journey of putting yourself out there will probably suck at times. It will be challenging, and you will have to push through a lot of difficult comfort zones. But the world needs to know about the awesomeness that is you. Just keep going.

You Are Already A Success.

Success means different things to different people. There are many measures of success out there that humans like to use as a yardstick. Make up your own. Don't chase validation by trying to fit someone else's measure of what success means.

Get Comfortable Being Uncomfortable.

You know when you know you are growing? When it is uncomfortable. Challenges are always uneasy, and we usually feel like we are not ready to face one. The only way to know for sure is to face it. When we decide to put ourselves out there, we are standing on stage and sharing our voice. Being ignored, booed, rejected, criticized, and judged is terror-inducing. You will have to get used to being uncomfortable if you are planning on making any significant impact in putting yourself out there.

Seek To Be Honest, Not Right.

The person who constantly needs to be right will miss out on much of what life has to teach them. They may alienate themselves from others. Arrogance repels, humility attracts. Chances are, if you are digging your heels in arguing with someone, it is because you are trying to get them onboard with your way of thinking. Your message gets lost when you do this.

Say what you got to say, then listen. You may change your mind about what you think is right or wrong. Either way, it's not a competition, it is a conversation. You may disagree, but an open dialog is more powerful than a confrontation.

Seek Honor, Not Popularity.

It's been said that our honor is "who we are," and our reputation is who people think we are. If someone is chasing fame and popularity, then it can all get jumbled and lost. This leads to a lot of people-pleasing and worrying about your reputation. People are fickle and judge you based on how they feel about themselves at that moment. What they think doesn't really have much to do with you, so you might as well just focus on being real.

Be An Innovator, Not An Imitator.

We are so used to being taught to follow the rules. We are asked which path we will take in life and discouraged from creating our own. The same thing happens in marketing. Don't let your fear stand in the way of your potential to create, innovate, or lead your own way of putting yourself out there.

When I decided I would begin my art career (after a little persistent nudging from Klee) I was given all kinds of opportunities to be part of projects or dreams that weren't mine.
I was being spread too thin and didn't have time to work on my own projects. Don't allow this to happen.

Like with art, if you are going to focus on marketing, focus on your projects and innovations. Find your own confidence to innovate. It will get much more attention if it has never been seen before than the typical boring marketing crap.

Do What Most Won't.

If you want to achieve something that most people struggle to succeed in, you have to be willing to do what they won't. If you're going to achieve what you haven't yet achieved, you must do what that old version of you wouldn't. If you want to be like everyone else, then do what they do.

Most people won't persevere, won't finish what they start, won't find the good, won't do what it takes, won't question their limiting beliefs, won't be solution-focused, won't do what scares them, and won't "be the change" they want to see in their world. Choose to be different. Choose to be a Rogue. Choose to be you.

Change Is Scary. Embrace It. Some of us resist change at all costs. We may do this because we fear that a change will alter the stability we feel. We can be habitual creatures who tend to feel a sense of safety and security when we know what to expect. The problem is that everything changes and evolves. Everything grows, and nothing will stay how it was.

Resisting change may lead to a comfortable stagnation in your life. Embracing and becoming comfortable with change allows you to expect the unexpected and not be controlled by fear. It will enable you to challenge yourself to believe that you will navigate change no matter what circumstances or situations arise.

It is important to remember when you put yourself out there because everything will change and evolve as you do.

I'm Afraid To Take The Risk. If You Don't, You Will Never Know What You Are Capable Of. People are fearful of risking rejection or failure when putting themselves out there. They worry that maybe it won't be worth it, or they'll end up with regrets. Taking a chance can feel incredibly risky. However, *not* changing can also be a risk. Let's be honest, life is a series of dramatic episodes that are always changing and in flux.

Taking a chance on yourself and following your dreams is a risk. Going against the grain is a risk. Creating an art career is a risk. Driving your car to the store is a risk. Everything in life is risky. We tend to forget that we take calculated risks hundreds of times a day in the most minor decisions.

We make determinations and predict outcomes all the time, but at the end of the day, big or small, they're all just guesses. Putting yourself out there feels risky because you may have spent many years talking yourself out of it.

The question isn't "is it risky?" because everything is. The question is, are you willing to face the risks? Do you believe that YOU have what it takes to persist through the suck?

Just to be clear, there is a difference between being reckless and recognizing risks. Irresponsible people don't even think about the dangers.

However, a Rogue Artist is well aware of the risks. Being willing to accept the consequences if things don't work out allows you to prepare.
As Rogues, we embrace failure. It's not the opposite of success.

It's a necessary component in growth. The opposite of success is not taking the risk and sitting still.

At the end of the day, we are either living boldly and shamelessly promoting who we are and what we do, or hiding from the world because everything seems risky. Live life, reach for the stars, and take a risk on who you want to be.

Act As If You Are Already A Rogue. Be the thing you want to be and ask yourself, "If I was a badass, who was bold, what would I do?" Then do it. The only way to get there is to show yourself that you are capable.

Be prepared for certain people who know you to act surprised when you do things that they think are out of character. That's fine, don't let someone else's perception of you keep you small. Have fun and see what happens.

Just Go For It. Whenever you're feeling hesitant or timid, make the first move. Just go for it before your brain gives you a chance to talk you out of it.

Be Unpredictable. Surprise the people who think they know you. Don't be afraid of trying new things. At least every week, do something, eat something, or try something you've never been brave enough to do. Just pick something and do it. This will build your confidence like nothing else.

Ask For What You Want. Don't timidly wait around for people to offer something to you. Just ask. There is nothing wrong with asking for what you want. The worst that will happen is that someone will say no.

Rediscover Your Rogue. Ultimately, we are born rule breakers and socially outgoing. We all have bravery coming out of our ears. It is not about what you do. It is about who you are. The only reason any of us are timid is that we constantly try to prove ourselves to others. Every interaction feels like we are on trial, but you are not. You are you, and YOU are a badass!

We all have our own gifts to bring to the world. It could be music, art, poetry, books, leadership, innovation, architecture, love, a smile, conversation, or anything. If these gifts are not making it into the world because you are afraid of doing what it takes to put it out there, you are doing the world a disservice.

The only way these gifts can manifest is by investing in yourself, believing in yourself, and being willing to go all the way. Persist through the suck. You have the power within you to leave the world a little different than when you came into it. Make that your mission, not chasing a buck.

You are special, you are worth it, and you can do anything you set your mind on. Everything we see around us was created by a human who persisted through the suck and held onto a desire to live a life beyond what most thought was possible.

Discover what makes you different, and then parade it around for the world to see. Call attention to it and love yourself for it no matter what others think. That is the heart of being a Rogue Artist. Go all the way. You have the power to do that. Tell your story, share your art, connect with other humans, inspire mutual excitement for what you do, and most importantly, blaze your own trail doing it.

So, PUT YOURSELF OUT THERE!

You deserve to be heard. Be bold. Be a Badass. Be a Rogue.

WAKE UP.
BE KIND.
BE AWESOME.
CREATE.
REPEAT.

Find out more about Rafi and Klee, their art, shenanigans, and books at www.RafiandKlee.com.

Made in United States
North Haven, CT
13 February 2023

32549454R00202